PARTNERSHIP & PO

Vince Cable was MP for Twickenham for twenty years, retiring in 2019. He was Secretary of State for Business Innovation and Skills (BIS) and President of the Board of Trade in the coalition government between 2010 and 2015.

He is the author of several acclaimed books, including the memoir *Free Radical*, the number-one bestseller *The Storm*, about the banking crisis, the novel *Open Arms* and, more recently, the non-fiction books *Money and Power* and *The Chinese Conundrum*. He is also a regular columnist with *The Independent*.

He was married to Olympia Rebelo, with whom he had three children, until she died in 2001. He married Rachel Smith in 2004, and together they have ten grandchildren.

Rachel Smith was born in Tanzania, youngest of five children of a colonial civil servant. She was married for 31 years to Dirk Kalis, a barrister and marina developer, and has three children. She worked as a teacher and then as a translator while the children were young and managed a small livestock farm in the New Forest for 35 years. She was a parish councillor for 12 years, serving as chairman of Brockenhurst Parish Council from 1988-91. She was also an active member of the SDP in the 1980s and, as chair, steered the local party through merger with the Liberals.

She worked in various capacities in developing affordable rural housing and chaired New Forest Villages Housing Association until 2018. She is currently joint president of Arts Richmond together with her husband. Her hobbies include painting and textile art.

Partnership & politics
in a divided decade

Vince Cable and Rachel Smith

To Debbie

Very best wishes

Vince Cable

THE REAL PRESS

www.therealpress.co.uk

Published in 2022 by the Real Press.
www.therealpress.co.uk
© Vince Cable and Rachel Smith

ISBN (print)   978-1912119257
ISBN (ebooks) 978-1912119479

Cover illustration: DYLAN KALIS

Acknowledgements

We would like to thank colleagues, friends and family for their support and encouragement during the production of this memoir. Amongst colleagues, our researcher Rory Reid deserves particular mention, having sorted and reduced the mountains of material in our attic. He also helped to decide what to publish and how best to organise the narrative and has been patient and polite throughout. David Boyle and Lesley Yarranton of the Real Press took on the job of final editing and publication. Without their professional expertise, the book would not have seen the light of day.

Friends who took the trouble to read the manuscript in early 2022 include Jackie Rowley, Duncan Brack, Dee Doocey, Alex Davies and Emily Walch. Their advice has been invaluable.

Our families are central to our existence. They have individually and collectively been a huge emotional support to us, especially during the turbulent decade covered in this book and particularly in periods of illness and stress.

Any errors or omissions remain entirely our responsibility.

To our families – and other political couples.

Contents

Foreword

Vince and Rachel conceived the idea of this joint memoir at the beginning of the first Covid 19 virus lockdown in March 2020. Vince had published an autobiography called *Free Radical* in 2009 and Rachel had self-published a piece called *My Life in Less Than 100 Objects* in 2016. Both started as memoirs for family and friends but found a wider audience.

Their motivation now is similar. At the very least, they would like those closest to them to be able to make sense of their lives. It is possible that there might also be some insights into a momentous decade in British public life.

There is a danger of it being a 'pantomime horse', as their personalities and writing styles are very different.

The lessons learnt in ballroom dancing are relevant: to have core strength both as individuals, and as a couple, and at the same time, to make your own shape in your own space, which together make an exciting and harmonious whole.

Introduction *by Vince*

The decade 2010-19 was a remarkable and intense period of modern history for the UK, and for me personally. It saw the first post-war coalition government; the European referendum and Brexit; the improbable Labour leadership of Jeremy Corbyn; the re-making of the Conservative Party from the period of David Cameron to Boris Johnson via Theresa May; the Lib Dems' rise to government and fall. Overseas there was Trump, the rise of China, wars in Syria and Libya. There was growing evidence and awareness of climate change. And the decade ended with the beginning of the Covid pandemic.

I thought I had captured the highs and lows of my own life, in and out of politics, in my book *Free Radical*, published in 2009 when the banking crisis was being played out and deep recession loomed. I was not to know then that I would play a part in the coalition cabinet for five years; suffer a traumatic defeat in my Twickenham constituency in 2015; regain it two years later; and then find myself as party leader for two years.

It is only after I retired from Parliament at the end of 2019 that I had the chance to reflect on the ups and downs of the decade and their significance.

The old adage that history is written by the winners was never more true than of the coalition government. When Nick Clegg led the Lib Dems into that government, it was a brave and decisive break from 65 years of single party rule. At times it now feels as if the Lib Dems have been airbrushed out of history. The coalition is routinely referred to as a 'Conservative' government and, in their weakened state, the Lib Dems have been unable to argue back. It is often forgotten that important policy initiatives, subsequently embraced by the Conservatives, originated with the Lib Dems and would probably never have happened without their work in government.

There was a sizeable group of Lib Dem ministers who played an important role in the coalition but mostly disappeared from Parliament and public life after 2015. Their work and that of MPs who gave loyal support goes largely unrecognised. I described in *After the Storm* some of the debates and tensions around economic policy, but there is a bigger story to be told.

The body of work they accomplished, often in the face of Conservative scepticism or outright opposition and now claimed as 'Conservative', includes: the 'pupil premium', big increases in the income tax threshold, the pensions 'triple lock' and 'stakeholder pensions', a revival of apprenticeships, same sex marriage, bank reform, industrial strategy, the renewables revolution – especially offshore wind – the prioritisation of mental health, the Green Investment Bank and the British Business Bank, shared parental leave. Many Conservative policies were resisted and blunted by Lib Dem ministers: even deeper cuts in welfare spending; the near-extinction of further and adult education; the removal of employment rights including the right to strike; the dilution of environmental regulation; greater restrictions on immigration of overseas students and skilled workers; bigger tax cuts for the wealthy; abandoning civil liberties.

When Lib Dems left the government, Cameron felt emboldened to hold the Brexit referendum, and lost it: perhaps the biggest and most disastrous consequence of the Lib Dems' demise.

Three unsuccessful elections for the Lib Dems followed the coalition but it remains as a significant 'third force'. The highly successful 2019 local election results re-established a substantial part of the local government base which was swept away during the coalition. The party found a new mission seeking to stop Brexit and was rewarded with outstanding results in the 2019 Euro elections. While the Brexit battle was lost, the party's credentials are well established for when the issue returns, as it will.

The Lib Dems are potentially a key constituent of a 'progressive' group of parties – with Labour and the Greens – whose ability to co-operate may well be crucial to an eventual change of government. Having led the party for two years during the very difficult period of rebuilding from near-annihilation, I saw at first hand the immense obstacles but also the possibilities for the party. A solid bedrock of committed activists, many of them schooled in the realities of local government, remains.

The recollection of events a decade or more ago relies heavily on my memory, prompted by Rachel's journals. They also rely on a large collection of press cuttings which I kept during the coalition years relating to events in which I was involved. Reliance on these sources produces a necessarily rather egocentric account of the period, but it has the advantage of producing a history which reflects both my lived experience and external perception of it. One disadvantage of a history drawing heavily on media references is that it exaggerates personality clashes and leadership issues relative to the serious debates on policy and approach within the Lib Dems, as well as within the coalition.

One of the themes of *Free Radical* was the importance of a hinterland in a political life and in particular a stable, loving family. I described in that book my marriage to Olympia, who died in 2001. I was then blessed with a second happy marriage (as well as three children and now three grandchildren from the first). Rachel provided emotional and practical support without which I would not have been able to undertake and survive the challenges of the decade. But I felt that I should not just acknowledge her role but that she should describe it in her own words: hence this book.

Introduction *by Rachel*

I started keeping a journal, intermittently, in 1996 – on holiday in Shetland. The first entry is a little watercolour of a beautiful – but dead – baby bird found near a beach. Twenty-five years later, there are nearly as many volumes, mostly written in haste.

As writer Wendy Cope says of her poetry: "I have emotion – no one who knows me could fail to detect it -/But there's a serious shortage of tranquillity in which to recollect it" (*Serious Concerns*, 1992).

And so it has been with my prose (mostly prose), none of it written with publication in mind. It was more to "catch the moment", especially during the events of 2010-2019, when we were near the centre of political life in the UK, and to process my thoughts and feelings at the time rather than unload them onto my nearest and dearest.

As other political spouses know, it's hard to support one's partner as well as to find a space to be oneself without inviting critical, often hostile, media attention. No names, no pack drill!

I was a political animal before I was a political wife. As a student in the 1960s, I was a passionate opponent of apartheid and also founded a university society to improve race relations in Britain. As a young wife and mother, I was a teacher and then a translator. In the 1980s, I was a parish councillor whilst running a small beef-rearing enterprise in the New Forest, a role which sparked my interest in affordable rural housing and was my job for the next 20 years. I joined the SDP in 1983 and chaired my local party through the merger with the Liberals after the 1987 election.

I re-met Vince in 2001, giving a talk about globalisation to the Lymington United Nations Association, with my 85-year-old mother presiding, after a 35-year interval (we had met for about 30 minutes at a charity lunch in Cambridge in 1966). I had been on my own for four years. He says he noticed my "good legs". I certainly noticed his blue eyes. We had a difference of opinion on home grown dairy products versus free trade and I challenged him to visit my farm.

We married in 2004, and, speaking for myself, have been extremely happy, notwithstanding the pressures of frontline political life.

The decade covered in this memoir was one of professional fulfilment for Vince and personal development for me. I managed to keep the strands of my rural, artistic and family life going whilst fully supporting Vince's high wire political act. It was only when "the music stopped" because of the pandemic early in 2020 that we found the space and time, if not exactly tranquillity, to write this joint memoir. The narrative is his, the 'asides' in *italics* are mine.

But what we share is the belief that how we are governed matters, and that the coalition was a better period of government than what went before or came after it. Words of the poem *Sometimes* by poet and novelist Shenagh Pugh capture that spirit of high endeavour which characterises politics at its best...

Does it all come flooding back? *Private Eye's* cover No.1349,
20 September 2013 (courtsy of *Private Eye*).

Part I

The British Weren't Used To This

Vince and Rachel with Nick Clegg at Lib Dem party conference in 2009 (*picture courtesy of Getty Images*).

Chapter One
Prelude to the coalition

The dawn of a new decade saw the British political class picking its way through the debris left by the parliamentary 'expenses scandal' and the twisted, burnt structures damaged by the financial firestorm of 2008. An election loomed in the next six months between an unpopular Labour government led by Gordon Brown, battered by the events of the last two years and exhausted by thirteen years in office, and David Cameron's Conservatives, struggling to escape the party's reputation for 'nastiness' and the divisions left by the Thatcher years.

For the first time in many years, the Liberal Democrats, led by Nick Clegg with me as his deputy, had the realistic prospect of a significant breakthrough and of playing a key role in reshaping British politics. For the activists and supporters who, for decades, had braved endless frustration and ridicule, and had been told to aspire to a valuable but limited role in local government at most, these were heady days.

The New Year was a good deal more auspicious for me than the millennium, a decade earlier. I had spent the beginning of the century sitting in an empty but welcoming church in Chelsea, tearful and mournful, while my wife Olympia recovered from an operation in hospital nearby in her long, losing battle against cancer. A decade later, I was settled and happy in a new marriage, to Rachel. And I was riding a political wave after years of national obscurity. I had suddenly acquired a high level of recognition from having warned of the financial disaster, which was being incubated as a result of reckless lending and growing personal indebtedness and from a largely apolitical commentary throughout the crisis.

This success was embellished by escaping the expenses scandal intact and being accorded saintly status as a result. I was lucky enough to have avoided the peccadillos and careful enough to have avoided the larger abuses which led to the humiliation of many MPs and the exit of some to political oblivion or prison.

A combination of my own puritanism and my efficient, scrupulously honest, constituency office in Twickenham had kept me out of the mire.

Politics can be a roller-coaster of implausible highs and painful lows and I was lucky enough, for a short period, to enjoy national recognition and approval. I should have savoured the moment more than I did, aware that the exhilaration of scaling a steep mountain is matched by the risk of falling off and the inevitability of descent.

I was also acutely aware that for some colleagues, let alone opponents, such publicity makes for envy and animosity. My attempts to communicate in a language which connected with the public led to occasional barbed observations that my popularity was independent of the party, and that perhaps I should try harder to use the party's slogans and 'lines to take' and appear less detached from the hurly-burly of tribal politics.

And I was causing problems for Nick Clegg, who was getting less and less favourable publicity than his deputy. I should say, however, that he was always good-natured, understanding and supportive, but I was aware of an undercurrent of discomfort beneath the surface.

I was given a weekly column in the *Mail on Sunday*. Some of my friends were horrified that I was straying so far from the liberal comfort zone of the *Independent*, the *Guardian* and the *Observer*. But it was an opportunity, never before given to a Liberal Democrat, to speak directly to millions of *Mail* readers over their cornflakes. The *Mail* team were professional and respectful of my independent voice.

On January 31 2010, I addressed the issue which was to dominate British politics for much of the decade to come: cuts, or what was later called 'austerity'. My piece was headlined: "The patient is on drip-feed; cuts will kill us now"[1]. For obvious reasons, the article – and press comment and speeches in a similar vein – were a major source of awkwardness and mischief when circumstances changed a few months later, in the febrile atmosphere of market alarm during the Eurozone crisis, and the coalition embarked on cuts right away. Back in January, I was conscious of the real dilemmas ahead: "I believe that government borrowing has to be reduced but the timing has to reflect the health of the economy... [Bond dealers] are obsessed with the county's credit rating and warn that we are in danger of losing our Triple A status which enables the government to borrow cheaply. They had to be taken seriously. But it would be reckless to plunge the economy back into recession through the immediate slashing of public services and jobs".

January 30 2010: Another week, another train. We are on a wonderful high-speed train to Liverpool: two hours to Lime Street (We were to have stayed with our good friends Richard and Jennifer Latto but they are rushing the other way to meet their first grandchild... so we are hosted by their friendly Lib Dem neighbours). We are here for a pep talk to the Lib Dem troops in Southport, a marginal seat with a Lib Dem MP (John Pugh), and then a fundraising dinner in Liverpool, long a centre of local government strength and now including a target seat.

We came to Euston via a big 'demo' in Richmond Park, a protest against parking charges in the Royal Parks.

---

[1] *Daily Mail*, 1 February 2010.

Vince and the neighbouring Lib Dem MP, Susan Kramer, had done the heavy lifting on this issue and were anxious to spike the guns of Zac Goldsmith, who had organised the meeting to make it into a Toryfest. It was a wonderful, crisp morning in the park and made a great start to the day.

February 14 2010: *Valentine's Day: Managed a break for both of us on the farm and a sentimental walk to the Hare & Hounds pub for lunch, where we went on our first date back in 2001. I am organising canvassing and envelope stuffing for the local Lib Dems in the New Forest, where East is a target seat.*

Then, two days on the farm in the rain trying to get silage to the cattle without getting bogged down in the mud. Have just read a DEFRA information pack which tells me I need to complete a Soil Condition Survey: alarming, given the state of the waterlogged fields.

I look forward to four days with V in London: a class at Kelly's Dancing School; dinner with Matthew (Lord) Oakeshott and Pippa; fundraising in Colchester; one of V's book launches for The Storm *at Fortnum and Mason. Then by train to Cornwall where we are promised a dinner dance at a fundraiser for Andrew George, our MP in Penzance.*

As the elections approached, the parties' generals prepared for battle. For the Lib Dems an increasingly pressing issue, given the closeness of the polls, was what we would do in a 'hung Parliament'. There were some well-oiled mantras to trot out in interviews to avoid answering the question to which a reply implying partiality would antagonise numerous voters leaning either 'right' or 'left' and, also, party members who valued our independence.

The party's spring conference in Birmingham on March 13 – 14 provided a test of discipline and an opportunity for members to air their anxieties. A warning shot was fired in the press by 'agony aunt' Claire Rayner, a high profile convert from Labour, who said that she was "appalled to hear Nick Clegg praising Margaret Thatcher and pleaded with him not to get into bed with Mr Cameron's party and appealed to him to stop flirting with the Tories or risk destroying his party".[2]

What Nick had done was to ask Chris Huhne to lead a group doing some scenario planning for a 'hung Parliament'. The assumption that I, and most of my colleagues, had been making was that any coalition or post-electoral arrangement would be with Labour. In terms of electoral positioning, a majority of our held and marginal seats were 'Conservative facing' and relied heavily on tactical voting by Labour supporters. Paddy Ashdown had built the party's recovery from near-oblivion 20 years earlier as a party opposed to the Conservatives. Charles Kennedy, when party leader, was even further removed from the Tories politically. Like me, he had an instinctive antipathy to the Tory party, even when we were in agreement with them.

Yet, when Chris presented his analysis to a group of us – an unofficial leadership team – in Nick's office, we all had to acknowledge the logic of a particular throw of the

---

[2] *Mail on Sunday*, 14 March 2010.

electoral dice which made working with the Tories numerically the obvious option. And co-operation with them had opportunities as well as threats. Nick made it clear that this option had to remain open; that we should acknowledge a common social and economic liberalism; and he had had conversations with Cameron anticipating this outcome.

I became involved in cross-party diplomacy as a result of a series of invitations to visit Gordon Brown for private chats in his rooms in Downing Street. I judged that he wanted a line of communication in the event of a 'hung Parliament'. He emphasised our common interests and my background as a Labour councillor in Glasgow and working for John Smith. For my part, I both admired his intellectual integrity and liked him; he was authentic and warm beneath the gruff exterior and somewhat vulnerable, talking about some of the personal pressures, constantly under attack including from many of his Labour colleagues.

He never mentioned my infamous put down of him in Prime Minister's Questions: that, beset by a series of crises 'he had morphed from Stalin to Mr Bean, creating chaos out of order, rather than order out of chaos'.

We maintained a dialogue until a few minutes before he resigned. I was able to report back his wish to keep open the option of working with us, should the electoral outcome require it. He feared for the legacy of the Blair/Brown years if the Tories returned. Beyond that I was puzzled as to what Gordon got out of the conversations until I saw a press comment later: 'According to Labour sources, these fireside chats were a form of therapy for Brown who trusted Cable implicitly. Cable, to his credit, has never spoken of them...'[3].

A source said: 'Gordon would moan to Vince about how unfair everything was. It started quite soon after he became Prime Minister. He would call Vince in, ostensibly to discuss economics, but he wasn't really looking for advice. I don't think he wanted solutions, just someone to listen.'[4] That seemed as good an explanation as any other.

March 13–14 2010: Conference. *We arrived late and tired at the hotel in Birmingham, V having insisted on doing his regular Friday advice surgery before we left. As almost always, it started early and finished late.*

We seem to be getting good coverage on the news channels. Nick's speech especially, which is great. I was a radio star myself, talking about being a political wife on R4's pre-recorded PM Programme *with Sandra Howard, Linda McDougall (wife of Austin Mitchell) and Carole Caplin (Cherie Blair's style guru). The questions we were asked to address were whether the party leader's spouse was part of the election package; how much coverage the BBC should give wives and partners; and what it feels like to be on the receiving end of media attention.*

In my case, I only became of interest as the killjoy wife who almost scuppered Vince's celebrated joke about Gordon Brown as I thought it was unkind. Sarah Brown, Samantha Cameron and Miriam Clegg were all very attractive and photogenic and I was pleased to be able to get in a plug for Miriam González Durántez, who manages

[3] *The Sunday Times*, 20 May 2010.
[4] *Sunday Times News Review*, 16 May 2010.

to combine her own high-powered job with a very young family and appearing glamorously at set-piece party events. An amazing number of people said that they had heard it.

In late March it was lovely to get back to the countryside, farming and gardening again. The cattle had to be wormed and we did their Blue Tongue vaccinations at the same time, after which we left youngster cows Helpful and Caramel in the little paddock to do some halter training over the next few days. In between, I did some canvassing in very Tory Brockenhurst with a team in good heart.

On March 24, Alistair Darling presented a pre-election budget which was expected to define the terms of the economic debate in the coming election. It had a few small tax sweeteners and spending pledges. But the Chancellor declined to spell out details of future spending cuts until after the election, which he warned would be the "toughest for decades". The fiscal deficit would be halved by 2014/15 and spending would carry twice the burden of tax rises.

In response, I echoed a consensus view as in the BBC summary: 'The IMF, OECD and EU say the plan lacks credibility. They want more detail and a faster timetable as does the governor of the Bank of England, Mervyn King'.

Four days later, the three contestants to be chancellor had a televised debate on Channel 4. I went into the debate as favourite, having topped a poll to be 'best chancellor' with 32 per cent public support as against 23 per cent for Alistair

Darling and 21 per cent for George Osborne.[5] George Osborne announced a plan for overall tax cuts, stopping a planned rise in national insurance. I attacked it as "utterly incredible" and prompting the headline "Darling and Cable join forces to attack Osborne over Tory plans for tax cuts".[6]

I had the easiest task as the 'plague on both your houses' spokesman and Ann Treneman noted: "only Vince, the pig in the middle, had any fun".[7]

The press was generally kind.[8] Even the *Telegraph*'.[9] Amazingly, and not without its dangers, there was even an endorsement from the editor of the *Daily Mail*: "Once again Vince Cable proved more convincing than Labour or the Tories in outlining how he would fill the terrifying gap opening up in the public finances."[10]

The bigger challenge was to help Nick get our poll rating up from just over 20 per cent. I thought I had helped get the poll ratings up from single figures at the beginning of 2009 to the low 20s, but the mundane truth was that our ratings depended on media exposure and we were getting more in the run-up to an unpredictable election. The harsh logic of the first-past-the-post electoral system was that even with over 20 per cent vote share we would do well to keep our current haul of 62 seats, out of 650.

The prospect of making progress hinged on the election campaign and in particular on Nick Clegg, largely unknown

[5] *Daily Mirror*, 24 March 2010.

[6] *The Times*, 30 March 2010.

[7] *The Times*, 30 March 2010.

[8] *The Guardian*, 30 March 2010.

[9] Benedict Brogan, 30 March 2010.

[10] 'The Lib Dem who gives it to us straight', 7 April 2009.

but intelligent, articulate, telegenic and a good communicator.

March 28/29 2010: We are on the train from Manchester after events in Rochdale, Oldham, Gorton and Cheadle. V has had a hell of a week again, having to switch seamlessly between completely different audiences. Tomorrow he has the chancellors' debate. His press officer wants me to be around the following morning as a 'soothing influence'. Then we escape for an evening at the cinema in Richmond: The Girl with the Golden Tattoo. *Afterwards, I can get back to the farm and training the heifers to be halter-led. I realise that calving is going to coincide horribly with the election.*

The election campaign was now in full swing on schedule for May 6. The Tories had a lead over Labour of five to seven per cent, but it was fragile. The Lib Dems were where we had always craved to be: taken seriously, potential king-makers if not kings. Where I was concerned, my job was to maintain economic credibility through what would undoubtedly be a tough few weeks of cross-examination. Nick took the unprecedented step of having both our heads on the side of his battle bus, which was generous of him and a big vote of confidence. At that stage, we assumed that I would be as much in the firing line as him.

To reinforce the economic message, we released a manifesto full of 29 detailed suggestions for savings of £15bn a year including some controversial items: reform of public sector pensions and curbs on universal pensioner benefits like winter fuel allowance. The core of our message was fiscal prudence combined with a commitment to basic public services while raising income tax thresholds – cutting marginal income tax rates for low earners – but paying for it by taxes on the rich: a tax on valuable properties, higher capital gains tax and inheritance tax. The plan owed a lot to David Laws who had been working with me for years to establish our economic credibility.

We got a lot of credit for being ambitious and explicit in spelling out cuts and having a 'progressive' tax message. The more perceptive critics, however, picked up on some of the weaknesses. Philip Stephens of the *Financial Times* attacked the tax threshold proposal both for its intrinsic weaknesses – only a small part of the benefit would go to very low earners – and for the optimism of the tax raising proposals to finance it;[11] Financial journalist Anatole Kaletsky also argued that 'despite this boldness, however, the Lib Dem numbers do not fully add up'[12] and even the supportive *Guardian* posed the question: "Did the Lib Dems get their sums right?"[13] But relative to the other two, we were positively heroic in confronting the 'elephant in the room', as I called it.

What received virtually no attention in the campaign was the macro-economic issue I had earlier raised in the *Mail on Sunday* article: the timing of the cuts and the risks of deeper recession. The criticisms were entirely about whether the numbers added up.

What worried me more than the largely fair criticisms

---

[11] *Financial Times*, 30 March 2010.

[12] *The Times*, 19 April 2010.

[13] *The Guardian*, 15 April 2010.

were the hostages to fortune which we were quietly storing up, should we find ourselves in government. In the chancellors' debate, I had given what I thought was an honest answer when I had said that no section of public spending could be completely protected from cuts, including the beloved NHS which infuriated Nick and his team. My comments were effectively disowned.

The disagreement went back to a serious row at party conference in the previous autumn when I had argued that we should make a virtue of the crisis and inevitable austerity while Nick, strongly supported by most of the MPs and our campaigns team led by Chris Rennard, argued that the election would be won on spending pledges and promises of tax cuts. The tension resurfaced later in the campaign when, exasperated by my negativity, Nick went to Glasgow and pledged on peak TV news, with a supporting hoarding, to oppose any, Tory-inspired, increase in VAT (which the coalition did within weeks). But the compromise between the two approaches worked well enough in the campaign.

Nick won the first leaders' debate on April 15 hands down. He was well prepared, confident and he used simple but effective techniques like speaking to the camera and replying to questioners by name. Over the following week, Lib Dem support shot up from 20 per cent to over 30 per cent and a couple of polls showed Lib Dems ahead. Some of our supporters started to get carried away with a belief that we were on the road to victory: 'Clegg-mania'. They underestimated the Tories' stockpile of ammunition and the resilience of Labour's core support.

I was sent around the country – from Cardiff and Cornwall to Liverpool, Hull and Aberdeen – to designated marginal seats and I largely left Twickenham in the hands of my agent, Dee Doocey, whose political and organisational skills were reflected in our run of successful results. She had overseen three of my four previous elections in Twickenham, where I had steadily progressed from a deficit of over 7,000 votes to a majority of just under 10,000. I knew there would be a well organised, highly motivated local team.

April 23 2010: St George's Day is celebrated in Whitton (in V's constituency) with St George's flags on white vans. I was out canvassing and met a lady on the doorstep who said, "I'm BNP, me" but when I offered her a leaflet about Vince, she said she "didn't mind old Vince".

Next day, there was a parade. It was a wonderfully colourful, ethnically diverse event, complete with St George, who looked North African or Pakistani, and his attendants who looked faintly like Maid Marion; kids on stilts being Turks, various dragons and all manner of minor characters. Very few uniforms, apart from cubs and brownies. And a black, cockney pearly queen. The whole thing set off for Whitton's main street, followed by the most beautiful pair of black horses with flowing manes and a carriage advertising Co-operative Funerals.

I did 550 leaflet drops in the four days I was there and my legs were tired and my feet sore.

The second debate, a week later, was judged to be roughly tied between Clegg and Cameron and after the debate, Lib Dem support started to fade. The Conservative press – that is to say most of it – opened fire on Nick and the Lib Dems with varying degrees of venom. A heavily qualified commitment to an amnesty for illegal immigration became a promise to allow unlimited immigration; our opposition to Trident was going to leave the country defenceless.

In the third debate, on the economy and tax, Nick was less commanding; Cameron was judged the winner and Gordon Brown was able to deploy his experience of crisis management. 'Cleggmania' was slowly deflating, and we seemed to have no response. Even in Twickenham, where I was well ahead, we could feel a drift back to the Tories. Election Day couldn't come soon enough.

May 3 2010: *Bank Holiday. Have been able to get to Twickenham after Bella's fifth calf (and first heifer) looks much healthier after several days of fitful feeding. Have canvassed twice – friendly in general. Got through another 400 leaflets. Will have done 1,500 by the end of tomorrow!*

V had gone to Aberdeen with his daughter, Aida, acting as aide, and returned for a big rally in Richmond where he did the warm-up speech for Nick Clegg. The rally was amazing: 400 people packed into a big Baptist church. A lot of enthusiasm. It doesn't really matter what Nick says at the moment; he is walking on water. V goes to Cornwall with Aida tomorrow and I finish my delivery rounds. Hooray! Dee is ahead of her schedule at the office so does not need me and I feel superfluous. And no news is good news from the farm, so I go and do some campaigning with V.

Election Eve: *Off with V to Kings Cross for breakfast at the Sourced Markets stall – served by my son Max's French* *girlfriend. Then to St Albans for some old-fashioned soapbox campaigning where Young Conservatives and Young Lib Dems were engaged in a stakeboard battle. By tickling the bare midriff of one of the Tories, I managed to get him to lose control of one of his two boards. Back to whistle-stop appearances in three north London constituencies, where there was a real buzz.*

May 6 2010: *Election Day. V is in the constituency doing the usual rounds of polling stations and thanking volunteers. He has the first slot on the BBC before the exit polls at 10 pm, which are awful: well below expectations and losing seats. We have Vince's older children, Paul and Aida and their spouses round for dinner and then the results. We struggle to keep awake. Our count is interminable. At 3 am V gets a call from Dee to brace himself for defeat. After the panic subsided – it was just a cluster of Tory votes in one polling station – we went across for the count at 5 am: instead of defeat, it was a majority of 12,000, up 2,000 on 2005! As we made our way home to sleep V (who had been an MP since 1997) was handed a 'Starter Pack for MPs'!*

We tried to go to sleep in the morning and V got up to make tea at 11 am, which never arrived. Instead, there was a long telephone call: Gordon Brown. V was the only person he could trust; must have a Lab-Lib pact or the Tories would call another election and wipe us both out. And then Clegg on TV repeating his statement of working with the party with the biggest number of seats.

Chapter Two
Seven days in May

The election result was sobering. We had 23 per cent of the poll, fractionally up on 2005, but lost nine MPs, gaining four others. Particularly painful was the loss of Susan Kramer in next-door Richmond and Julia Goldsworthy, my deputy in the economic team, in Cornwall: two very talented women in a parliamentary team already very male. Despite the roller coaster of 'Cleggmania', we had finished the campaign pretty much as we started it. But our private frustration was overshadowed by the fact that for the first time since the mid-1970s there was a hung Parliament.

The morning after began with a call from Gordon Brown. Against expectations, the Tories hadn't won an outright victory and were a long way short of a majority. He thought the arithmetic allowed for a Labour-Lib Dem coalition and urged me to get Nick Clegg to set the talks in train. I urged him to speak to Nick directly.

He also raised an issue to which most of us had failed to pay attention during the election: the growing crisis around Greece and the Eurozone. He seemed genuinely concerned about the issue and the risk that Britain could soon be sucked in. When I got hold of Nick to relay the conversation back it was clear that there was little interest in any negotiations with Labour which allowed Gordon to stay as PM.

In the afternoon, I was asked to go into HQ in Cowley

Street. When I got there, I discovered that a decision had been made to start talking to the Tories in line with Nick's pledge during the campaign to negotiate with the largest party in the new Parliament. A negotiating team had been assembled: David Laws, Chris Huhne, Danny Alexander and Andrew Stunell. I had a slight feeling of being sidelined, but reassured myself that, like Nick himself, I had a bird's eye view of the negotiations and that the four negotiators were ideal for that role.

With little to do, I played around with the parliamentary arithmetic which was changing during the day with new declarations, chatting to colleagues about options. It seemed likely that a Lib Dem-Labour coalition could get to 315 with the Tories on 306. But there were 29 others. We could probably attract another eight (SDLP, 3; Plaid, 3; Green, 1; Alliance, 1) with Sinn Féin (5) not voting.

That left the DUP (eight) who were very dubious allies and more likely to support the Tories. The balance (8) was of Scottish Nationalists. Allying ourselves with the Nats could be incendiary, however. At best the 'rainbow coalition' would be a pantomime horse with several attachments and be at the mercy of Ulster confessional politics and Scottish nationalism. It wouldn't work. I realised then that we had no alternative but to deal with the Tories in some form and had to live with the unpalatable consequences.

May 7 2010: I sit through Friday watching the box. We are in serious talks with the Tories. Extraordinary. The overlap in policy terms is really very small in my opinion. So, we are in a Dutch auction for our support. Gordon offers us more and more. But it is clear, if nothing else, that he has 'lost' the election since the Conservatives have 50 seats more than him. The legacy of Blair reneging on the PR promise in 1997 is coming home to roost.

By Friday evening, we had had enough of being doorstepped by TV, so we went to V's daughter Aida's house instead. They asked us to stay the night so, while Aida got V to a 9 pm meeting at Cowley Street, I went to Twickenham to get overnight things. In the morning, V dashed off an article for the Mail on Sunday, *sitting in bed over morning tea. I helped to get four-year-old grandson Charlie dressed; he is lovely but a bit of a monster at the moment, no doubt sensing the drama unfolding around him. I was becoming desperate to get to the farm, so I took V's car back to Twickenham while Aida posted him back to Smith Square for a parliamentary party meeting.*

They were greeted with a 1,000-strong demonstration by the Electoral Reform Society, anxious to make sure that PR was on the cards. The Tories are wholly intransigent on the issue, offering only a committee to talk about it, the last thing we need. We went through all that when Roy Jenkins led the SDP. Then there is Trident and Europe – and I fear we may have to sit through the foxhunting debate again.

There is a much looser arrangement possible, in theory, called 'supply and confidence' where we only support things we agree on – but that is pretty much the same as minority government.

By Saturday morning the crowds of journalists and TV cameras had begun to build up outside the front door in Twickenham. Rachel and I had devised an escape route via the back garden into a cul-de-sac out of sight of the main road: a solution which was to prove a life saver when I later encountered the more serious media invasions after the crises around tuition fees and Murdoch.

Once in central London, the main focus of attention was a meeting of our new team of MPs to gauge their reaction to the talks with the Tories. The message from the leadership was that we had to explore all the options. These included a coalition with the Tories. We could offer a 'supply and confidence' arrangement but the Tories would go to the country at the first opportunity to get an overall majority, citing Lib Dem obstruction, and we would be toast; so, let's get the best deal we can. Unfortunately, the Tories were being obdurate on the issue which mattered most for the Lib Dems: PR. At that stage a lot of colleagues thought a deal with Labour could be salvaged; but overall, they could see that the Tory option was much more plausible.

Sunday morning: another call from Gordon. He had already understood that Clegg wanted him to agree to step down before serious discussions could take place. He accepted that in general terms and I had to stress that Nick wanted clarity on his intentions.

We moved on to the Eurozone. He had all kinds of ideas for solutions building on his leadership at the G20 meeting two years earlier. His passion was obvious and I was amazed that he could focus on the details of EU fiscal policy and Eurozone monetary policy in the middle of a UK political crisis of which he was the centrepiece.

May 9 2010: Sunday morning on the farm. Sorted out passports for the new Dexter cattle: Charcoal and Rachel (the calf, not me). The heifer looks less likely to calve than it did a week ago. But my dog is pleased to see me and the May blossom is just beautiful. I shall go and look at the Bluebell Wood in a minute. For me, being in London is like swimming lengths of crawl. I can do it, having learnt how to breathe in a three-stroke rhythm, but eventually I tire. Whereas being here is like swimming breaststroke. I could do it indefinitely. But I need to get back to be with V for his birthday today (which he hates to celebrate).

Calls came in from Whitehall: The Head of the Treasury, the BIS Permanent Secretary, Cabinet Secretary. Did I appreciate the severity of the financial and economic crisis? The Treasury Permanent Secretary, Nick McPherson, I had met a few months earlier when it had been judged that the Lib Dems needed to be included in pre-election planning and briefing. He came across, on first meeting, as a rather absent-minded, bookish, university professor. He was anything but: Eton and Balliol, a very sharp mind, though with deeply conservative instincts on financial matters, born of a career trying to stop politicians spending public money.

He made the case for any new government showing immediate seriousness in cutting spending. I was more persuaded of the same argument by Gus O'Donnell, the Cabinet Secretary. I had encountered Gus as a fellow lecturer in economics at Glasgow; he was a highly regarded economist and was the perfect civil servant, setting out options fairly and dispassionately.

The concern essentially was that speculation against Eurozone countries could spread to the UK, given the scale of UK deficits – the biggest in the developed world, thanks to the scale of the UK bank collapse. Britain had a flexible exchange rate, unlike Greece, but an uncontrolled fall in sterling would destabilise the economy, push up inflation, cutting real wages and probably lead to increased interest rates on debt. I was given to understand that the Bank of England governor, Mervyn King, shared these concerns.

He was also operating a highly expansionary monetary policy to support demand and offset the deflationary effects of fiscal tightening. The message was unmistakable: the country faced a serious crisis of external confidence over and above the financial and economic legacies of the banking crisis. It was imperative to have a stable government very soon and a credible plan to demonstrate seriousness about the fiscal deficit.

In the circumstances, faced with the seemingly unanimous views of the economic establishment, I felt that it was no longer reasonable to hold out on the narrow issue of whether a round of deficit reduction measures should take place within weeks rather than months. I signalled to our negotiators that this should not be treated as a red line. Instead, they should concentrate on getting strong commitments on bank reform – splitting off the investment bank 'casinos', bank lending through the nationalised banks, progressive taxation of capital, as well as the party's wider agenda on PR, the environment and civil liberties.

On the crucial issue of cuts, I insisted on a carefully worded phrase about reducing the 'cyclically adjusted, structural, current deficit' which was the agreed formulation of the Darling Plan. The problem with such nerdish language was that when, later, the Treasury embarked on 'mission creep', slashing public investment, few fellow Lib Dems appreciated the significance of it and quietly acquiesced in the most economically damaging aspect of the cuts programme.

May 9 2010: Sunday (later). Fed V while he fielded endless calls including one from the PM, one from the Chancellor and one from the Treasury Permanent Secretary... The country needs a government quickly but there is a chasm in policy terms between us and the Tories. There is a letter through the door from a constituent who sees V commuting on the train and says he is appalled at the thought of Lib Dems propping up Cameron and Osborne in government. That is my own initial gut reaction. But the arithmetic is such that someone is going to be 'propped up' or there will be no sustainable government.

We went for a walk along the river to Richmond and back, then V's daughter Aida, husband Stephen and grandson Charlie dropped off a birthday cake for V who is 67 today. He wants to forget his birthday but agrees to take the cake into London for the next - 11 pm - meeting to share with the team. It ended at 1 am the next morning. It hadn't gone well judging by V's steely look on his return, with lots of concerns about the Tory offer.

I could see what they were fretting about. I think that there is the moral authority for a Lib Dem-Labour government, based on 52 per cent of the popular vote; but it needs the nationalists as well. The Conservatives will no doubt be outraged and ask the Queen to invite them to form a government – or perhaps they will up their offer to us.

When I turned on the news, there was a story about a

soldier – unnamed – killed in Afghanistan. I worried about my friend Kate, whose son is out there on the front line, but mercifully (for her) it turned out not to be him.

Hope of a lie-in was dashed by an early call from Gordon Brown. He had telephoned Nick Clegg who was willing to talk to Labour in principle since the talks with the Tories were not going well. The issue of his standing down promptly was, however, the key obstacle for Nick. I also expressed pessimism about forming a stable government with Labour despite my genuine preference for that option.

We argued about the parliamentary numbers, but he was insistent that, with goodwill from the Lib Dems and Labour conceding PR, a government could be formed. We had to stop the Tories forming a government and playing games with the economy at a time of maximum danger. The Greek crisis was getting out of control and he wanted me to sign up to a public statement setting out the steps that needed to be taken at a European level to stabilise the economic situation.

The ideas made a lot of sense, but they assumed a British government to take them forward. The trouble with a lot of politicians is that they don't see the wood for the trees of process and prosaic detail. Gordon's problem seemed to be the opposite: he saw the wood but not the trees.

Monday: another day sitting around waiting for feedback from the negotiating group and from Nick Clegg on his talks with Cameron. We gathered that Cameron was willing to offer a referendum on AV: not the AV+ which had been the conclusion of Roy Jenkins' commission on electoral reform and a version of which was operating well enough in Scotland. Even the diluted proposal was causing leading Tories to have kittens. Our side was inclined to accept it as a deal breaker.

Meanwhile, preliminary talks with Labour were going nowhere: it was reported back that Mandelson and Adonis were keen; Balls and the two Milibands, however, had made it clear that they were not interested. The pendulum swung back to an agreement with the Tories and that was the recommendation when Nick reported back to MPs in the evening.

I had been quiet in previous caucus meetings, reflecting the fact that my heart and my head were in different places. But I judged that now was the moment to speak up. I made the case for suppressing our adversarial dislike of the Tories. We should trust Nick Clegg's judgement and accept the facts of parliamentary arithmetic which led to the conclusion that a coalition with the Tories was the only way to establish a stable government at a time of economic emergency. Moreover, Lib Dems could achieve something in government: far more than shouting from the sidelines.

Anonymous colleagues reported afterwards: "Cable seemed devastated. You could see from his face that he felt betrayed. He had tried terribly hard to keep Labour in play and they didn't seem to be serious. He had been at his whiteboard, trying to figure it out but he realised it was just not going to happen. I think he was gutted. Cable's speech had a decisive effect on the MPs."[14] I don't know if I did; but I thought my tone of reluctant acquiescence in the coalition, in the wider national interest, reflected the mood of

---

[14] *Sunday Times News Review*, 16 May 2010.

colleagues and supporters in the country.

The next day the Tory coalition agreement was finalised with little more fuss. The Labour talks petered out with accusations of bad faith and lack of seriousness on both sides. The main issue was over when Gordon Brown should go to the Palace to resign. He hadn't given up. In one embarrassing exchange in Nick's office, he was on the mobile asking me to make Clegg see sense while Nick was sitting a few feet away. He said he wanted clarity from Clegg so that he could resign with some dignity, but Team Clegg thought he was looking for excuses to stay on.

It was a great pity to see his prime ministership ending amidst such confusion and acrimony. In the event, he went shortly after and Cameron was asked to form a government.

The next step was to persuade the full Lib Dem parliamentary party of both houses formally to accept the newly printed, finalised, coalition agreement. There was some sharp dissent from Charles Kennedy who feared it would kill the party in Scotland. Ming Campbell was equally unhappy. Paddy Ashdown spoke twice, once against a deal then, when he had seen the coalition agreement, enthusiastically in favour of it. At the end there was overwhelming support.

We moved on to the formation of the coalition government. My role was settled in a five-minute interview with Nick Clegg. I made my pitch to be Chancellor, but he had already agreed that the top three jobs – Foreign, Home, and Chancellor – should go to Tories. Perhaps that was inevitable given the disproportion in Parliament and new government – one Lib Dem to six Tories.

I had the choice of being Osborne's No 2 as Chief

Secretary, responsible for public spending, or the Business Department. I am sure vanity played a part in my rejecting the first, and a feeling that I had expressed many times publicly that Osborne would be difficult to look up to in the way that I could with Tories like Ken Clarke who had been a successful chancellor. Also, the bits of the Treasury which really interested me – responsibility for the banks and overall economic strategy- were not on offer; they only wanted a Lib Dem to be seen to wield the knife and impose spending cuts.

Richard Littlejohn in the *Daily Mail* noted: "Vinny had the choice to go to the Treasury as Chief Secretary but flunked it because he couldn't stomach the opprobrium which will accompany the necessary cuts".[15] Had I been offered a serious economic policy role at the Treasury I would have grabbed the chance.

So I accepted the business department, but asked for banking and financial services to be returned there, as it had been in the days when John Smith had been Secretary of State. At least it was worth a try and I made it clear in interviews that I had accepted the job on that basis. What Nick and I should both have thought more about was the fact that the biggest responsibility of BIS was universities. The fees time bomb was ticking and the coalition agreement for Lib Dems to abstain on a vote on fees took no account of the fact that there could now be a Lib Dem Secretary of State in charge. We discussed an obvious compromise which involved my taking the banks to BIS and hiving off universities to a Tory-led department. But Cameron had

---

[15] *Daily Mail*, 14 May 2010.

insisted that there was to be no moving of the Whitehall furniture. And the mere suggestion that I take responsibility for the banks caused apoplexy in the City and had Osborne and the Treasury manning the barricades.

It was agreed the following day that I would have a key role in bank reform alongside Osborne, but financial services remained with the Treasury. The alternative to accepting the arrangement was to walk, which would have been seen as petulant and incomprehensible. I consequently found myself responsible for a department which was much changed from the place I had worked in two decades earlier and which I had, at one point, argued was unnecessary and should be abolished.

While the argument about my responsibilities was still being sorted out, I walked across from Nick's office in Parliament to meet David Cameron in 10 Downing Street. and confirm my appointment, causing the first of many talking points by setting off back on foot followed by a car which I hadn't known was there for my benefit. Eventually, in front of the assembled cameras, a policeman bundled me into the Jaguar and we went off to a quick round of introductions to the core staff at BIS, who I was soon to get to know well; to take stock of the magnificent office overlooking Westminster Abbey at the top of 1 Victoria Street; and then to be whisked off to the Palace to swear an oath, become a privy councillor and acquire a couple of artefacts which went with being Secretary of State and President of the Board of Trade – which I never saw again. Apparently, they were locked in a departmental cupboard.

Events were moving very fast. I hadn't appreciated until later that while I was getting used to the floor plan and fittings in 1 Victoria Street and finding out where the loos were, Clegg and Cameron were launching the new coalition in the Rose Garden of No. 10. It took a while to sink in but when I saw a repeat and the news coverage my heart sank. It was wrong. It was too much of a love-in: two centre-right politicians singing from the same song sheet and sounding as if they belonged to the same party.

In my view, we were working with the Tories reluctantly, in the national interest, to deal with a real crisis and that was what the public would understand and forgive. There was no love lost and we were very different. My disagreement with Nick, shared with many colleagues and party supporters, over this interpretation of the coalition would repeatedly surface in the years ahead and cause a great deal of grief.

At the time, however, the Rose Garden event seemed to capture the public mood. A *Sun* poll showed that 60 per cent of the public liked the coalition; only 33 per cent were opposed.

May 12 2010: *Last night, the five days 'without a government' ended with the disappearance of Gordon Brown at 7 pm, to go to see the Queen. The British are not used to this, but to my mind it was a bit like the five days without aeroplanes last month, when the unpronounceable Icelandic volcano erupted and spewed ash all over British airspace, grounding air traffic for a week and giving us blissfully quiet skies. Then the Poet Laureate Carol Ann Duffy wrote a great poem about ash and the unaccustomed hush and the way we could hear birdsong properly again.*

Being government-free has a somewhat similar effect:

no government exhortations, initiatives or policy statements make it very restful, at least for a bit. Perhaps, changing the metaphor, I should write a poem about the inter-regnum: from the ashes of a disappointing election, a phoenix of apparently consensual politics seems to have arisen in the form of the coalition. Instead of the cacophony of warring words, there were huddles of negotiators emerging blearily from time to time and stage whispers from the sidelines. Carol Ann Duffy talked of ash and hush. This is hush and dash and rash, but a genuinely new shape is emerging.

What a day it was yesterday. Vince went to see Alistair Darling – apparently neither he nor the chancellor fully understood what the meeting was for – and I rushed down to the farm to check up on the new additions to my herd. It wasn't easy getting the cattle in and we had a few hairy moments with the calves before they were safely tagged. I tried to follow the events in Westminster on the TV, saw Gordon Brown falling on his sword and an hour later Cameron going to the Palace with his wife Samantha, visibly pregnant. Brave stuff! The moment when the Lib Dems could have thrown out the Coalition Agreement has passed but I worry particularly about the promise of a vote on proportional representation.

Today's Six O'Clock News tells me V is doing 'Business and Banking'.

The day after swearing-in, there was a cabinet meeting. It was a bit like the first day at a new school for a new set of pupils. There was a lot of friendly banter and nervous introductions to people who, a few days earlier, we had regarded as mortal political enemies. I managed to crack what was described as the 'first joke of the coalition', saying that my experience of marrying into an Indian family had made me aware that our Indian friends' arranged marriages could be just as durable as love marriages (though my own was very much the latter).

As a demonstration of good intent on the economic front we all agreed to take a 5 per cent pay cut. When the cabinet was over, and the formal photos completed, I returned to 1 Victoria Street to discover that David Cameron wanted to make an impromptu visit, a strong signal that he valued my participation in the coalition. Hundreds of staff were decanted into the street outside to greet him and we both made friendly speeches. I earned the accolade from him of being an 'absolute star'.[16] He was a good actor and almost sounded as if he meant it.

I have two images going around in my head. One is of the Lib Dem liberty bird caught in the branches of the Tory blue and green logo, with some damaged feathers fluttering to the ground, but nonetheless setting about building its nest there. The other is of that yellow bird being forcibly stuffed with a Trident missile, like a foie gras goose.

Meanwhile, I had some fun choosing pictures online from the government art collection for Vince's BIS office and spoke to V's principal private secretary. He needed to know if I wanted to go on foreign visits with Vince, to

---

[16] "The new Cabinet's first meeting", *The Independent*, 14 May 2010.

which I said "a few, please". V and I quickly concluded that, if I did, I must pay for myself, although the PPS seemed to think a work role could be found for me.

Chapter Three
The business of government

After the flattery and the mutual backslapping, onto the business of government. The first step was talking to Osborne. I learnt on day one the protocol of the cabinet: those lower in the pecking order always visit those above them, hence the need to visit the Treasury.

There were two big issues of substance. One was banking reform: setting in train what was to become the Vickers Commission. The banks hated the idea: 'The thing that worries us most is the new commission to investigate whether banks should be broken up. In opposition, Cable was a harmless irritant... now this measure has left the industry on edge.'[17]

For the next few months, there would be continued speculation over where bank reform might lead: "Chancellor to face pincer movement over banks' break-up".[18]

The other issue was capital gains tax (CGT) which had become a serious bone of contention. Our party policy was to align income and capital taxes since there was a great deal of scope for avoidance by exploiting differences in rates. This would involve raising the lowest CGT rate from ten per cent to 40 per cent. There was outrage from second

---

[17] *Sunday Times*, 16 May 2010.
[18] *Financial Times*, 14 June 2010.

homeowners and the bosses of private equity firms, one of whom said: "We all vote Conservative and we're ending up with worse tax treatment than if Gordon Brown had stayed in power."[19]

Osborne was willing to compromise (the uniform CGT rate became 28 per cent). I came to enjoy the conversations with him; he was more engaging in private than in public. I also noticed the other person in the room, who was to become a key figure: Rupert Harrison, a clever and utterly self-confident man (a former Eton head boy, like Cameron). I realised I needed someone of similar stature to take on the Treasury.

Back at BIS, I began to realise the scale and complexity of what I was taking on, over and above the coalition politics (and my constituency). For years, I had operated with a small, tight, team at Westminster: a couple of researchers, a press officer and a sounding board for ideas in the form of Matthew Oakeshott, our spokesman in the Lords with a good understanding of financial issues based on his experience in fund management. Now there was a department of over 3,000 in the HQ alone and an archipelago of well over 70 quangos plus the universities, colleges, Royal Mail and Post Office.

The first shock was to discover that I had a private office of six civil servants dealing with different aspects of the department's work; to keep me fully briefed; to fill my Red Box with recommendations for decisions to be made every night; and then to make sure the decisions were acted upon. I was assured that there was more than enough work to keep

---

[19] *Sunday Times*, 16 May 2010.

them fully occupied. I quickly realised that, unlike in *Yes Minister*, it was the Private Secretary who was the key figure advising and helping the minister on a daily basis, with the Permanent Secretary one stage removed.

My first Private and Permanent Secretaries were Richard Abel and Simon Fraser, very capable civil servants who had been close to Peter Mandelson. I judged that they wanted and needed to move on, enabling me to have a team motivated to support me and the new government. In particular, I wanted a strong private secretary, preferably with a Treasury background, and a woman.

I got one: Jo Crellin. She made all the difference to what was going to be a very bumpy ride and, between periods of maternity leave, covered most of my time in office. With her help, I built up a great team, mostly women and ethnically diverse.

The next priority was political advice and support: the Special Advisers (spads). Old timers (and Rachel, with her civil service family background) are critical of the spad system, believing that it sidelines the civil service. I disagreed and considered spads to be absolutely essential. So much of the decision-making was 'political' as between ministers and their respective departments and parties. It was better to have that political role given to people recognised as political rather than inviting civil servants to dabble in party politics. That applied above all in the coalition.

I was lucky to get Giles Wilkes, who was economically literate and very bright and, having made a lot of money in spread betting, didn't see the job as part of a party career ladder but, rather, enjoyed the intellectual challenge. Katie

Waring was a clever policy analyst who was to prove invaluable in dealing with the immense complexity of the universities' brief.

What I lacked initially was someone to deal with the press. The easy informal relationships with journalists I had enjoyed in opposition disappeared as I was sucked into the daily grind of government. Publicity was sparse and increasingly negative. I began to realise why good 'spin doctors' matter. Eventually (in early 2012), I managed to recruit an outstanding spad, Emily Walch, who turned around my relations with the press along with several exceptional departmental press officers – Fiona Cookson, Alison McLeod and Jo Robotham. And when Giles and Emily moved on at the end of the Parliament, I was able to recruit two more effective spads – Vanessa Pine and Ashley Lumsden – and was even allowed the luxury of a personal economic adviser, Leo Ringer, recruited from the CBI.

One of the awkward aspects of coalition government was that there were fewer jobs to go around. The Conservatives had a dozen or so people who were expecting to become ministers and whose ministerial jobs had gone to the Lib Dems. Cameron had a clutch of disillusioned, bitter, mainly right-wing and Eurosceptic, MPs who would make trouble later.

The Lib Dems also had too many people for the jobs available. I had to point out to Nick's team that some front-line Lib Dems had been somehow overlooked in the provisional appointments, notably Ed Davey and Norman Lamb. I grabbed Ed Davey for a junior minister role in BIS and Jo Swinson to be my PPS, an unpaid role linking ministers with their party backbenchers. Norman was to step up when Ed joined the cabinet after Chris Huhne was charged with perverting the course of justice and therefore had to stand down.

Indeed, that was one of several misfortunes which robbed us of major talents but led to upward mobility within the Lib Dems: David Laws lasted only a few weeks after accusations related to parliamentary expenses.

The loss of those two proved, however, to be seriously damaging in terms of our effectiveness in the coalition. David had a serious, financial and economic brain and, whilst his instincts were fiscally conservative, he had the intellectual self-confidence to take on 'groupthink' and in particular the orthodoxies of the Treasury.

He later managed to put through significant education reform, notably by introducing the 'pupil premium'. Chris was a first-class economist who was also a formidable debater, able to intimidate Conservatives and departmental officials alike. He managed to put through important changes in electricity regulation which enabled the emergence of renewables (and nuclear).

By far the most important of my new Conservative colleagues was David Willetts, the universities minister, who had, not unreasonably, expected to be in the cabinet as a Secretary of State and had finished up as my Number 2, an indignity which he carried with great forbearance. He was exceptionally bright: the fabled 'two brains'. He was also a very likeable man: easy to deal with, good-humoured and devoid of pomposity.

Our first meeting, however, signalled the big problems ahead: he had immersed himself in university issues over several years, knew everyone of significance in the sector and had a clear road-map of where he wanted to go, including implementation of a report by Lord Browne, best known for his role at the energy company BP, which he had jointly commissioned with Peter Mandelson to prepare the ground for higher tuition fees.

By contrast, I knew next to nothing about the politics and financing of the sector beyond a conviction that my own party's tuition fee pledge and wider fees policy were mistaken and unsustainable. And my gut prejudices were that there were too many university (as opposed to further education) students and that was where we should be looking for cuts; and that universities were unacceptably complacent and provided poor value for money in their teaching. Unfortunately, these were views with which David passionately disagreed. Serious trouble ahead.

Looking back, it is hard to take in the sheer pace of our lives at the time. At the farm, we were haymaking and opening my small, walled garden (created in 2007/8) in aid of the local Air Ambulance, part of a village effort which raised £2,500. By the time I rejoined him, Vince had been negotiating the "emergency budget" with George Osborne early in the week but also doing Question Time *and a three-hour constituency surgery and its follow-up with Sandra Fayle, his very competent case-worker. Plus his Red Box. The weekend included an hour's dancing class and the local Lensbury Club Ball.*

On Sunday, V was on Andrew Marr *so set off early to rendezvous with his new spad to discuss the interview before going to the studio. On his return, there was a 'friendly' media interview with the* Mail on Sunday *to do with home-grown potatoes in grow-bags. The* MOS *sent Toby Swift from BBC's* Gardeners' World *to judge. There was a photographer and they all took it very seriously and for a long time. I had sweated for days over the garden to get it presentable. Our own potatoes were what my father would have called "fiddlin' an' small"!*

Family life was squeezed into the gaps: fetching V's son Hugo (who was working in Singapore at the time) from Heathrow on Saturday and having all Vince's children and two grandchildren to lunch on Sunday. By the time we went to a jazz festival in Bushy Park in the afternoon and a charity concert at Marble Hill House in the evening, we were seriously tired, so we skipped the supper in favour of sleep. For me, the sartorial codes, involving lots of changes of clothing, are enervating.

As the new government settled down, views about the coalition tended to polarise. The centre-left and left were hostile – often vituperatively so – and the Conservative-leaning press (most of it, in other words) saw the Lib Dems as cuckoos in the nest, me in particular. Even sympathetic observers were pessimistic about the future for the Lib Dems: "who will be squeezed once the first flush of enthusiasm fades... the arrangement may allow Labour to claim a monopoly on the centre-left".[20]

It became clear that the Lib Dems had collectively under-estimated the tribal character of British politics. Nick organised what he believed was a helpful seminar with

---

[20] Philip Stephens, "Cameron risks career, Clegg chances party", *Financial Times*, 12 May 2010.

leading European Liberals who told us all about consensual coalition politics and how to operate within it. They seemed to be from another planet.

I was also able to take stock of my own role in the coalition. I was not at the centre of coalition decision-making; it was clear that Nick Clegg and David Cameron wanted me on board the ship but not on the bridge and made that clear later when a quad emerged of Nick, Danny Alexander, David Cameron and George Osborne to resolve disputes in the coalition. Nor was I to have control of key decisions on the economy.

The upside was that I had a very big department with the potential to do a lot with the powers I had. And my personal popularity had held up with an approval rating of +24.[21] That mattered, not for reasons of personal vanity – though I am sure that played a part – but because it gave me a valuable, if depleting, asset which I could leverage to get things done. I was also difficult to sack. I could carve out an independent and critical voice within the coalition, however irritating to some of my Tory colleagues.

Making a success of this role required having a strategy for the department. Helped by the civil servants, I set up a process which involved speaking to all the 3,000+ head office staff in Westminster Central Hall with a TV overflow to staff in Cardiff and Sheffield, defining half a dozen policy or legislative priorities, repeated annually, followed by quarterly meetings with the top 200 and regular meetings with the top dozen directors.

One of the main challenges was to raise the self-

---

[21] *The Guardian*, 3 June 2010.

confidence of the department which was used to being treated as an adjunct to the Treasury and very much second-class citizens, especially in the years when Gordon Brown was chancellor. I was appalled when I first assembled staff to develop plans to get banks lending to business to find that they simply parroted the Treasury line that nothing could be done or said to upset the bankers. I was determined to bring in people like Lord Oakeshott, who were not so easily intimidated.

BIS officials had never quite recovered from the humiliation when Alan Johnson had renamed the department PENIS to reflect a new focus on Productivity as well as Enterprise, Innovation and Science. But there were some nuggets of gold: officials who had vast, accumulated experience after years of toiling anonymously in the department and were passionate about their specialist knowledge of particular sectors. And Peter Mandelson had undoubtedly boosted the department by bringing in post-18 education, including universities, though the new department had yet to gel and universities were in open revolt about the vulgar insult of being classified as 'business' rather than 'education'.

The first big challenge was the round of immediate cuts and taxes, to raise £12 billion, about half from in-year spending cuts. Seen from a big picture perspective, this didn't seem a particularly serious problem: involving well under 1 per cent of public spending. However, the way in which Whitehall operates made this an extremely difficult problem, as I soon discovered.

Officials insisted that vast areas of the department were off-limits for a variety of reasons: 'ring-fences' of various kinds; rigid staff contractual arrangements; commitments to various institutions like universities, which had to be honoured come what may. The fact that I was new to the departmental brief and knew little about many of the programmes and projects made it difficult to argue back.

I established that there was a whole set of commitments which had been made by Peter Mandelson, on behalf of the outgoing government, without value-for-money approval from the officials. They included the refurbishment of Blackpool Tower and others with a blatant political objective.[22] Ken Clarke had described my predecessor as 'like a Bourbon monarch going round in his coach throwing out gold coins'. This was an obvious place to cut.

Unfortunately for me, this list of questionable projects contained a proposed loan to engineering firm Sheffield Forgemasters for high-spec nuclear reactor equipment. The civil servants were divided on the economic justification for it. The project went on the bonfire of cuts. The word Sheffield should have set alarm bells ringing but I discovered too late that the very aggressive Sheffield Labour Party, together with the UNITE union and with the support of the *Sheffield Star*, was launching a vitriolic campaign against Nick Clegg, the MP for Sheffield Hallam, blaming him for the cancelled loan, and did him a good deal of political damage.

This was a big, bad mistake which I regretted, and I undoubtedly let Nick down. But it reinforced my determination to get some early changes in staff and have my private office looking out for elephant traps. Any manual

---

[22] Dominic Lawson, *Sunday Times*, 30 May 2010.

for incoming ministers should stress the need to scrutinise the small print of submissions from officials who, however impressive, are not primarily concerned with ministers' careers.

I made my first ministerial speech at London's then Cass (now Bayes) Business School explaining and justifying the government approach to the deficit: "If deficit reduction comes too rapidly, there is a danger of deeper recession and even bigger deficits. But, like the governor of the Bank of England and, like the OECD, I have changed my view on this. I have been persuaded that early action is necessary and that is what we are doing".[23]

I acknowledged that compensating measures needed to be taken to stimulate the economy through monetary policy, to bring pressure to bear on banks to increase lending to small firms and to implement other 'supply side' measures. The issue of bank lending was crucial since the standard Keynesian arguments for boosting demand through spending broke down if lack of credit prevented an expansion of output and investment

The Cass speech was also an opportunity to define the basic philosophy behind my approach to the work of BIS. The *Financial Times* gave a fair summary: "He has a vision for an active industrial policy – but it is market-led and organic, not statist... robustly liberal".[24] I majored on the 'dysfunctional' nature of the banking system' and the need for sticks as well as carrots to get finance flowing to business, especially small and midsize enterprises

---

[23] *The Guardian*, 4 June 2010.

[24] "Britain adopts an industrial policy", 4 June 2010.

(SMEs).[25] The speech received extensive coverage: "the Vince marathon – like a Castro speech with jokes".[26]

It achieved my objective of setting an overall framework for the department, working with business as the 'department of growth', but up for a fight with the banks over their lending policies.

The first wave of cuts created the platform for the June budget. The main action was the increase in VAT, which Nick Clegg had, unfortunately, committed the party very publicly to opposing during the election campaign. It was assumed in the press that I was opposed to the VAT rise: not so, it would have been one of my first steps as chancellor. There were so many exemptions for the essentials of life that the Institute for Fiscal Studies (IFS) called VAT "slightly progressive". The budget also lifted income tax thresholds and introduced the pensioners' triple-lock which ensured that, throughout the years of austerity, there was no return to pensioner poverty.

These were important Lib Dem priorities about which the Tories were, at best, lukewarm, though the public message was all about Conservative authorship. The budget was predictably attacked by – mainly Labour – critics as if it were the Slaughter of the First Born, but I had no problem defending it either in Parliament or on *Question Time*, with a hostile audience. Peter Hitchens pointed out with uncharacteristic matey-ness that: "If Vince had joined the coalition with Labour that he'd have preferred, he'd have

---

[25] *Metro*, 4 June 2010.
[26] Ann Treneman, *The Times*, 4 June 2010.

had to go through roughly the same performance."[27] The budget was a prelude to a full spending review and the cabinet was given the framework within which we were to negotiate for the next few months. The agreement across the coalition, which I had opposed, to ringfence big chunks of the public sector meant that the exercise promised to be painful for unprotected departments like mine.

There was also a subtle but significant moving of the goalposts. I had been careful to define, in the coalition agreement, what the objectives were: to cut the current deficit in the budget, and the structural element in it. By the time of the spending review, the Treasury had managed to redefine the coalition objective as being to cut all government borrowing for whatever purpose including capital spending – because 'that was how the markets saw it'. Yet capital spending was the key to economic recovery because of its linkages to the rest of the economy, mainly through construction, and it now faced serious cuts.

When I protested, it was clear that Nick and Danny Alexander, our new man at the Treasury (after David Laws' enforced resignation), had gone along with the Treasury arguments. One person who did get the point was Osborne, who agreed that cutting capital spending was the most economically damaging way to execute a programme of cuts. But, as we were to discover, he was 100 per cent political and saw every twist of policy as an opportunity to drive a political bargain.

In this case, he offered to reverse the public investment cuts if I agreed to back him in cabinet, demanding ever

---

[27] *Mail on Sunday*, 27 June 2010.

deeper cuts in welfare spending. I was not willing to do that and was left with the choice of soldiering on or walking out over an essentially technical argument few would understand.

There was relief from 'soldiering on' in the form of regional industrial visits and trade promotion overseas. My first was to Crewe to the Bentley factory operating at 40 per cent of capacity in the wake of the crisis but surviving in the UK and a rich source of high skill employment. Many other visits followed, and I developed a genuine enthusiasm for the manufacturing industry, inspired by the craftsmen and the managers and owners I met.

On Teesside, I went to the mothballed steel plant shortly to be taken over by a Thai firm: the source of much future drama. I saw the National Renewable Energy Centre (NAREC) wind turbine testing facility, to be a key contributor to the coming wind-power boom. And in Derby, I met the most skilled labour force in the country, at Rolls Royce, but was warned by chief executive Sir John Rose of the precariousness of the business when financial markets were so short term in outlook.

There was, in the manufacturing industry, a fierce determination to survive, born of years of battling the prevailing pessimism about manufacturing and the near-death experience of the crisis when credit lines were cut and markets collapsed. The best of the companies were world-class. A bonus from the visits was that the regional media were usually very interested in the visit and positive, in contrast to the metropolitan cynicism of the lobby. I relished the days away from the daily grind of back-to-back Whitehall meetings. It was also an occasion to meet local

Lib Dems and I sensed the growing apprehension of the grassroots at what the coalition was going to do to our city strongholds in the north.

And then there were the overseas visits. In marked contrast to the Brexiteers' later vision of virgin territories outside Europe, waiting to be explored by British companies freed from the shackles of Europe, what was blindingly obvious from the numbers was that, even within the EU, Britain lagged badly behind other EU countries in exporting to the big emerging markets: China, India, Russia, Indonesia and Brazil.

Fortunately, David Cameron shared my enthusiasm for raising our profile in the so-called BRIC group of countries (Brazil, Russia, India and China) and we planned a series of visits with business delegations to achieve that. We started with India, which gave me the opportunity to revive old Delhi contacts as well as to fly the flag while using my knowledge of the Indian economy. There was one delicious moment when I had to rescue Cameron on Indian TV after he was ambushed by hostile Indian journalists asking about Theresa May's unhelpful comments on student visas. But the visit was almost insultingly brief.

It wasn't long before another visit was scheduled: Brazil. The programme looked like an exquisite form of torture: endless meetings against the background of wonderfully interesting cities. I invited Rachel, who was keen to come. She would, of course, have to pay her way and not benefit from taxpayer subsidy. Even so, some of the civil servants were surprised. But I took the view that too many marriages were sacrificed for political careers and public duty. Early mornings and late nights combined with constituency work at weekends meant that I rarely saw my wife. On the visits, there was at least some downtime.

After three months of intense drama around the spending cuts and the politics of the coalition and getting to know the department, I wanted to make a serious contribution to address what I saw as the main reason for the economic crisis and the most important policy issue: the banks, to make them safe and get them lending to business again.

There were massive obstacles. The department was deferential. The Treasury officials were extraordinarily complacent: there was no real problem; the bankers of the City were the country's pride and joy – our main export industry and budget support; criticism, let alone action, was deeply unhelpful (I exaggerate only slightly). To cap it all, one of Alistair Darling's less positive legacies was putting the nationalised banks, mainly RBS and Lloyds, under an arms' length body – UK Financial Investments (UKFI) – whose members seemed determined not to let 'politics' invade 'operational matters,' which in practice meant practically everything.

Osborne did appreciate that bankers were toxic (and particularly toxic for the Tory party as he acknowledged in cabinet) and went along with modest reforms. And he was egged on by leading Tories: David Davis (with whom I had written a strongly worded cross-party report, also with John McFall) and John Redwood (who wanted to split up RBS). One would have thought that a 'crisis of capitalism' centred on the banking system would have generated political and intellectual radicalism on the Left rather than the Right, with lots of ideas for bank reform. Not so.

Labour was developing a narrative that the fiscal consolidation – austerity – of the government was entirely driven by ideological, free-market, bigotry combined with a wilful disregard for Keynesian economics; that it was designed to undermine the public services built up under a Labour government. Whilst such notions were undoubtedly motivating some Conservatives, it was breathtaking that, on the Left, the banking crisis and its crippling effects on the budget and the credit system, was just airbrushed out of history. The nearest we came to an alternative view was Ed Balls' campaign against bankers' bonuses which, by this point, had fallen dramatically in any event but were still a red rag to the bull of public opinion.

In developing a challenge to the inertia of the financial and government establishment, I had only my spad, Giles Wilkes, and the benefit of ideas coming through the morning press from good economic journalists like Martin Wolf on the *FT* and Alex Brummer on the *Mail*. I was also keen to make use of Matthew Oakeshott's financial experience. I arranged for him to have a security pass to come into the department to offer advice, despite fierce resistance from officials who hated the informality of the arrangement and regarded him as trouble.

I met the bank chiefs regularly, alone or with Osborne. Initially, the leader of the group was John Varley of Barclays who behaved towards me like an old-style colonial governor faced with a local 'terrorist' from the independence movement: a mixture of extreme distaste, apprehension and incomprehension. Neither of us knew then that he would face criminal charges in relation to the attempts to forestall nationalisation, over which Matthew and I had given him a hard time when we were in opposition.

The new head of Lloyds, Antonio Horta-Osorio arrived with clean hands but sullied his reputation at the outset by demanding an extraordinary salary and bonus package which then set a benchmark for the top banks. But he was subsequently helpful and went out of his way to prioritise business lending and to keep me in the loop.

The newcomer at the top table was Stephen Hester, who had replaced the disgraced 'Fred the Shred' Goodwin as CEO of RBS. We did not hit it off. He had two concerns: what he saw as the overriding priority to clean up the RBS balance sheet: an important task which he was, clearly, good at. The other was to defend his own financial package which had to be bigger than his competitors'. My concerns with bank lending to small and medium-sized business and the growing scandal around the activities of the Global Resource Group – which preceded him – he regarded with barely concealed irritation. We had less to do with Douglas Flint at HSBC, which had kept clear of the bank collapse.

There were several overlapping issues to deal with. The first was to settle with Osborne the composition and mandate of the commission to look at bank structure. Osborne treated it as a genuinely joint project: the commission included my nomination of radical reformers including Martin Wolf of the *FT*, Martin Taylor a former Barclays banker who had spoken out for reform, and Clare Spottiswood, a consumer champion; I accepted his favourite investment banker, Bill Winters; and we had a respected academic chair – John Vickers.

The second and more difficult problem was bank lending. The banks were refusing to lend to SMEs which they regarded as high risk and were liquidating their portfolios of SME loans to raise cash to boost their cash reserves. So, thousands of exporters couldn't export, builders couldn't build, growth companies couldn't grow and start-ups couldn't start because of a lack of access to finance. The government guarantee scheme was insufficient to cover the risk and too complicated.

Later, I would get some money from the Treasury to start the British Business Bank but, at this stage, I was reduced to haranguing the banks in private and public, demanding that they set and observe net lending targets. I was joined, at least in exhortation, by the chancellor in a public warning: "We'll change rules to make you lend."[28] The banks replied that any patriotic duty to save British business was trumped by bank regulation, including exceptional high-risk weights for business loans. Adair Turner, the regulator, and Mervyn King at the Bank of England told me the rules were immutable. The British regulators blamed the EU and the EU blamed the Bank of International Settlements in Basle: one of the several cases of major decisions being determined by obscure accounting regulations which no one could change to deal with new facts. The bankers hit back not just at me but at the Prime Minister and the governor of the Bank of England. As the departing chief executive of Lloyds put it: "Daniels: Forcing us to lend won't work."[29]

Then there were bankers' bonuses, especially for the investment bankers, which had an incendiary effect on a

---

[28] *Daily Mail*, 2 August 2010.

[29] *City AM*, 5 August 2010.

public increasingly chafing against hardship produced by the said bankers, but which Hester and Varley, in particular, tried to protect (the latter on behalf of his successor, the notorious Bob Diamond, among others). I wanted a transparent bonus disclosure system, but compromised with Osborne on a scheme which revealed the numbers of pay-outs above a certain level per bank and which an assiduous journalist could use to identify the biggest bonuses.

A particular headache was the pay at the top of RBS, as a nationalised bank. Cameron, in particular, hated my 'banker bashing', but agreed that Hester couldn't just behave as if the financial crisis had never happened and had to be reined in. The matter was taken out of the hands of UKFI and with Osborne and Clegg we hammered out a deal in Cameron's office. Hester bitterly resented the 'interference' but didn't walk away.

We were, however, dealing with an amoral culture rather than an individual. And it was a culture that appeared to accept no responsibility for the fact that rewarding reckless behaviour had led to the taxpayer footing the bill for the collapse of banks. I thought the public was in a mood for the greediest and most culpable bankers to be hung from the lamp-posts. But there was no criminal route to prosecute them. Osborne shared my frustration that a Financial Services Authority (FSA) report into the failure of RBS was kept secret.[30]

We brought in legislation covering reckless behaviour

---

[30] "Cable demands details of FSA's secret report into RBS collapse", *The Guardian*, 8 December 2010.

but too late for the villains of 2008. I sought investigations by the regulator and Companies House into the directors of RBS, but I knew it would take years of plodding inquiry and legal appeal to nail any fault. The baton passed from me to parliamentary select committee hearings, where the offenders would have their reputations trashed, if nothing more. But I was reassured that what the critics called 'puerile banker bashing' had support from thoughtful business commentators.[31]

August 2010: *After an intense early summer of taking on the banks, V desperately needed an August break: a week in a cottage in Burgundy which we had 'won' in a Lib Dem fundraising auction. Blissful peace, sleep and good French food interspersed with exercise, cycling along the nearby canal and visits to historic Burgundian towns like Beaune.*

The only interruption was a telephone call to V's phone from Arcadia Group chairman Sir Philip Green complaining about V's comments in the press on his tax avoidance. No idea how he got the telephone number. But he gave V a long harangue on how much he was contributing to the UK economy and how V needed his services to get his department operating as efficiently as Topshop. People like him always seem to think that the government of business is the same thing as the business of government.

The last week of August was a welcome breather on the

---

[31] "Don't go soft on the bankers: Vince Cable is right to keep his foot on the throat of the bankers", *Daily Mail*, 27 November 2010.

farm, but busy. The beef distribution to customers had to be rearranged because the butcher was running late with vacuum-packing it all. But Applejack the bull loaded quietly to go home to his owners on Wednesday and my friend Gail helped me sort beef on Friday morning, before setting off for London with the last trays of meat destined for customers there (and clothing suitable for Brazil!).

I accompanied V on his Brazil trip: not cheap (since spouses, rightly, have to pay their way; but it means we get more time together and I am useful in my "Figaro" role as valet and barber). And I was keen to see a bit of South America, a continent I'd never been to. Arriving at Sao Paulo, we had four police outriders to escort our convoy of three big black cars with darkened windows. At one point we were driving the wrong way down motorways in the face of oncoming traffic swept out of the way by the outriders. Somehow, we reached the consul's residence – in a nice bit of this enormous city (population over 20 million) on a slight hill. The consul's attractive wife Dilsa is Brazilian and was warm and welcoming.

From the British Centre V, did a 'Town Hall' meeting by video link with Brasilia and Rio. Finally, we got an hour of 'down time' with a quick swim in the pool at the residence; then a reception for 150-200: filling snacks as dinner, meeting people doing business in Brazil or wanting to, all seemingly wanting a piece of V.

The next day, museums for me and the Stock Exchange for V with a quick visit to the cathedral before flying to Brasilia. The phalanx of drivers, guards and outriders were causing chaos, waiting for the secretary of state to set off for the airport. Eventually, the police outriders decided they wanted a photograph with V at the steps of the cathedral and this stirred the interest of the public, including the rough sleepers and various soapbox orators attacking politicians of all persuasions and nationalities.

After a day and a bit in Sao Paulo, another day and a bit in Brasilia. The embassy is a stunning modern house with a beautiful garden. Then I got to see the sights while V did ministerial visits. Late lunch and off to Rio.

Finally, Rio. Copacabana is not a disappointment: a wide, long, beach with perfect sand. Our hotel suite has fabulous views over the bay. The favelas creep up the steep hillsides behind us, like reverse lava flows. We are getting used to vast double beds, but this has a double-width bath, too- and a sauna room!

On to dinner with the consul general, mainly with people from the petro-world, then a late-night visit to a samba place with live bands and dancing. Next day, I got the chance to sample the beach; people kept warning us about the violence but it felt extraordinarily safe, with the beach immaculately maintained and unobtrusively policed.

Last day – Saturday – is the end of V's programme, so we set off to see the city with a driver and a guard, insisted on by the embassy. Not disappointed by the Cristo Redemptor statue; it is monumental but beautiful, the surface tessellated, not bland concrete as I had feared – and there are stupendous views. After ambling around the cobbled streets of Santa Teresa we got to the amazing cathedral. V loves the peace and timelessness of churches. This one is dark inside so that stained glass windows are the only source of light. From the outside it is like a giant *spaceship and very dark but inside it is cool and a haven from the heat and bustle of the city.*

On the way back to London I am upgraded to business class, courtesy of the Brazilian airline VARIG, which is bliss.

The key political event of September was the party conference season which, this year, would be in Liverpool for the Lib Dems. This was the first time to take stock of the coalition together with our activists.

But that was not straightforward. As ministers we were surrounded by security and missed the easy informality of fringe meetings. There was also a concerted attempt to have us and the Tories singing from the same song-sheet.

The White Elephant; Steve Bell in *The Guardian*, 23 September 2010 (*picture courtesy of Steve Bell*).

We were asked to share our speeches. Mine horrified No 10. I had a personal call from David Cameron asking me to remove the more provocative bits. I gave some ground on the language but kept the substance.

I thought it was crucial to highlight the battles we were fighting, the differences between the parties, and our distinctive identity. I thought our members appreciated my speech, but the Tories hated it and the Tory press went to town on it, particularly my comments on bankers and unaccountable businesses: "On banks I make no apology for attacking spivs and gamblers who did more harm to the British economy than Bob Crow could achieve in all his Trotskyite fantasies, while paying themselves outrageous bonuses under-written by the taxpayer", "I am shining a harsh light on the murky world of corporate behaviour" and "capitalism takes no prisoners and kills competition where it can".

The press was divided as between critics of my 'puerile banker bashing'[32] and supporters.[33] There was some recognition of the need to cheer up our own troops.[34] Serious business commentators were supportive: "Ignore the screams of rage, Cable's spot on over spivvery"[35]. But I earned the accolade "anti-Business Secretary"[36]; and there were lots of satirical jibes: "Comrade Cable tests the coalition's cohesion with capitalist attack."[37]

---

[32] Alistair Osborne, *Daily Telegraph*, 23 September 2010.

[33] *Daily Mirror*, 23 September 2010.

[34] Matthew Engel, *Financial Times*, 23 September 2010.

[35] Chris Blackhurst, *Evening Standard*, 27 September 2010.

[36] City *AM* and *Daily Telegraph*, 23 September 2010.

[37] *The Scotsman*, 23 September 2010.

The *Mail* ran a feature 'Was he a Marxist?', but concluded that I wasn't and wrote a supportive editorial 'Not all bad, Vince.... Wasn't there much truth in Vince Cable's controversial speech to the Lib Dems?'[38] David Cameron pronounced himself 'relaxed', recognising that 'Vince is Vince'.[39]

The speech was also the backcloth to my announcement of consultations on takeovers and executive pay which were to provide the evidence base for reforms to come to fruition the following year.

There was, however, one event the significance of which passed me by at the time. I was invited to have dinner with the *Telegraph* and was surprised to find not just the editor but members of the corporate board representing the owners. They wanted to talk about Murdoch. I was at that time sitting on the application for News International to take over the remaining shares in BskyB on which I was to adjudicate, but had at that stage thought little about it as I waited for interested parties to make submissions. I said very little. But I picked up some of the fear and loathing of Murdoch amongst what we cheerfully dismissed as 'the Tory press'.

September 18–22 2010: *Party conference in Liverpool. We had a tyre blow out on the way up – luckily at a reasonably quiet time on the toll road – but not good for my nerves or our schedule.*

Last day. Vince gives the final speech and he's set off to

---

[38] *Daily Mail*, 23 September 2010.
[39] *Daily Telegraph*, 25 September 2010.

do telly etc. He hasn't had a working day of less than 15 hours. I have to go and get the spare tyre sorted.

We had supper with the Times journalists on Sunday night and the Mail on Sunday gang on Monday. The latter included Suzanne Moore and Peter Hitchens, one on each side of me. Talk about upper and nether millstones! I immediately liked her but he seemed to be a rather unhappy character, pretty right-wing but anti-war in Afghanistan.

The only thing we had in common was Worthing where we had each spent a bit of our childhood. Having read his brother's book Hitch 22, I knew the extraordinary story of how his parents had kept secret the fact that his mother was Jewish (seemingly to gain acceptance in their social milieu) and her tragic and probably unintended suicide.

September 30 2010: I have not been sleeping well this week, provoked partly by dashing up to London to be at supper with party colleagues – at V's request – to discuss strategies for surviving the spending review, which seems a bit like the old lady who swallowed a fly, then a spider and then a bird, then a cat, until she swallowed a horse and was DEAD, OF COURSE.

He is swallowing very unpalatable stuff on tuition fees but wants to walk away if he is required to decimate all further education and science. The Treasury is bound to play hardball until the last possible minute. Everyone is urging him to stay at least until after the referendum on fairer votes in May.

Chapter Four

A season of disasters

We returned from Liverpool to the final stages of the spending review. I was better prepared than for the first round of cuts, with a first-class private office led by Jo Crellin, my spads in place and a good negotiating team who realised that I was there for the long term; and I had a positive vision for BIS. I accepted that there would be severe cuts; indeed, the outgoing Labour government had pencilled in 25 per cent cuts for the department. But rather than shave the same amount off everything, I set out some priorities to protect or increase (or cut less than the norm).

One was an enlarged programme of vocational education through apprenticeships. Regard for post-school education and training had been in decline for decades because of the aspiration of middle-class families to send their children to – heavily subsidised – universities. The bias was deeply embedded in Whitehall since almost everyone was a graduate and expected their children to become one. My commitment to apprenticeships was inspired by my father, who had devoted his professional life to vocational training in Further Education colleges for the building industry. Fortunately, a Tory minister in my department – John Hayes – shared my passion and helped me fight the battle over funding priorities.

Another priority was adult education. Most Treasury and BIS officials had no interest in it and lazily assumed it was all about basket weaving for middle-class women. I was made aware by my mother, a factory girl, who left school at 15 and who later had serious mental health problems, of the therapeutic effect of discovering education in adult life. Moreover, the idea of continuous education seemed the obvious way forward in a society faced with rapid technological change and the need to reinvent careers. To the bafflement of officials, I saved some adult programmes.

They were equally baffled that I prioritised the Post Office network. I had campaigned for years as a local MP and a Lib Dem spokesman against the run-down of the network under successive governments which were depriving many communities of an essential service. With Ed Davey, I secured money to modernise the service and enable it to provide financial services as the banks retreated. The shocking, false, allegations of fraud against some postmasters based on computer error was at the time subject to court proceedings and had hardly surfaced as an issue.

My other priorities included funding for high-cost subjects in universities: science, engineering and medicine. This seemed to me far more important than subsidising tuition for all or packing in more students regardless of aptitude or commitment. Nonetheless, I found myself in an unwanted row with the science community, whose budget was protected by a ring fence, when I decided to prioritise business-oriented innovation.

I discovered that there was a bizarre Whitehall convention which treated publicly funded research (in R&D) differently from development. It helped to explain something which had long mystified me: why the world-famous National Physical Laboratory in my constituency (a D) was faced with financial crises at a time when money was being poured into research (R). I sought to level up the treatment which, because it benefitted D at the expense of R, prompting Nobel Prize winners to write angry letters to the *Times* and besiege Downing Street with calls.

The argument was defused when Osborne came up with more money for the pure scientists. I put more money into the government-funded innovation agency Innovate UK and initiated a national network of innovation centres which became the Catapult network. This was helped by a conversation which I recalled with the journalist, Will Hutton, who had managed to get through to me on my mobile phone in my first day in the office, recommending that, if I didn't do anything else, I should read a report by a Cambridge venture capitalist called Herman Hauser on the need to apply the German Fraunhofer model of innovation centres in the UK.

Painful though the cuts were, the negotiations were thought by the department to have produced a far better outcome than it had initially feared, and I got some credit for defending the department's turf and establishing clear priorities. There was, however, one discordant note. The acting Permanent Secretary, Philip Rutnam, had led the very able negotiating team but then put a piece of paper in front of me to sign, seemingly designed to give him some form of absolution from responsibility for adverse consequences of the cuts.

Other civil servants told me that it was unheard of. I refused to sign; then heard no more about it. But almost a decade later, when Rutnam was Permanent Secretary at the

Home Office, he was sacked on the instructions of Priti Patel who was then accused of breaking the ministerial code for 'bullying'. I don't know what happened there but have a fleeting sympathy for the Home Secretary. In due course, he was replaced by Martin Donnelly, who proved to be a good and supportive permanent secretary.

I learned, too, that Conservative colleagues across government varied greatly in their commitment to implement the promised cuts. Dr Liam Fox at Defence claimed to be a fiscal hawk, but lobbied publicly – with his generals – for more money for defence. The right-wing press had orchestrated leaks from the chiefs of staff blatantly lobbying for special treatment. This led me to attack the military in a cabinet meeting when I called for the chiefs to resign or be sacked. I obviously crossed some invisible red line since David Cameron, visibly shaken, asked me to see him privately later. He appealed to me not to tell the press what I had said and, while I honoured the request, the episode opened my eyes to his deeply conservative instincts.

At the other extreme was Eric Pickles, who wanted the biggest cuts in his own department, Communities and Local Government (DCLG), as soon as possible. The consequences for local government and social housing are felt to this day. There was a particular difficulty for me in that our departments co-financed the Regional Development Agencies. I shared his scepticism about the value of some of the RDAs but wanted to keep reformed agencies in the north east, north west and Yorkshire, which served a necessary regional development function and to scrap those in the south.

Pickles revelled in his reputation as a blunt no-nonsense Yorkshireman and came to my office to tell me very firmly that he wanted to scrap the lot immediately and wouldn't contribute anything to the funding; so the system was entirely closed down, causing BIS a major headache in unscrambling assets and liabilities and leaving a big gap in regional policy.

In its place, Nick Clegg managed to mobilise some money for a regional growth fund, run out of BIS, to be based on the recommendations of a business panel led by Michael Heseltine. It funded some excellent projects, alongside private investors, but was temporary and limited in funding. What remained of decision making in the regions were some largely voluntary Local Enterprise Partnerships (LEPs), which lacked funding and institutional support. All of this contributed to the malaise in north-south relations which contributed to Brexit five years later. The post-Brexit, post-pandemic, preoccupation with 'levelling up' and 'building back better' involves yet another attempt to reinvent the wheel of regional policy.

The corollary of my prioritisation was that some things were deprioritised. Amongst them was the straightforward subsidies for university teaching. The crisis over tuition fees was slowly building, but I had alerted Nick Clegg and my Lib Dem colleagues to the fact that there was absolutely no way that we could avoid raising tuition fees unless some device could be found to rebrand the fee-loan repayments as a graduate tax, which, in effect, they were.

Arguments raged behind the scenes and Osborne set up a task force in the Treasury to explore the scope for some accounting device to enable universities to be funded by graduate contributions later in life which were not called 'fees'. But the timer on the unexploded bomb was ticking.

Late October 2010: *Last weekend, Vince was in meltdown, having heard on the radio that the defence budget reduction is a mere 7 to 8 per cent instead of the 15 per cent agreed in cabinet – a reward, as V saw it, for bad behaviour as Liam Fox and the military chiefs of staff have been voluble in the press for weeks. He requested a phone call with Osborne who claimed he had tried to speak to V on Saturday afternoon but didn't get through until 10 pm on Sunday, by which time he had 'found' £400 million for V's science budget without him even asking for it! On Monday, he came home at midnight and said another £36 million had been added to his budget to defuse the row.*

But the budget settlement had resulted in the Lib Dems being forced to do a U-turn on university tuition fees and, as the minister responsible, there is damage to his reputation. He knows that he argued in the shadow cabinet before the election to accept the need for universities to be funded by higher graduate contributions but was overruled and had then had to follow Nick Clegg in signing the pledge to vote against higher fees, albeit not on camera like the other MPs.

We called in at Shirley Williams' office. She had asked to see him and quizzed him pretty sharply about the whole tuition fees strategy. It's hard to recall that she goes back so far, having grappled with these issues in the first Wilson government. She is now 80 years old. She had some shrewd and creative suggestions for dealing with the gap between the Russell Group and the 'lesser' universities.

When V referred to the complexity of university funding, she glared at him and said "Vince, I do know. I was the Education Secretary for two years".

The final stages of the spending review were emotionally draining which was unfortunate since the really big battles were still to come over tuition fees, Murdoch and the economic strategy in the face of what looked to be a 'double dip' recession. But I was able to take some satisfaction from the endorsement of parts of the press which had hitherto been personally critical as in the *Times* applauding the achievements of the coalition after six months.[40]

I was, however, anxious not to lose sight of why we were engaged in this painful process: the history of the crisis and its aftermath. The Tories had developed a simple narrative that we had a budget problem because Gordon Brown had wasted vast amounts of money and left a big deficit behind. Like Labour's equally dishonest story that it was all the fault of the coalition, it conveniently overlooked the havoc caused by the banking crisis which accounted for almost all the deficit.

Unfortunately, some leading Lib Dems were starting to echo the Tory message which was not just wrong because it

---

[40] "The strains of the Comprehensive Spending Review were almost entirely in the blue corner. Liam Fox's special pleading at the Ministry of Defence tested the patience of No. 11 Downing St as did Iain Duncan Smith's half-baked plans for welfare. Meanwhile, Vincent Cable's stature and that of his department were enhanced by his handling of the spending round" (Editorial, *The Times*, 30 October 2010).

reinforced a false history, but was helping to gloss over the real causes of the banking crisis: the credit boom which preceded it and the anti-social behaviour of some in the banking community. I tried to set the record straight at the Confederation of British Industry's (CBI'S) annual conference as a background to launch an initiative to rein in executive pay.

The right-wing press was predictably excited.[41] The public spat did, however, bring to the surface what I regarded as a big victory when Cameron told the CBI that the government would delay selling shares in RBS and Lloyds so that it could influence the banks' lending policies. And Osborne, at the same CBI conference, announced his proposed tax on bank balance sheets which was designed as a form of insurance premium to pay for the fact that the taxpayer was carrying the risk of banks being 'too big to fail' (and he was attacked for it by the CBI Director General). I was the most strident critic of the banks but, at this stage, Cameron and Osborne were pushing in the same direction.

But while I savoured these little bits of good news and good publicity, I was having sleepless nights worrying about the coming crisis over tuition fees. The arithmetic coming out of the spending review was stark: tuition fees, paid through the fee-loan system, would have to rise to over £8,000 to make the numbers add up. An educational and political issue was being dictated by public accounting conventions; a straightforward payment to universities for

---

[41] "Cable mocks Tories on recession" (*Daily Mail*, 26 October 2010) and "Cable dig at PM over downturn" (*Daily Telegraph*, 26 October 2010).

teaching was 'public expenditure', but a payment to universities which came indirectly via a loan to students did not (other than an amount set aside for defaults on the loans).

The alternatives were all unpalatable: we could slash the number of students qualifying for fee-loans, and therefore in practice for university admission, which David Willetts and Nick Clegg and almost everyone else except me would not consider; take an even bigger, probably terminal, bite out of FE colleges and apprenticeships which I was not willing to do; remove all the grants and loans for student maintenance, which would have killed off the possibility of low-income students going to university, which none of us were willing to do; or to sacrifice both research and high cost STEM subjects in the interest of subsidising fees, which Willetts and I were not willing to do. So, we were left with higher fees and the problem of the Lib Dem pledge.

We had joined the government to embrace the world of tough choices but were stuck with commitments made in the world of perpetual opposition. Ever since the Blair government had introduced tuition fees, Lib Dems had opposed them and unsurprisingly found a good response on university campuses. I had long regarded the policy of universal free tuition, initially in a minority of one amongst Lib Dem MPs, as a serious obstacle to being taken seriously on economic matters and I found the arguments of Labour ministers compelling. There had been a growing number of shadow cabinet allies, including Nick Clegg, keen to drop the policy in the 2010 manifesto. Despite the best efforts of Nick and Danny, however, party activists fought back and insisted on keeping it in the manifesto..

Nick's team then decided to get some political credit out of the defeat by having Nick, very publicly, signing the National Union of Students' pledge not to raise fees. David Laws and I initially refused to sign. It was then pointed out that, as deputy leader, my refusal would be portrayed as a display of disloyalty only a few weeks from an election. I reluctantly signed, but kept well away from cameras. I have berated myself ever since for not standing my ground which would have caused a nasty row at the time, but might have spared the party the agonising consequences of a collective breach of the pledge.

In government, I had two strategies to deal with the problem: one was to negotiate with Willetts the best compromise available to make the fee-loan system 'progressive' by lifting the threshold at which graduate repayments started and otherwise sugaring the bitter pill for students. There were weeks of fraught discussions trying to juggle numbers within public sector balance sheet conventions to get an acceptable policy.

The other ploy was to describe the policy as a 'graduate tax' (which it was). I had been trailing the graduate tax idea for months but there were some practical problems, at least with a pure graduate tax. A low tax on all past graduates might have been sellable politically, but would have involved retrospective taxation and, anyway, there was no database of graduates; so it had to be a tax on new graduates. Then, either the tax was a national tax which went to the Treasury and removed the autonomy of universities which David Willetts was not willing to compromise on; or it was paid to individual universities which could, legally, only apply a 'fee' not a 'tax'. Then there were EU students who could legally be charged 'fees' but not 'taxed' because tax was not an EU competence.

The *coup de grâce* was delivered by Lord Browne, whose report on student financing featured a trenchant attack on the idea of a national graduate tax. He invited me to dinner at his beautiful house in Chelsea, decorated with exquisite art and sculptures. In his impeccably mannered, rather precious, way he explained that I risked taking on not just the combined weight of the universities but also him, if I persisted with this bad idea. I was not sure if he ever got my point that I was not remotely concerned with overturning centuries of university independence, the legacy of Tudor monarchs and Oliver Cromwell, but simply to find a form of words which would help us to deal with an awkward political problem.

I looked for a year's delay to find the solution, but Willetts was preoccupied by timetables; the universities had to print next year's prospectus with the level of fees. Like train timetables in 1914, there wasn't the flexibility to stop a war. Then parliamentary draftsmen opined that there was no way of presenting 'fees' as a form of graduate tax even if that were the reality. So the accountants, lawyers, parliamentary clerks and printers sealed the exit doors and I had to prepare my colleagues for their fate. Like Gulliver on his travels, we were not defeated in some epic battle of policy ideas but by being tied down by large numbers of pieces of string.

In the meantime, there was time for trade diplomacy and a visit to China with Cameron to meet the President (Hu Jintao) and others. I savoured every minute of the all-too-brief China visit which rekindled an interest from a decade earlier, carrying out scenario planning in China for Shell prior to massive investment.

Then, out of the blue, came an invitation from the BBC to perform on the Christmas edition of television's *Strictly Come Dancing*. There was no precedent for serving cabinet ministers to get involved in events of this kind, but I thought it was a risk worth taking, even if a few colleagues would disapprove.

October 22 2010: *Royal Banquet for the Emir of Qatar.* *The official car wafted us to Windsor Castle. The flower arrangements stunning and the company glamorous. I managed a minimalist curtsy without falling over my trailing skirts. The Emir was a rather large gentleman with a very beautiful wife wearing a stylish turban.*

The Queen seemed tiny and silvery white – white skin, white dress, diamond tiara – and the Duke was very wiry and tanned, like a retired jockey. Later they were in a procession in which the leading participants included a bejewelled Camilla (whom I had last met many years before in her blue jeans at her home in Wiltshire), the rather red-faced Duke of Kent and the very regal Princess Royal, who had opened our affordable housing in Brockenhurst in 1991.

I had someone labelled the Earl Marshal (EM) on my right and the Qatari ambassador on my left. When I asked the EM for his family name, he muttered something double-barrelled that I didn't quite catch, but later it transpired that he was the Duke of Norfolk – Eddie Norfolk as he disarmingly put it. He was extremely pleasant, and we had a good conversation about farming and land (I didn't dare ask how many acres to compare with my smallholding).

An officious waiter insisted on moving my programme towards the middle of the table, which was at least ten feet across. Unfortunately, there was butter attached to the underneath which then sat there when I retrieved the paperwork, an eye-catching small yellow pyramid. Eddie said not to worry but I did and eventually got a kind waiter to clear it up.

I noticed that the men on each side of me also did the wrong thing about the toasts: raising their glasses when the toast was announced rather than waiting until after the appropriate anthem was over. It was easier to enjoy now that the formalities were familiar: speeches first and then a brisk pace set on serving the meal, bagpipers circling around the hall twice to indicate the meal at an end and drowning out further attempts at conversation, followed by coffee in the next room. And the Great Hall is well worth a mention. If the table was ten feet wide it must have been 200 feet long, with at least 150 people round it. This is in the restored north wing, complete with knights in suits of armour seeming to burst out of the walls and heraldic devices over the entire vaulted ceiling.

November 9 2010: None of V's aches and pains put him off from accepting an invitation to dance on the Strictly Christmas Show. So far, this has involved having a medical and one practice session with Erin Boag, his lovely partner, at a gym in Kingston. I glimpsed a furtive paparazzo trying to catch them in a compromising *embrace as we left!*

On Saturday, he left for Beijing on his five-day visit to China. Today, the PM joined him there. Some of the press are presenting this as a 'trade versus ethics' issue, with the Chinese artist, Ai Weiwei – the one whose ceramic sunflower seeds are currently several inches deep on the floor of the Tate's Turbine Hall – getting almost as much air time as Cameron. V looks tired in the few glimpses I have seen of him.

Back in London the main task ahead was to manage the launch of the fee increase and to get the parliamentary party ready for the inevitable explosion around student fees. As to the first, the politics of the university sector was complex and difficult. There were three main 'mission' groups, plus Universities UK, trying to present a common view, together with the students' union, the NUS, riven by factional left-wing politics, the Student Loan Company in Glasgow, which had recently come close to collapse because of administrative failures, and the funding body Higher Education Funding Council for England (HEFCE), which came closest to understanding how the system actually worked financially.

The most influential mission group was the Russell Group: the elite. They had vastly disproportionate influence, reflecting the Oxbridge culture around the top of Whitehall. They also had a very glamorous and capable woman who ran the organisation and seemingly had the male vice-chancellors twisted around her little finger. They not only had a strong sense of entitlement but were in a grumpy mood because of Theresa May's hostility to overseas students, one of their main sources of income, and because the spending review had involved some loss of income, even with higher fees. The mid-range universities were more reasonable and appreciated that we were trying to help them.

Another very grumpy bunch was the Million+ group, including some of the newest universities. Their chair was a rather militant vice-chancellor from Bedfordshire (Luton, in fact) who gave me something of a rant with the standard Left critique of the evils of student debt and that everything in education should be free, etc. On the principle that poachers make the best gamekeepers I appointed him – Les Ebdon – to head the regulatory body overseeing university admissions policies, much to the fury of Michael Gove, who tried unsuccessfully to get the PM to block the appointment of a known 'lefty'.

As for the students, I had met the NUS executive in Liverpool and it was clear that – as Labour or far left activists – they were going to squeeze maximum campaigning opportunities from the discomfort of the coalition and Lib Dems in particular. They hinted that they would moderate protests if we stayed below £6,000. Even if we could trust them to honour the hint, the numbers didn't add up without savaging FE which didn't seem to concern them.

The party was committed in the coalition agreement to abstaining on any vote on tuition fees. I could hardly abstain on my own policy (though I unwisely left that option open in an interview). As Matthew Parris noted in his *Times* column, 'his offer to abstain if all other Lib Dems did so was one of those offers you don't expect to be taken up and it won't.[42] I offered Nick Clegg the prospect of introducing the policy, letting him and the rest of the Lib Dems abstain. He knew my true feelings about the Lib Dem pledge and, anyway,

I had sufficient political credit stored from my various outbursts during the coalition to be able to weather the storm. But Nick was adamant that I should not be in that position. I wasn't sure then, or later, whether he was trying to protect me or was afraid that I would expose our disagreement over the handling of the pledge.

Another reason was feedback from the whips that, with some Lib Dems committed to voting against come what may, and some Tories also wanting to oppose the fee increase, the numbers were not there to allow collective abstention. So the parliamentary group would split three ways.

University fees, public spending cuts and the banks were testing the limits of my appetite for punishment. But I could see another fight coming over another of my responsibilities: licensing for arms exports, an issue where I had established a somewhat priggish reputation in opposition.

My past caught up with me when I had a call from David Cameron telling me that my appointment had caused deep unhappiness in Riyadh. The Saudis had been greatly offended by my campaign in Parliament, working with the *Guardian*, to expose corruption around the Al Yamamah arms contract originally signed by Margaret Thatcher and continuing to provide thousands of jobs in the aerospace

---

[42] *The Times*, 4 December 2010.

supply chain. The government's new anti-corruption legislation would curb future 'commission', 'facilitation payments' and 'hospitality'. I saw no problem having a 'selfie' with the ambassador but declined to add Saudi Arabia to my travel itinerary.

I drew comfort from the appointment of a new trade minister in the department: Stephen Green. I had met him when he headed up HSBC and was impressed by his thoughtfulness and decency (he was an Anglican priest as well as a banker). We discussed the somewhat queasy ethics of the arms trade and the criteria – the 'consolidated criteria' – governing licences.

We concluded that it was better to take responsibility rather than wash our hands of it. He was later to discover that God and Mammon did not mix well when his reputation was tarnished by a money-laundering scandal on his watch at HSBC.

Shortly after, I got an invite to a secret location in London to address a gathering of industrialists, ex-spooks and arms dealers, several of whom would be perfectly cast for the role of villains in Le Carré's *Night Manager*. I was able to reassure them that they were keeping the British economy afloat. I was also able to surprise them with my pedigree; 35 years earlier, as a First Secretary in the Foreign Office, I had played my part in kitting out the armouries of various Latin American states.

November 2010: My life is seesawing between our posh-urban-political life together and my scruffy-rural-farming life alone. Last month the banquet, this month the bog. The latter included visiting the state-of-the-art slaughterhouse at Laverstoke, halter-training calves, concluding the sale of two breeding cows and burying my dog, Lucy, the border collie I'd had for nearly 16 years. As all dog owners know, this is distressing stuff, especially as her lifetime spanned the period in my life from apparently happily married to divorced and on my own for four years, through to happily married again.

She had padded to and fro without mishap from my old home 300 yards away to my new one for four years, though increasingly deaf and doddery; but on Friday she was hit by a lorry. As I was in London without a car, it took me a while to get back by train so my son Dylan had taken her to the vet. With a broken leg and internal injuries suspected, we jointly decided to let her go. It's easy to say "where there's livestock, there's deadstock" but it's tough when it happens. I wrote a piece called "We all loved Lucy" and circulated it to the family. We buried her in the bluebell wood.

Another issue was heading to crisis point. James Murdoch called me, notifying me formally of the bid for BskyB. More and more submissions were coming in, mostly hostile. There was a lot of comment in the non-Murdoch press, especially the *Guardian*, highlighting the importance of the issue and the dangers of the 'Foxification' of the media. At that point I was detached, happy to be guided by evidence and careful to make no public comment. I had no particular beef against News International and the *Times*, in particular, had been fair in its coverage of the coalition and my role in it.

However, one day at City Airport I bumped into Claire

Enders, a media consultant, who asked if I had read her submission. I confessed that I hadn't noticed it amongst the dozens of others and undertook at least to read it. I did so subsequently, and it was a brilliantly clear and persuasive paper dissecting the issues around plurality. It helped to persuade me that I had no alternative but to refer the issue to the competition authorities via the regulator, Ofcom, which I did.

I was, however, beginning to worry about what was happening behind the scenes. Reports reached me of Lib Dem parliamentarians being approached by News International lobbyists trying to find out about my views and warning that if I was unhelpful this would be reflected in the treatment of the Lib Dems in the Murdoch press. The public attention, however, was on the Lib Dem fees drama with a parliamentary vote set for December 9.

December 6 2010: *We have been doorstepped again by journalists on Saturday and this morning (Monday). I am proud of my plan to foil them. I appear at the front door in my wacky hat to go for a paper at the newsagents opposite while V goes through the back door and escapes to the station through the grounds of a nearby church.*

December 7 2010: *There are two young women looking as if they are journalists at the door again. I went to get the paper at 9 am and sent them away. They were indignant: they had been there since 6 am in temperatures well below zero. I told them to go home and get warm.*

The student fees issue –or graduate contributions as we prefer to call them – is getting very ugly. It is a defining moment for the coalition and the Lib Dem party. Today is the parliamentary party meeting when a strategy has to be decided ahead of the vote on Thursday raising the cap on fees to £6,000 but extendable to £9,000 for universities with an acceptable admissions policy promoting social mobility.

I wish that this wasn't the battleground. It looks and feels awful. The proposal as I understand it is to take away the subsidy for university tuition except for Science, Technology, Engineering and Maths (STEM) subjects and to put all the money into the Student Loan Company for loans which students pay back later when they earn £22,000 or more. The effect is to reduce the government deficit but not government debt (under complicated government accounting rules).

December 8 2010: *When the BBC journalist asked how V was getting out of the house on the doorstep this morning, I asked him whether he had missed seeing the helicopter. I had lunch with Catherine Fenton, subeditor of the* Mail on Sunday's You *magazine. They wanted me to do a piece on my life for the column called* This Life.

The day of the parliamentary statement and vote was every bit as bad as I had expected. I read a statement against a wall of noise from the Labour back-benches and tried to justify the policy against the background of constant reminders of Lib Dem policy. It was a long way short of being a great parliamentary performance beyond the minimal achievement of getting through it.[43] There was a massive revolt in the vote. 21 colleagues voted against and five abstained with eight Tories also rebelling. Amongst our Lib Dem rebels were Charles Kennedy and Ming Campbell, both chancellors of Scottish universities (where the policy didn't apply).

Much worse was to come. There were riots in Parliament Square and, amongst other excesses, Nick Clegg was burnt in effigy, an indicator of the personal viciousness now being directed against him by extremists opposed to the coalition. The following day (Friday) I went to the local university: St Mary's in Twickenham. There were some heated but civilised exchanges. Then, when I went to my advice surgery nearby, I found a hundred or so demonstrators at the door (who, I discovered, had come from central London) and a couple of police officers trying to keep order.

I got inside with some difficulty to meet constituents with problems, but they were clearly frightened by the banging on the doors and windows and the abusive chanting. To try to defuse the situation, I agreed to see a delegation of half a dozen and we had a forceful but peaceful conversation, apart from one severely disabled man who I recognised from TV the previous day alleging police 'brutality' and who maintained a non-stop harangue. Eventually, I got them out of the office to join their comrades outside, by which time my constituents had fled, apart from two women. My staff were still inside with a local policeman, who looked lost and overwhelmed by events.

My PA was trying to signal to me that there was

---

[43] *The Guardian,* 10 December 2010.

something not quite right about the women, but I was too preoccupied to notice (they had put down local addresses which Joan Bennett, my PA, did not recognise and suspected were false). I was happy to keep talking to them in order to give time for the demonstrators to disappear and the subjects they raised – Osborne's proposals on child benefit and the impact on women of 'the cuts' – seemed innocuous enough.

I was sufficiently charged up to give vent to my feelings about aspects of coalition policy and issues that were coming up, like the BskyB decision when I let rip at the Murdoch empire, still seething after the intelligence I had been given that Lib Dem MPs were being intimidated by threats of what would happen if I made the 'wrong' decision.

I had no reason, at the time, to suspect that they were journalists with hidden microphones, though I realised afterwards that I had said too much. I went home hoping that the worst was over. I assumed, rather naively, that I was not being spied upon (I later discovered that my phone was being hacked and my rubbish bins were being examined for incriminating material).

December 12 2010: V had the most awful time last week introducing the Universities Bill to allow fees to rise from £3,300 to a maximum of £9,000. There were riots in Parliament Square in which some students and policemen were seriously injured.

There is something viscerally terrifying about watching mounted police in action.

The mood is very ugly with professional troublemakers hijacking the student protests. Then there are the indignant middle classes, vociferous in places like Twickenham. V's back pain is an exact barometer of the amount of stress he is feeling and is not good again. We now have two young policemen at our front gate. One of them said to me: "I didn't know this was where he lived", to which I replied: "Nor did anyone else till they saw you".

I went with him into London today. The European commissioner Michel Barnier was in town for the weekend at short notice and wanted to meet V to talk about the single market. We were on our way to a Lib Dem fixture, so I tagged along. V had described him as dry, but he was full of Gallic charm towards me, doing that clicking of heels combined with lifting my hand and simultaneously bowing, which is irresistibly appealing. If he was surprised to see me there too, he didn't show it and I can do a bit of French. He was quite didactic about what he would, and would not, tolerate, especially from the 'American protectionist lobby'.

It emerged that there is a small army of officials trying to make the EU single market work – on issues like professional qualifications and intellectual property rights – and as the originator of the single market he wanted the UK setting an example – which was where V came in.

The stress and agitation were preventing me enjoying what should have been the treat of being on *Strictly*. I had a good routine; Erin was a great coach and partner; and she was complimentary about my dancing technique. But in trying an ambitious lift I hadn't realised how unfit I had become after months without proper exercise and dislocated part of my spine trapping a nerve. The pain was very unpleasant but intermittent and I was getting through the day and the practice sessions. I just had to hold it together for a week or so until the pre-recorded programme.

When the day came, I was put at ease by the leading characters: Bruce Forsyth in particular was warm and engaged and good company, as was Anton Du Beke, who gave me hints on posture and noted, fairly, that my hold was worse than my footwork and needed attention. I had a disastrous dress rehearsal with numerous errors but was lifted by the atmosphere of the live show. The noise was tremendous, but the experience of cheering rather than jeering was energising. Erin was really reassuring. And I had Rachel and Aida in the audience willing me on. I got ten from Len and came second overall – not that it mattered. One sour note was of press reports that party high command was unhappy that I had chosen to appear, which earned me an unlikely ally in Ann Widdecombe.[44]

But foxtrotting to 'Walking in a Winter Wonderland' was soon eclipsed by a Murdoch meltdown. I had an early warning of the trouble ahead when I had a visit from the editor of the *Times,* James Harding. He wanted to talk about the BskyB application. I thought it odd for an editor to be sent on an errand of this kind, but I was well disposed to him, not least because he had produced a wonderful big picture on the front page of the *Times* of me dancing with Erin.

I didn't tell him that I had already referred the case to the competition authorities which was the key decision

[44] "Clegg Told to 'Get a Life' over Cable Row", *Daily Mirror,* 20 December 2010.

point. Ofcom would almost certainly refer the matter to the Competition Commission which would carry out an extensive and, probably, time-consuming review of plurality which was what I wanted but where News International did not want to be.

As the days went quietly by until Christmas, I had a call one evening from Nick Clegg's press officer who had seen the front page of the next day's *Telegraph*. Several of my colleagues and I had been exposed by an undercover reporter saying unflattering things about Conservative colleagues in the coalition. I had talked about having a 'nuclear option' of resignation, which sounded boastful. The story filled the rest of the press the next day but wasn't especially damaging, except perhaps to the reputation of the *Telegraph* for its sneaky reporting.* It was embarrassing but a 24-hour story.

The next day I was hosting a Christmas lunch for my private office staff when Jo Crellin said that a new story had broken on the BBC. Robert Peston had access to an extract of the *Telegraph* recording, where I had talked about being 'at war with the Murdochs'. The *Telegraph* had tried to keep it back but a journalist – possibly the editor, Tony Gallagher, who went on to edit the *Sun* – had passed it to the BBC.

Jo was really alarmed since this appeared to

---

* I was quoted as saying: "I could kill the Coalition says Cable" (*The Sun*, 21 December 2010), "Cable: I'd Bring Down Coalition" (*Daily Star* and *The Herald*); "Vince Cable quit threat to coalition" (*Daily Mirror*); "I could end coalition threatens Cable" (*Daily Express*), and much else in the same vein.

compromise my 'quasi-judicial' role as a minister. Within minutes a statement of apology had been prepared and I was whisked off to see the prime minister, who said it created a very difficult position; I was not to resign but someone else would have to take over the BSkyB case and similar duties in future.

I was too shell-shocked to respond to this rapidly moving sequence of events and to mobilise a defence. Still, it was a humiliating situation and the more so a day after the boast about my 'nuclear option'. Katie, my spad, was sent out to keep the baying media pack at bay. The advice from her, Jo and others close to me was to lie low for a while and regroup after Christmas; easier said than done since our home in Twickenham was now besieged by an army of cameras and reporters.

December 21 2010: All hell has broken loose over V's head in the media. It worried me yesterday that this was about to happen when the press reported the story of the Daily Telegraph *sting and the comments about fighting a war with only a nuclear option.*

V has just rung and says the whole thing has escalated because he commented on Murdoch. He arrived home pursued by cameras. It seems that towards the end of the recorded interview he described himself as waging war on Murdoch, so he has been taken off the Murdoch case. This is being described in the media as 'humiliation'.

December 22 2010: On the front page of all the broadsheets: 'Cable unplugged' etc, with cartoons of him as a suicide bomber. Several cameras at the gate and I explain that V is staying in Twickenham, as planned, and is not giving interviews. I tell myself that these are only journalists, not cattle, and they have been told not on any account to lay so much as a finger on me.

With the help of the police, we only just manage to get away without injury from the scrum at the front of the house to a local pub where V had organised a Christmas lunch for his Twickenham staff.

December 23 2010: *Mercifully, we are to go to my daughter Zoe's home for Xmas in Scotland and we manage to get away from the house in a taxi. I see the paper with a headline 'Mrs Cable Stands by Her Man' – with photo. Idiotic. Anyone would think he had been chasing other women, not caught in a nasty sting operation slagging off Murdoch. I hear that the* Sun *is even nastier: "Coward Cable hides behind his wife". The Murdoch press in action.*

The whole thing is awful: the day of the Cameron/Clegg joint broadcast to the nation. Now Vince is taken off the case in the Murdoch decision. Jeremy Hunt replaces him and is on public record as being pro-Murdoch so is no less 'biased'. I have to admit to a sneaking admiration for the speed and finesse with which David Cameron acted. I also feel that this may be a blessing in disguise: a poisoned chalice has been removed.

We arrive in Scotland to the village near Perth where Rachel's daughter and her family live. It seems a different world. No chasing press. We have heart-warming but limb-freezing walks in a bitterly cold winter; go tobogganing in local parks with Rachel's grandchildren against the background of ice floes in the Tay; and return to hot food and mulled wine with friends, who couldn't care less about the 'scandal' of speaking too freely off the record, but have vaguely concluded that I am on the side of the angels.

I did my best to calm down and make sense of what had happened. I spent time on the phone to my family and to my Lib Dem colleagues seeking advice but really wanting reassurance. The general consensus is: 'Hang in there; the storm will blow over.' And on Christmas day, the *Strictly Christmas Special* was on TV. My friends tell me that, outside the commentariat, that is what the public will remember. As it did. I am still asked about the show ten years on.

Then, off to a week's skiing in Courchevel. The world looked altogether a better place from the slopes.

Chapter Five
Frost, friction and feuding

January 2011: The big news back here at the farm is that Aslan the cat (aka 'fat cat') has condescended to move in with me – a little over four years since I moved from next door! He has been fed in the garage all that time. It's actually not so much affection for me as missing the dog, with whom he was very matey. He looks extremely sleek after three weeks of the new regime and snuggles up to me on the sofa, moulting and making me sneeze.

The return to the office in the New Year was, however, frosty: the Tory-supporting press thought (gleefully) that I was finished or much diminished; the *Guardian* and left-leaning press thought that the opportunity to curb the Murdoch press had been blown by my indiscretion; the civil servants felt that the department had been punished because the boss spoke out of turn. The one piece of press coverage which I liked, and made me laugh, was in *Private Eye* in its wonderful 'Coalition Academy' report from the 'headmaster':[45]

'Mr Cable has been relieved of his duties as the master in charge of media studies. This was because he was overheard in the staffroom toilets being very rude about one of our most respected sponsors, Mr Murdoch... I have naturally

---

[45] *Private Eye,* January 2011

written Mr Murdoch a personal letter of apology and I very much hope that Vince will do the same, if he is not too busy making a fool of himself on the dance floor.'

It was clear, moreover, that something was afoot when Andy Coulson stood down as Cameron's communications director. I had myself always found Coulson very helpful in defusing potential arguments with Number 10, but ugly rumours were flying around about him.

For the Lib Dems, and not just me, this was a time for humility and self-abasement. Nick had decided that the way to detoxify the fees issue was to grovel and apologise. He made a rather toe-curling video which became a comic hit on YouTube. I and other colleagues were told to seek out groups of young people to apologise to. We were like the teachers required to wear dunces' hats during Mao's Cultural Revolution.

I felt angry rather than apologetic and probably came across to my group of outraged teenage Red Guards as rather arrogant and patronising. In my view, we should have adopted the formula suggested by our colleague Simon Hughes that we got 2/10 for the politics of fees but 8/10 for the policy, apologising only for the pledge, not the policy.

A score of 8/10 was, perhaps, generous since David Willetts and I had already identified two weaknesses that were appearing: the effect of the Treasury's insistence on a high interest rate – Consumer Price Index (CPI) plus 3 per cent – which was bound to magnify, unnecessarily, the cumulative debt for students; and the weakness of the mechanism we had devised to stop universities charging the full amount for lower cost and lower value courses.

Overall, however, the policy achieved its objective of

paying for university education without up-front fees and in a 'progressive' way: in fact, fewer students would be paying at all than under the pre-existing Labour arrangements. But few were listening to such arguments.

The bigger political argument was a growing crescendo of criticism of the coalition's economic policy. The economic indicators were worrying: negative growth in the fourth quarter of 2010. I tried to counter the flow of negative argument through a piece in the *New Statesman*[46] which attracted a considered response from economist David Blanchflower and economic historian Robert Skidelsky.[47] Both sides drew a kindly-worded rebuke from distinguished economics journalist Sir Sam Brittan: 'Both articles were on a much higher level than most of what passes for economic debate. But these could have stood on their own without enlisting a dead man in support.'[48]

I wrote Osborne a personal letter urging a more radical approach to stimulating demand to head off a serious 'double dip' recession. He never answered but in subsequent meetings, it was clear that he now recognised a need to hold back fiscal contraction until growth was restored. Public spending cuts were postponed, the effect of which was to make the government's timetable closer to Labour's Darling Plan.

The issue of bank lending and bonuses came to a head with the so-called Merlin agreement, brokered by Barclays chief executive John Varley on behalf of the big banks,

---

[46] "Keynes would be on our side", 17 January 2011.
[47] Flatteringly titled "Vince Cable is working. The Coalition isn't", 24 January 2011.
[48] *Financial Times*, 4 February 2011.

which was an attempt to draw a line under 'banker bashing' by making specific quantitative commitments on SME lending, restraining bonuses and transparency on pay.

The banks also tried to buy a little goodwill by putting money into the prime minister's Big Society Bank and a private Business Growth Fund to provide equity to growth firms (the latter subsequently proved to be a great success). The agreement fell some way short of the commitments to net lending targets that I had been pushing for and attracted justified criticism. Nils Pratley argued in the *Guardian*, "Merlin is a sell-out, not a settlement".

Matthew Oakeshott described the deal as 'pitiful' and resigned his spokesman role in the Lords: 'The Treasury's negotiating tactics have not been very good... Most of them couldn't negotiate their way out of a paper bag and this has not been as tough a deal as it should have been.'[49] In BIS, we had pushed the Treasury as far as they were willing to go. And some commentators saw merit in a weak agreement.[50] After Murdoch and Merlin it was good to get away again: East Africa. Lots of trade promotion, but a chance to see my old haunts from the sixties and Olympia's brother and family.

February 9 2011: *Rang V to find out that there has been a meltdown: Matthew going on the news saying the government's dealings with the banks were 'a total failure... arrogant and incompetent'. By 7 pm, Matthew*

---

[49] "Sacked for telling the truth about banks", *Daily Record,* 10 February 2011.

[50] "Merlin's magic may yet work a banking miracle", *Sunday Times*, 6 February 2011.

had gone and we had Danny Alexander saying it was 'by mutual consent'. V fears their friendship may be permanently damaged.

February 21 2011: On our travels again. It was grey and damp when we left London. This time Nairobi. V has gone to a round table meeting on corruption. I am sitting on the verandah reading and writing in a beautiful garden with a breeze blowing and just one small cloud in a blue sky.

Before dinner, we go off with the high commissioner's wife, Alison, to see the Karura Forest on the outskirts of the capital, where V lived in a remote dwelling when he worked here. Alison is a really live wire who has turned this wild but disappearing forest into an asset. She has got Barclays Bank to fund people to be guards and guides instead of stealing from visitors.

Next morning, we were up at 6.30 am for the drive to Tanzania. I got to see Moshi, in the shadow of Kilimanjaro, where my father was district commissioner before independence and where I spent two years of my childhood, aged five to seven. The road between Nairobi and Arusha was being 'fixed' (V says he was involved in negotiating aid funding to complete the road 45 years ago). It is 80 per cent finished on the Kenyan side but only 50 per cent done in Tanzania. It also took well over an hour to clear the Nairobi traffic jams so instead of five to six hours on the road it was more like eight.

The early months of 2011 were politically quiet in terms of coalition disagreements, but events were taking place which did not attract much attention at the time but would blow up spectacularly later. The Health and Social Care Bill was introduced into Parliament without fanfare and little recognition amongst Lib Dems of the trouble it would cause. Andrew Lansley had introduced the idea of NHS reform as part of a process whereby each of us with operational departments set out our plans for legislation, in turn, at cabinet.

When Lansley's turn came, he spoke for an eternity in a language of NHS acronyms few of us understood. Cameron neatly summarised the discussion by acknowledging that Lansley seemed to understand what he was doing, even if the rest of us didn't. It was something to do with giving doctors more autonomy relative to bureaucrats: seemingly a good idea and uncontroversial. If only we had known.

I contributed my own bad mistake by going along with an idea coming out of a 'supply-side' reform initiative to scrap unnecessary 'red tape'. I was supposedly in charge of a cross-government 'one in, one out' project for regulation and under constant pressure from Number 10 and the small business lobby to demonstrate progress.

Ministers, and especially my Lib Dem colleagues, kept coming up with ideas for legislation or more regulation, most of which I happened to agree with – like rules for abolishing compulsory retirement coming from Steve Webb in the Department for Work and Pensions or environmental improvements coming from Norman Baker and Andrew Stunell. Tories, like Theresa May, also wanted more regulation for their own reasons, for example, to extend immigration controls. And Treasury ministers wanted more regulation to stop tax evasion. So we had lots of 'ins' and no 'outs'.

My lack of fervour on the deregulatory front was causing some embarrassment to the department and, to demonstrate seriousness about deregulation, I asked for something uncontroversial. I accepted a recommendation from officials and Ed Davey, the relevant minister, to extend from one to two years the period in employment before employees could sue for unfair dismissal; together with a list of measures designed to reduce the numbers coming to tribunals with frivolous cases. The theory behind the unfair dismissal reform was that employers would be more likely to hire people if they knew that they could dismiss those who were underperforming.

The measures were designed in part to shed my reputation for being the anti-business business secretary with key groups like the Federation for Small Business and the crop of business start-ups, who were expecting 'pro-business' deregulation to lift the country out of economic stagnation. There were pats on the back from right-wing newspapers.[51] It became clear in the months that followed, however, that I had seriously alienated moderate and constructive people in the Labour movement like Frances O'Grady, deputy general secretary at the Trades Union Congress (TUC) and that I had not appreciated the extent to which anti-union legislation and technological change had already weakened the position of labour.

Simultaneously, Tory ministers were pushing publicly for tougher anti-strike laws to deal with occasional disruption on the trains and underground which resonated

---

[51] "Coalition right to help job-creators", *City AM*, 27 January 2011.

with the London commuting public even if the proposals were impractical or counterproductive. The union movement was becoming seriously hostile to the coalition as a whole, as I discovered when I went to speak to a hostile GMB union conference in Brighton.

I was to change tack on labour issues, arguing strongly that we should be pro-business and pro-worker (and pro-union), but that message certainly didn't get across initially. I realised how easy it was to get the balance wrong. Like other business secretaries I had scheduled – usually quarterly – meetings with each of the five business federations and numerous individual companies. On the other hand, there was a meeting every few months with Frances O'Grady and with union reps on industrial visits when I insisted on seeing them; it rarely occurred to visit organisers that I might want to see anyone but the management.

And then there were the big set-piece events like the speeches at Mansion House dinners, which were carefully studied for any 'anti-business' criticism of the City or corporate behaviour. Part of the price the unions paid for their affiliation to the Labour Party was that they had no voice when Labour was out of government, even when we needed to hear it.

March 2011: A long hair-do in the morning in preparation for V's Trade and Industry speech at the Mansion House. I wore my Roberto Cavalli dress and the Kalis family's 'crown jewels' (given to me by my sisters-in-law after their mother died) and felt the part. V's speech has had too many cooks in its composition, and he was rewriting it in the car on the way there. I don't know how he can be so nonchalant, but it comes out both coherent and fluent. Audience of several hundred businessmen seems content.

We left promptly after a super dinner as V's back was giving out: a Strictly *legacy. After the Lib Dems' Welsh conference there is a week to go before an epidural and then some intensive physiotherapy.*

Another unexploded bomb, this time with a very long fuse. It concerned Prince Andrew. I didn't have particularly strong views on royalty. I was seeing more of them as a privy councillor, which reinforced my respect for the Queen's dignified manner, sense of duty and endless patience; and my liking for Prince Charles, who quietly prosecuted genuinely good works and also identified me as a fellow member of the exclusive club of those developing a career when most people have retired.

Prince Andrew asked me to come to the Palace to discuss how he could best help promote exports. He seemed genuine enough but appeared desperate to find something useful to do. Rumours about his extravagant tastes, taxpayer-financed jaunts and dubious friends like the child sex offender, Jeffrey Epstein, were already in circulation. When I was later asked if Prince Andrew should continue as trade envoy, I offered a noncommittal 'no comment' which earned a headline: 'Cable refuses to back Andrew as trade envoy.'[52] The dubious friend who triggered the press interest happened to be a friend of the ousted President of

[52] *Mail on Sunday*, 6 March 2011

Tunisia, Zine El Abidine Ben Ali, the first casualty of the Arab Spring.

The Arab Spring had begun in the New Year leading to a revolution in Tunisia in January, the overthrow of Egyptian President Mubarak, the outbreak of civil war in Libya and the attempted overthrow of President Gadhafi and, beginning in March, unrest in Syria. The main action initially concerned Libya leading to a proposal, endorsed by the United Nations, for military intervention on the side of the rebels.

When the issue came to cabinet, we Lib Dems fully supported military action. The armed forces, represented by General Sir David Richards, chief of the defence staff, had a careful and cautious approach with no suggestion of British troops on the ground, as in Iraq. The action was in support of US President Obama's and French President Nicolas Sarkozy's commitment to air strikes, and there was a strong legal opinion in support based on a UN resolution. Had we known then that the civil war would be still going strong ten years later, we might have been less gung-ho.

March 20 2011: The war in Libya is dreadful. It is called the 'Libyan Conflict' in the papers as if to sanitise it. But today an American plane came down and the two pilots ejected safely; then the Americans piled in to get their guys out and wounded a group of Libyans who were trying to help the pilots. One Libyan has lost a leg, but they were still willing to thank the Americans for trying to help them. I am more of a peacenik than V. My friend Jane P and I are amazed that only 15 MPs voted against the engagement and V said the cabinet was unanimously in favour. So easy to get in; so hard to get out.

And the death toll from the Japanese tsunami stands at 21,000 today. After 11 days they are gradually getting in control of their nuclear power stations but clearly some radioactivity has spread. Such things make our national domestic problems look relatively minor.

The Arab Spring was in lockstep with a volatile British spring as unhappiness over government cuts and economic stagnation spilled over onto the streets. At the end of March, hundreds of thousands marched in London to protest against cuts and the demonstrations turned violent, an early warning of what was to come in August. There was also a souring of the mood inside the coalition. The issue was immigration.

The prime minister made a speech expressing concern over the level of immigration and restating a Conservative pledge to cut net immigration to the 'tens of thousands' which he presented as coalition policy, though the Lib Dems had never signed up to it. I said publicly that the speech was 'very unwise' and 'risked inflaming extremism'. The reaction from the right-wing press was furious.[53] Even the more restrained editor and columnist Matthew D'Ancona demanded: 'Cable broke the rules, and he should have been sacked.'[54]

Nick Clegg waded in in full support, reminding the critics that collective cabinet responsibility applied only to agreed

---

[53] "The Prime Minister should sack Vince Cable right now", *Daily Express*, 18 April 2011.
[54] *Sunday Telegraph*, 18 April 2011.

policy, which this wasn't. I particularly enjoyed *Private Eye's* Coalition Academy's take from the headmaster: "'I did not expect this perfectly reasonable idea (a cap on the number of foreign students in the school) to be met by Mr Cable spray-painting on the wall of the staff-room toilet the words "The Headmaster is a fascist".'[55]

I had more allies than the critics realised. Theresa May's relentless chipping away at non-EU migration was seriously alienating the business community which faced big obstacles to obtaining visas for highly skilled specialists and executives. World class scholars from overseas were refused visas, leading the vice chancellor of Oxford University to demand a meeting with the PM. The most serious problem was the attempt to curb drastically the number of overseas students, supposedly to stop abuse (of which there was undoubtedly some). The Home Office assumed, with little evidence, that 50 per cent overstayed after graduation, grossly inflating the numbers of 'net migrants'.

Overseas students had become a critically important contribution to university income (because they paid uncapped fees) as well as enriching university life in their undergraduate and post-graduate roles. (I was always conscious that I had married one; the first ever student, either British or from abroad, to register at the University of York was my late wife Olympia). I received a lot of support from David Willetts and other Conservative ministers and we saw off the more extreme proposals; though a lot of damage was done to the reputation of the UK abroad, especially in India.

---

[55] *Private Eye*, 2011.

What made the coalition arguments more bitter was that battle had been joined on the Alternative Vote referendum. The proposal was modest and somewhat short of proportional voting. But it was one of the concessions we had obtained in the coalition agreement and we had to fight for it, especially as the Tories were determined from the outset to destroy it with the ruthless 'politics of fear' we were later to see deployed *so* effectively in the Scottish referendum, the 2015 election and, less successfully, in the Brexit referendum. Nick Clegg described the Tory anti-AV campaign as full of 'lies, misinformation and deceit'.

It was blindingly obvious that we could only win by mobilising the support of Labour and I agreed to share platforms with Ed Miliband, the new Labour leader, which produced another paroxysm of rage on the Tory side, especially when I led in the *Guardian* with 'Vince Cable: vote yes to AV and end Tories' dominance'. Followed by "Business Secretary calls for 'progressive majority' of Lib Dem and Labour voters".[56] This was described as 'open revolt' and 'Cable fires up attack on Coalition'.[57]

The campaign was doomed, however. Not only were the Tories adamantly opposed but Labour was lukewarm, not wanting to be associated with the Lib Dems, and with some of the Labour opponents of electoral reform, like its former party chairman John Reid, openly endorsing the anti-AV side.[58]

I appeared at a packed AV debate in London alongside

---

[56] *The Guardian*, 23 April 2011.

[57] *Sunday Times*, 17 April 2011.

[58] "Labour 'spitting blood' over Reid's backing for Cameron on voting reform", *Independent*, 19 April 2011.

Ken Livingstone and against Michael Howard; we won easily but that was not the mood nationally. We lost 70:30 in the referendum. On the same day there were calamitous local election results with Lib Dem councillors being decimated in areas where they had provided good local government representation for years.

The Lib Dems had produced some outstanding local government leaders who were running formerly Labour-controlled big cities: among them Mike Storey and Richard Kemp in Liverpool, John Shipley and David Faulkner in Newcastle, Howard Sykes in Oldham, Gerald Vernon-Jackson in Portsmouth and Abby Bell in Hull. Now these political strongholds were being swept away. We knew the blow was coming which didn't make any easier the hollowness of our old slogan: 'Where we work, we win'. And the longer the coalition lasted, the more the blows would keep raining in.

Buried in the bad news was a virtual Lib Dem wipe-out in Scottish parliamentary elections, where the Scottish National Party (SNP) swept to power. Those warnings from Charles Kennedy and Ming Campbell about the impact of the coalition on Scotland had proved horribly prescient. A decade later the consequences still reverberated.

April 17 2011: Vince got embroiled in a row over a speech from Cameron on immigration. While the speech was mostly 'measured' in Chris Huhne's assessment on

Question Time *Cameron talked about 'mass immigration',*[*]
*which is not the case; and he talks about cutting 'net
immigration' well below the current 150,000 while no one
is actually counting the people – especially students – who
leave to go back home. V was incandescent because they
have just carefully negotiated modifications to the
Conservative policy and Cameron was presenting his 'cap'
(under 100,000 net) as <u>coalition</u> policy, which it isn't. The
universities also need foreign students' fees and businesses
need to get their skilled people in and out.*

*Politically, the run-up to the local elections is proving
divisive which is no bad thing because the parties need to
be distinctive, but the AV campaign is getting quite messy.
Nick Clegg trotted out the least convincing argument
today: that it would remedy the expenses scandal.*

April 24 2011: *Domestic politics is getting very sour
ahead of the local elections and referendum, with Dave and
Nick having several spats about how people get
internships en route to plum jobs. Nick says it's not okay
and Dave says it's fine and he intends to go on giving them
to friends and relatives. Nick cares strongly about social
mobility and sees this argument as a personal attack.*

V had a major article in the Guardian *on Saturday
saying the progressive non-Tory majority must unite
behind AV or the Tory hegemony of most of the last 100
years on a minority vote will continue. All this is helping to*

---

[*] 'Mass immigration' only happened later in 2015
following the Syrian refugee crisis, which chiefly
affected the European mainland.

produce a toxic brew. Sadly, it looks as if the AV referendum will be lost... which may embolden the Tories to have an autumn election.

April 25 2011: *The media is full of the wedding of Prince William to Catherine Middleton. I will go up to London and watch it there on V's telly.*

In the meantime I go leafleting with John W on the Waterside, our most hopeful area in the New Forest District Council elections. I am a candidate: this time strictly a paper candidate. We expect to do very badly.

May 5 2011: *We did, though I got nearly 30 per cent of the vote in Brockenhurst even as a paper candidate. Better than four years ago (John W tells me it was 20 per cent then). But the overall result was awful for the Lib Dems – eight district council seats lost: nationally 700 losses including loss of control in lots of towns and cities.*

The immediate aftermath of the referendum was a fractious cabinet meeting in which Chris Huhne created a scene, throwing the 'No' campaign literature onto the table in a dramatic denunciation of the Tories. He referred in particular to leaflets, backed by the Conservatives, which denounced Nick Clegg over higher tuition fees, a policy they had advocated and supported.

The anger was genuine and justified but it seemed to me to be pointless complaining after the event. They had done us over and we needed to be even more on our guard and forcefully independent in future.

I felt for Nick Clegg, who had been comprehensively

shafted by Cameron, whom he had trusted. This was one punch-up I decided to sit out and to concentrate on the next batch of problems coming down the track: bank non-lending, executive pay, short-term time horizons in the City, and the need for a coherent approach to the multiple problems facing industries like motor vehicles, aerospace and steel. And a trip to Japan and Korea to pursue trade diplomacy.

The first coalition birthday: David Simonds in *The Observer* (*courtesy of David Simonds*).

May 26 2011: The banquet for President Obama. After the dinner we mingled over the coffee and found ourselves in a room full of politicians – though the crème de la crème of the government and Obama's team seemed to be somewhere else. Sad because we lost Hillary Clinton, amongst others, who looked like royalty and would have been really interesting to talk to. Only the hard-working

Princess Royal and that old waxwork the Duke of Kent came through to our bit.

I sought out Sarah Brown because I felt bad I hadn't written when they left Number 10. She had looked after me for an afternoon when V had one of his 'secret' meetings with Gordon. We then spoke to John Major and Norma (who were delightful) but not Tony Blair and Cherie. He was a perma-tanned ghost of his former self and stayed well in the shadows. She looked agitated.

The rumours that Wills and Kate would be there proved to be false. Michelle Obama is spectacularly attractive close up as well as warm and friendly, though I felt she didn't need the false eyelashes which are a growing trend amongst younger fashionistas. When I said I was honoured to meet them as we shook hands, I meant it.

My son, Dylan says he saw us on the telly, me with my anxious face on. The Queen said to Obama by way of introducing V: "This is our Business Secretary – he does a lot of, you know, business."

May 30 2011: *Arrived in Korea yesterday after a fraught Friday and Saturday. V did* Any Questions *in Saffron Walden and I went too. We got back at 11 pm. Then off first thing to a Twickenham advice surgery before heading to the airport.*

We got to Korea on their hottest day of the year so far to be met by the ambassador and the UK Trade and Investment (UKTI) boss and whisked to the residence. Greeted by Fiona Uden, the ambassador's wife. They had met when she was a dancer in a company visiting Korea many years before and were delighted to be posted there.

In due course, there was dinner with a dozen businessmen from the Chamber of Commerce and several Koreans working for British companies. We were exhausted and almost fell over at the coffee stage.

There was then a hot and sleepless night made worse by breathing difficulties brought on by the yellow dust blown in from the Gobi Desert in China. I wondered whether our bed had been the one used by Charles and Diana on their last trip together in 1992 when they had opened the new office building in the compound and whether they too had slept badly, poor things.

V has a full-on day for official duties including the opening of a huge, new factory – a Korea-UK joint venture making high-tech vacuum pumps – and came back with a commemorative pump weighing well over a kilo. I had a lovely morning with Fiona in the Palace grounds. Then to the Samsung headquarters, where the company had cleverly organised a welcome with pictures of V projected all over the walls of the building.

Finally, to the demilitarised zone between North and South Korea in the company of a US colonel, which is an extraordinary experience. Particularly chilling are the border cabins where North Korean guards are a few feet away, looking at us totally without expression. We were encouraged to stare back and not look down.

June 7 2011: *There followed an amazing few days in Japan, as house guests of the Ambassador, David Warren. I was provided with a companion to do train journeys and bus tours while Vince was busy all day in meetings. My diary entries are far too long to recite here, but it was* *humbling to see signs of the recent tsunami and gratifying to know how much (now) Sir David and his staff had contributed to the recovery from it.*

I am back at the farm, catching up. V rings from Twickenham very early. He has been woken at 5.30 am by a 'Wake up to Climate Change' campaign. They banged on the door and two young women had cameras ready to snap V when he answered. Then they left but wrapped his door and porch in CRIME SCENE tape. He had the wit to remove most of it before TV cameras turned up, prompted by the protesters. He hadn't slept anyway: back issues. I pointed out that since flying back from Korea and Japan, he had spent nine hours travelling to speak at Hay-on-Wye; then the next day to Brighton to speak to the GMB union, where he was heckled. I think he is in denial about the stress of delivering messages he only half agrees with.

Chapter Six
Renaissance

Life at, or near, the top of politics is characterised by high highs and very low lows, both exaggerated by the refracted light of media coverage. I had had six really bad months: tuition fees, Murdoch, the bitter exchanges over immigration and AV. And the feeling – regret? guilt? – that the project I was involved in and had helped to create was having seriously damaging side-effects on poorer people and was contributing to the political demise of good, hardworking, party colleagues.

And there was the steady drip-drip of hard cases at my weekly advice sessions, including some of the million and a half people claiming invalidity benefit now receiving letters telling them to attend work capability assessment, resulting in ridiculous disqualification in many cases. Although we had a minister in DWP, Steve Webb, who was doing excellent things on pensions, we didn't seem to have any influence over some dreadful welfare policy changes designed to save money. Then the sky opened up to a succession of good news events.

The first was an opportunity to boost the car industry and help to save thousands of jobs at the General Motors – Vauxhall – factories at Ellesmere Port on Merseyside (cars) and Luton (vans). The industry had taken a terrible battering in the wake of the financial crisis contracting by over 30 per cent in 2009 and seeing the UK content of cars falling from 60 per cent to around 40 per cent. The year 2010 had seen a big recovery with 27 per cent growth to 1.3 million vehicles. Peter Mandelson's car scrappage scheme had undoubtedly helped, as had the creation of an Automotive Council to give cohesion to the industry.

I had been quickly convinced of the importance of the industry and had developed a relationship with Indian magnate Ratan Tata, whose company owned Jaguar Land Rover and his UK adviser Lord Bhattacharya (Tata had been mortally offended by a comment of Peter Mandelson which he had interpreted as linking Indians with corruption. Tata definitely wasn't corrupt). I approved loans or guarantees to Nissan and Ford to secure their investments. And the visit to Japan, meeting the top people in Nissan, Honda and Toyota had reinforced my belief that there was both a lot at stake in the industry and a big potential for the UK.

General Motors (GM) had suffered badly from the crisis and was looking to close one of its European factories which boiled down to the UK or one of two German – Opel – plants. The UK was favourite for the chop, having relatively high costs and a seemingly weaker commitment to the industry than Germany. We decided to fight.

BIS had a team of motor industry specialists who inspired me with their enthusiasm and knowledge. We were fortunate, too, in the union leader: Tony Woodley. He had been head of the TGWU (Transport and General Workers' Union before it folded into McCluskey's UNITE and knew the industry backwards; was willing to work with anyone who could help his members; and was a brilliant negotiator. His job was to persuade his members of the need to move to higher productivity work practices to cut costs.

My job was to persuade GM that the UK government would do all in its power – heavily circumscribed by state aid rules as well as lack of money – to support the industry. The company was surprised and impressed by our commitment. I sought to convince the chiefs of the European car companies as a group, at a conference in London, that we had a strategy for the industry and then flew to the USA to persuade Dan Akerson, the chief executive of GM, to stay, and invest more, in the UK.[59] The combined effort was a success. GM opted for the UK over Germany. The win greatly bolstered my standing in government, in the department and with the union. Also, it reinforced my growing belief that we needed a coherent industrial strategy rather than piecemeal intervention.

Two more major industrial issues drew me and the government further into intervention. Traditional, strict, narrow, public procurement rules led to the loss of a contract to build trains for the Thameslink line for Bombardier in Derby when the contract was won by Siemens who would manufacture them in Germany. As many as 1,400 jobs in Derby plus many more in the supply chain would go if Bombardier closed. There was outrage in the press and Parliament. The respected business columnist in the *Mail*, Alex Brummer, thundered: "We NEVER fight for the best of British".[60] The *Sunday Express* blamed the EU.[61] The role of BIS in such situations was largely passive

---

[59] "Cable goes to Detroit to woo car chiefs", *Financial Times*, 8 June 2011.
[60] *Daily Mail*, 6 July 2011.
[61] "How the EU railroaded British train workers", 10 July 2011.

and officials expected to do no more than to organise a task force to help find alternative jobs.

When I went to Derby to meet company representatives and unions and convey this news, the reception was extremely hostile, especially from a vituperative Conservative leader of Derby City Council.

I resolved to intervene with Philip Hammond, whose department oversaw the procurement, and we had an impromptu meeting on a street corner after cabinet. We wrote a joint letter to the PM seeking approval for a wholesale review of procurement to give support to UK supply chains.[62] To Hammond's considerable credit – I had hitherto written him off as a dry, Tory accountant – he managed to cobble together some work to keep Bombardier going and the protocol was overhauled to make it more like German-style protected procurement if not as overt as the French system. The plant was saved.

Then I was confronted with a proposal to make a £32 million loan to Westland Helicopters (owned by the Italian firm Augusta) to develop a civilian helicopter. I had already got to know Westland through a factory visit organised by my colleague, the local Lib Dem MP, David Laws. The recommendation to fund Westland came from the Regional Growth Fund chaired by Michael Heseltine and we had the delicious irony of the man, who had resigned from the Thatcher cabinet quarter of a century earlier over its failure to support Westland, now promoting a fresh plan to revive the company.

---

[62] "Lost £3bn. train contract prompts Cable to voice concern in letter to PM", *The Guardian*, 1 July 2011.

My willingness to get behind the loan was contrasted unfavourably with the earlier refusal of the loan for Sheffield Forgemasters.[63] The criticism was just. We – or I – were moving to more interventionist industrial policy but in a haphazard and reactive way.

Then the news broke about News International and hacking. *The Guardian* and then other newspapers revealed the extent of illegal phone tapping of the mobile phones of celebrities, politicians, and high-profile crime victims over the last decade by the Murdoch-owned *News of the World* (many years later I discovered that I was one of them). The stories also revealed the closeness to the Murdochs of senior Tories from the prime minister down, with numerous meetings including many while I was considering the BSkyB application and subsequently.

The *News of the World* ceased publication after 168 years in circulation. The BSkyB competition enquiry collapsed and the carefully crafted compromise which Jeremy Hunt had been working on became irrelevant.

The News International disaster fed a spate of 'Vince Cable is back' stories.[64] A particularly gracious piece by journalist Matthew Norman in the *Independent*[65] offered an apology which was both personal and, more important, a recognition of the decision making: "Had he not defied coalition pressure and referred the BSkyB takeover to Ofcom, as he justly enjoys reminding us, it would have been an irreversibly done deal before the Milly Dowler story

[63] "Cable Under fire Over Westland Loan", *The Times*, 21 July 2011.
[64] *Independent on Sunday*, Matt Chorley, 31 July 2011
[65] 27 July 2011.

broke". The reversal of personal fortunes revived leadership speculation in the Lib Dems. Nick Clegg remained friendly and equable, as ever, but his outriders were on coup alert and made it clear through the spad network that I was being watched for signs of disloyalty.

As it happens, I had little interest in his job. I did not have his ability to soak up endless punishment whilst smiling or any interest in negotiating with the Tories on numerous issues outside my comfort zone.

July 16 2011: The political news is that Rebekah Brooks has resigned as the chief executive of News International. People come up to V in the street and say 'well done' or 'you were right about him' – or even 'you got him'. The local newspaper (the Richmond & Twickenham Times*) had, as its headline this week, 'CABLE'S COUP'. And I rather liked an article elsewhere by novelist Margaret Drabble, which morphed 'News Corp' into 'News Corpse'.*

We have what I have come to see as a quiet Saturday. 6 am reading and papers in bed, 7.30 am wife gets tea, 8 am, wife gets cuddle, 9 am breakfast, 10 am journalist arrives for interview. 10.30 am photography for interview. 12 pm family – eight of them – for lunch, 3 pm walk to constituency event in St Margarets, 4.30 pm drive to another constituency event in nearby Hampton Hill and then on to Harrow Lib Dems BBQ. Speech, 7 pm leave Harrow. 8 pm back home and paperwork until 10 pm. No Match of the Day *in July.* MOTD *is essential to V's wellbeing and a key fixture in the ministerial diary. He rarely goes to big games: connected with his having been a few yards from a disaster at Ibrox in Glasgow in the*

1970s, when a hundred people were trampled to death. But he loves the game and seems to have an encyclopaedic knowledge of players and teams.

The personal dramas and the relentless, multi-faceted work of BIS tended to overshadow the bigger developments in the government and in the country. The publication of the Dilnot Commission on long term care in July offered a solution to an increasingly costly and divisive issue. Both sides of the coalition agreed that this was the best formula yet produced to balance different interests and pay for the care of an ageing population. But the Tories never followed through on the agreement we had reached and, when they found themselves in power in 2015, Theresa May, disastrously, re-opened the arguments.

The row over a 'dementia tax' contributed generously to her failure to win the 2017 election convincingly.[66]

The appalling massacre of teenagers in Norway on the July 25 by a neo-Nazi was a reminder of the violence lurking not far beneath the surface of our placid European societies. London then erupted with riots which lasted the best part of a week, causing widespread damage, spreading to provincial cities.

Parliament was recalled and we had COBRA national emergency meetings of the cabinet. There was a lot of instant wisdom and plenty of people blaming government cuts; but the causes were deep-rooted and owed a lot to pent-up frustrations about deprivation and discrimination

---

[66] The Tories eventually acted on this issue in 2021, but in a way that seriously widened inequality.

in inner-city, mainly black, communities which had been made more acute by the rise in unemployment after the financial crisis.

August 8 2011: *TV cameras in the front and back gardens. Rioting in London. Simultaneously, international panic about the financial situation. The USA has been downgraded from Triple A. Spain looks like joining Greece, putting the Euro into crisis again. V did his avuncular reassurance thing.*

August 10 2011: *Waiting for a taxi. We have been 'allowed' to go on holiday. I am relieved. V has been holding the fort for two weeks along with William Hague while Cameron and Clegg were on holiday at the same time and London burns; fires raging in Croydon, Hackney and Ealing. Probably cock-up rather than conspiracy but I harbour a suspicion that Cameron didn't want Nick to be seen acting in the role of Prime Minister. Who knows?*

We got a sense of the febrile atmosphere in London yesterday when a young, clean-shaven white man started shouting aggressively at V in the middle of Kingston when we were out shopping: "The government are traitors and scumbags". The papers are full of indignation at the young rioters and describe the Met police as too 'liberal'. V spent last night phoning a lot of businesses that had been badly affected; one boss told him that the real danger is the professional thieves moving in behind the looters and making off with really valuable stuff. I find that I am really agitated and so glad we have stuck with plans to get away to Ireland for a break.

When the crisis had subsided, Rachel and I headed for Ireland and a trip around the coast of north and south from Belfast to the Antrim coast, and on to Donegal and Connemara. Although there were drier and warmer places to spend a summer, there was something special about Ireland: the physical beauty of the coastal areas, the hospitality and warmth of the people on both sides of the border.

We had a brief reminder of the politics. We arrived in Derry, were stopped by the police from walking on the walls and were mystified by the absence of people from the city – until we turned a corner to meet the Apprentice Boys' Parade. I was recognised by some of the marchers, but the shouts in my direction were good-natured if alcohol-fuelled.

When we retreated to a cafe some way from the festivities a deathly silence fell until the barman, who recognised me, asked if I would like to meet his 'friends' in a yard outside. I was nervous of meeting what was almost certainly a militant republican group, but they were friendly enough and explained that they were in town to protest about prison conditions. When a passing reporter showed particular interest in a British cabinet minister talking to republican activists, we made ourselves scarce to enjoy the endless expanse of empty beaches on the coast nearby.

That summer the political centre of gravity had shifted within the coalition. Journalist Rachel Sylvester in the *Times* noted that: 'The coalition see-saw tips to the Lib Dems... the hacking row and a retreat on health reform have allowed the junior partners to lord it over their Tory allies.'[67]

---

[67] *The Times*, 2 August 2011.

Nick Clegg had managed to dilute the NHS legislation where it threatened to open the floodgates to private contractors.

She credited me with challenging seriously the Treasury orthodoxy and promoting in government a 'Plan A+' based on public investment and growth. And there was the imminent publication of the Vickers Report of the Independent Commission on Banking. Only a few weeks ago, bankers were relatively confident that the chancellor would see off the demands for radical reform. In the current political climate, they could no longer be so sure.

It was now clear where the Vickers Commission was heading as a result of its interim work. It was not going to push for a total split of 'casino' or investment banking from retail banking but was still pursuing a far more radical solution than the banks wanted: ring-fencing the two sets of activities to prevent recklessness in the 'casinos' dragging down banks which were hitherto 'too big to fail'.

The impact would depend on the details and timing. There was a degree of cross-party consensus that this was a reasonable compromise, though the press was inclined to dramatise the differences.[68]

When the report was formally launched there were predictable responses. *The Telegraph* was opposed – "Banks digest 'harsher than expected' proposals" and "reforms to cost £7 bn because of stronger regulation". *The Guardian* was cynical: 'Osborne's answer to the bank crisis – in 8 years' time', though its business columnist Nils Pratley was enthusiastic: "at last a route back to safer

[68] "Osborne and Cable at war over bank reform", *The Independent*, 31 August 2011.

banking". The *FT* was very supportive: "A necessary reform of British banking" and "Vickers plans shake up the City". As was the *Times*: "Banking on Vickers." The *Sun* concluded that "the banks can't complain at the shake-up coming their way." The *Mail* was broadly supportive, but its columnist Alex Brummer was critical of the long phase-in: "No excuse for this dangerous delay."

Overall, my view was that it wasn't a bad outcome: a partial victory, which needed to be consolidated in the months ahead in the face of constant foot-dragging by the banks over technical detail. Osborne accepted the recommendations, no doubt calculating that he could persuade his friends in the City that it could have been far worse. I accepted them as a useful, modest, step forward. And, as a Lib Dem I could point to something positive from the coalition: not just damage limitation.

Chapter Seven
Harsh political reality

There was now, after Vickers, a concrete result to put before the autumn Lib Dem conference in Birmingham. But it was a modest offering alongside the deep unhappiness in the party. Conference would be dominated by councillors and ex-councillors: as many as 700 had been massacred in May. There was the prospect of a repeat next year and the year after.

A *Times* Populus poll[69] showed that, while support for the coalition was holding up in general (60 per cent approved of it and 48 per cent thought it was doing well, albeit down 11 per cent over the year), Lib Dem supporters, who thought the coalition was doing badly, had grown from 15 per cent to 46 per cent. The off-stage unhappiness was reflected in the comments of party president Tim Farron, who asked about a possible 'divorce' from the Conservatives before the next election.

He was slapped down by the Clegg team for: 'peddling juvenile nonsense'.[70] His question was perfectly reasonable but better aired privately with colleagues first. Moreover,

---

[69] 14 September 2011.

[70] *The Times*, 20 September 2011.

* The commentator who captured at least the first bit was Quentin Letts of the *Daily Mail* – "on a minister at his most morose: glum Vince a moose munching the last grass of autumn", 20 September 2011.

there seemed less appetite for sedition and more for rallying round the leadership in difficult times.

I had the task of rallying the troops, keeping faith with the coalition on the basics and reminding the activists what we were achieving or stopping, deploying such political capital as I retained to that end. To my pleasant surprise, my personal standing with the electorate measured in approval ratings had remained largely intact: second in the government, just a little behind the prime minister.

Whilst this was reassuring, it was also dangerous when there was open speculation about the party leadership. And it invited attacks as when the *Sun*, having somehow got hold of my tax files in Grimsby, claimed that a few weeks' delay in paying a VAT bill amounted to 'tax avoidance'.

But what raised a cheer and really impressed the troops was that I was rated the least popular Lib Dem amongst Tory supporters. That was the trick I needed to keep going: keeping our distance from the Tories, while continuing to work with them on the essentials; being sombre about the economic threats we all faced while producing some positive outcomes.

September 18 2011: Asian Achievers Awards. I was surrounded by dazzling women, mostly in saris.

Off early next morning for party conference at Birmingham. Staying on the 18th floor of the Hyatt Hotel with a magnificent skyscape. V's speech today. Went well but quite a lot of carping and unflattering cartoons. He was on the go from radio at 6.45 am until Newsnight at 11 pm.

Increased security at the party conference, as seen by Morland in *The Times* (*courtesy of Morland*).

I got into a spot of bother after making some vox pop comment to Martha Kearney about the cuts, tweeted around social media as an attack on the government when what I had actually said was that too many people assumed that the 25 per cent cuts were happening now when many were backloaded over four or more years. The comments followed me around and the Mirror *had a story on 'Conference Comrade': Me.*

October 2 2011: *Yesterday I was flicking through the pages of the* FT Wealth Magazine, *which comes with the* FT *on a Saturday and came across a picture of a spiky-blue-haired damsel sticking her tongue out behind CLIMATE CRIME SCENE tape in* **our** *porch, clearly taken the day Vince was woken at 5.30 am on that day in June by this* self-appointed eco-warrior. The article was headlined 'Not Too Posh to Protest' and revealed that the girl in question was the granddaughter of a baronet. I was incensed enough to write to the editor suggesting that they find her a day job and pay for fashion shoots on our premises in future.

October 29 2011: *After the conference season we embarked on another grand tour, this time to Singapore, Indonesia and Vietnam.*

Both Hanoi and Ho Chi Minh City are hugely deferential to VIPs: VIP lounges, bouquets (enormous) on arrival and departure, motorcycle outriders and police escorts for the ambassador's car. But UK politics is never far away and there is a disaster unfolding back in the constituency.

Some papers, which should have been shredded (and there is a system for doing this with a bespoke contractor), have got into a recycling bag which is put out at night for collection early the following morning. An 'anxious constituent' has been picking through the bags over a nine-month period and has unearthed letters with details of constituents (one with mental health issues); V's engagement diaries, mostly out of date; some canvass returns; "Clegg and Cable" chocolate wrappers and other nonsense.

The details of the exposé are all over the local paper and the Sun has a 'scoop' (we suspect they are behind the bin monitoring as a retaliation for the Murdoch 'scandal' last December). V issues an apology for release back in the UK via his spad, Katie, to head off a newspaper storm over data leaks. But we missed a night's sleep and are exhausted, with another round of meetings in Hanoi tomorrow.

A few days after returning, we had another nasty surprise: a Sun *front page headline: 'Vince Avoids Tax'. All over the news bulletins. I receive a book on the doorstep –* Bookkeeping for Dummies *– from a* Sun *reporter who looks very pleased with himself. V is very agitated but deals with a heavy round of questioning extremely well.*

It turns out that the Sun *has got hold of his tax file in Grimsby (How? More Murdoch revenge?) and all that is involved is a £500 charge for a late VAT return a few years earlier when we hadn't realised that* The Storm *would become a bestseller: hundreds of thousands of small businesses have the same issue. But he worries about the cumulative, insidious damage affecting his hitherto strong support in the constituency. When he got home, he was still very tense but did what he does best: got his head down and worked on BIS questions and other homework.*

Back to business as usual: battles in the coalition. I had already supported reform of the tribunal system and extending the period before workers could claim 'unfair dismissal'. But a separate set of proposals put forward by venture capitalist and Tory donor, Adrian Beecroft, prompted by the Prime Minister's adviser Steve Hilton, wanted to go much further. He introduced the idea of 'no fault dismissal' which meant that workers could be fired at will, subject to the payment of compensation.

The scope for abuse and bullying by bad employers was obvious and the compensation proposal vague, so I decided to fight the report. Nick Clegg joined in, making it clear that this was a Lib Dem issue. The reaction outside the conservative press was hostile to Beecroft; in the *Independent,* journalist Andrew Grice denounced "A New Return to Victorian Values".[71]

It was difficult to separate our own more limited steps from Beecroft, though some journalists in the business press could: "Beecroft's plans for ousting staff drones is a bad one... but proposals hatched separately by Mr Cameron's coalition allies... deserve their own place in new employment legislation."[72]

Cameron and Osborne chose to beat a retreat on Beecroft: "The chancellor and prime minister are aware that they risk retoxifying the Conservative brand if they preside over the removal of basic workers' rights".[73] A Lib Dem gain but the publicity didn't get much beyond the inside pages of the *FT*, while our broadly sensible and limited but unpopular proposals on tribunals received wide coverage.[74]

In retrospect, we should never have gone down that road at all. I sought to rebalance our approach by trailing our plans to tackle 'fat cat' executive pay in the New Year, which generated their own controversy.[75] I proposed to use shareholders to restrain more greedy executives.

---

[71] "A New Return to Victorian Values", *The Independent*, 24 November 2011.

[72] *Financial Times*, 27 October 2011.

[73] *Financial Times*, 9 November 2011.

[74] "Easier sacking plans are fair to staff-Cable", *Metro*, 23 November 2011.

[75] "Back off, Mr Cable – let the shareholders approve CEO's pay", *Evening Standard*, 24 November 2011.

A more fundamental issue was the state of the economy. There was little sign of more than minimal economic growth and the new figures were showing over a million young people, aged 16-24, out of work. A recurrence of the Eurozone crisis was bringing recession to our biggest trade partner and spooking the financial markets. Monetary policy was not succeeding in boosting demand. The idea of some of my Conservative colleagues that supply-side reform – planning changes, employment law reform, bits and pieces of deregulation – would magically stimulate growth was laughable, even if it could have helped a bit in the very long run.

I wrote a pamphlet advocating a Plan B, called a 'Plan A+', involving a substantial boost to public investment, and got a frantic call from Osborne one midnight saying I was tearing up the government's economic policy and it would end the coalition. I finished up writing a resignation letter, still sitting in my files, but didn't send it; it seemed a futile gesture and Osborne assured me that he would reschedule the cuts to offset the downswing in the economic cycle.

We jointly announced a £50bn programme of capital works – using money from private pension funds – in the form of toll roads, power stations and homes. But a Treasury source then killed its macroeconomic purpose: 'We will not be changing the government's capital spending envelope and we will not be issuing new bonds to fund this.'[76]

The press were aware that there was a good deal of tension behind the scenes though the precise points of

---

[76] *Sunday Times*, 13 November 2011.

friction varied ('fresh details emerged of coalition infighting over their plans to get the economy moving with Business Secretary Vince Cable dramatically ruling out Tory proposals to freeze benefits').[77]

The political divisions were turbo-charged by the issue which has split the UK ever since: Europe. At a European summit, action to stabilise the Eurozone crisis was stymied by David Cameron exercising a veto over any moves to stronger co-operation, which did not explicitly safeguard the interests of the City of London. This opened up what columnist Mary Ann Sieghart in the *Independent* called: "The new divide at the heart of the Coalition."[78] Eurosceptic newspapers were uninhibited in putting the boot in: "Sulking Lib Dems and an unhappy union..."

I took to the TV studios to attack the prime minister's historic EU veto. Nick Clegg had not been consulted and he also launched "a furious attack on Cameron's conduct at the summit".[79] The Conservatives saw the episode as an opportunity to rehearse their pessimism about the euro.[80] But on a personal level, the *Independent* was right to report that there was no question of my resigning – a rumour which flitted round the Twittersphere – and that Nick Clegg and I were totally united on the issue.[81] The bigger story was

---

[77] *Daily Mail*, 14 November 2011.

[78] *The Independent*, 12 December 2011.

[79] *The Times*, 12 December 2011.

[80] "The Eurozone will not survive another year, warns Boris", *The Independent*, 19 May 2011.

[81] Mary Ann Sieghart, "We can't expect decisions from two parties so much at odds", *The Independent*, 12 December 2011.

that this was an issue about which Nick felt passionately and for which he had impeccable European credentials. The argument was a harbinger of a prolonged and deep divide over Europe.

December 8 2011: *Having a quiet patch on the farm. V came for the weekend but had to leave early to canvass at a by-election in Feltham, next door to Twickenham.*

Still ridiculously mild but we did give the cattle their first bale of hay.

V decides to spend the time between New Year and the rest of the recess clearing his study. At least five years of paper cuttings and other flotsam and jetsam have accumulated to a point where it is no longer possible to get into the room. We finish up with three trips to the rubbish dump and – remembering the Sun *"scandal"– a big pile for the shredder.*

February 2 2012: *Just before I leave the farm for Twickenham, I hear that the CPS is going to prosecute Chris Huhne and Vicky Pryce for 'perverting the course of justice'. This is a personal tragedy as well as a political disaster for the Lib Dems. I have been earnestly hoping that the CPS would decide that there was not enough evidence to bring charges. She is still giving her annual drinks party but I called in earlier in the day instead. To my surprise she seemed to be taking it all very calmly. She had resigned from her job as chief economist at BIS when Chris became Energy Secretary to avoid conflict of interest as a spouse, but now she had filed for divorce so would soon no longer be a spouse and he might well have to* *resign. The next week we go to Les Arcs in the French Alps for a week's skiing with Aida and her family. Glorious but very cold: minus 20 degrees C.*

Recovering from a broken wrist at Christmas and increasing right hip problems, but I do well after a shaky start and V is now very confident on 'nice' red runs. But he fell badly again today in bad weather, while I stayed indoors, and has now hurt both legs.

After a quiet period, there was an outburst of publicity – mostly bad – around a leaked letter I wrote to the prime minister making a call for an industrial strategy. I had been getting to know Michael Heseltine who had an office along the corridor as part of his work with the Regional Growth Fund. His main reporting line was to Cameron and Osborne, but he had some sympathy with what I was trying to do, particularly around the car industry following the success with GM. And I, in turn, had great admiration for his independent mind, his restless energy – he was almost 80 at the time, a decade older than me – his communication skills and sense of mischief.

In one of our meetings, he suggested that I should confront the prime minister with a proposal for an ambitious industrial strategy and we drafted together a letter setting out the arguments in quite trenchant terms. A week later, the letter appeared in the press. On this occasion, I was blameless, though everyone assumed it was me. We never got to the bottom of the leak.

The press seized on the letter and particularly the purple passages, which Michael had prompted, such as the penultimate paragraph: "I sense that there is still something important missing: a compelling vision of where the country is heading beyond sorting out the fiscal mess and a clear and confident message about how we will earn our living in future."

The letter was widely assumed to be an attack by me on the coalition and another example of my propensity to make trouble: the point of it – to make the argument for a proper industrial strategy – was lost. We had 'Where's our vision? Cable on warpath,'[82] 'Cable slams his coalition for its lack of leadership,'[83] 'Cable accuses government of lack of 'compelling vision' in leaked letter,'[84] 'Cable lashes coalition.'[85]

I tried to redirect the attack onto 'backward-looking' Tory right-wingers and their "ridiculous and bizarre claim that the key to economic growth in the UK lies through more business deregulation... old-fashioned, negative thinking which says that all the government needs to do is to cut worker and environmental protection, cut taxes on the rich and stroke 'fat cats'.' This earned the ironic headline: "Twickenham's Karl Marx shakes off a bruising week and vows to keep fighting."

Retaliation was swift in the form of a particularly vicious set of quotes in the *Mail on Sunday*[86] by unnamed Conservatives claiming to be incensed about my leaked letter and by my 'trying to drive a wedge between the prime minister and George Osborne' (over the Mansion Tax).

---

[82] *Daily Mail*, 7 March 2012.

[83] *Daily Mirror*, 7 March 2012.

[84] *The Guardian*, 7 March 2012.

[85] *The Times*, 7 March 2012.

[86] *Mail on Sunday*, March 2012.

"They have launched a counter-attack claiming that Mr Cable is lazy, and they say some Lib Dem ministers agree."

It was bad publicity, but I had learnt that bad publicity was an occupational hazard, was sometimes merited and had little impact on the public.

Those commentators who engaged with the issues were divided on largely ideological lines. The *Telegraph* editorial[87] concluded: "Closing the productivity gap through supply-side measures is the best policy for business, yet Mr Cable barely mentions it... It is time for the coalition's Jeremiah to move on". Commentator Allister Heath in *City AM* argued: "Industrial policies are doomed to fail."[88] But columnist Margareta Pagano in the *Independent* was very supportive noting that "Cable wrote his letter to the PM the day after Sir John Parker called on the government to do more to create a long-term strategy to guide UK plc... industry is now so sophisticated it needs forward planning." And those somewhat detached from the Punch and Judy show of party and personality politics got the point.[89]

On this occasion, what mattered was not the press comment but the quiet work of civil servants and spads behind the scenes. I also had the support of Nick and Danny. The letter had been cleared in No 10 and 11 Downing Street when it was first sent. I was pushing on an open door.

A cabinet meeting had been fixed to discuss the specific proposals and when it took place there were a few predictable but half-hearted objections from one or two of

---

[87] *Daily Telegraph*, 7 March 2012.

[88] *City AM*, 7 March 2012.

[89] "Britain's woes cry out for an industrial policy", *International Herald Tribune*, 8 March 2012.

the more ideological Tories, but Cameron and Osborne had clearly put the word around not to create difficulties. They understood that there had to be a narrative to counter the continuing trickle of bad news: job losses from BAE Systems after a lost Typhoon contract; closure of an aluminium smelter in the north east; unemployment creeping up month by month. Deficit reduction was losing its appeal as a rallying point.

We had been talking about a 'growth strategy' and there was a cabinet sub-committee dedicated to that subject but the 'supply side' reforms favoured by the Tories were either unacceptable to the rest of us (Beecroft) or of questionable merit (planning reform) or comically irrelevant (removing very obscure regulations).

By contrast, some visible industrial success stories, enabling senior members of the coalition to appear with hard hats alongside an assembly line, fitted the bill. And success stories were beginning to appear, especially in the car industry: I was able to announce at the Geneva motor show that Nissan was launching a new model, creating 2,000 jobs; JLT was creating 1,000 new jobs on Merseyside; the GM plants were now out of danger. The sense that the government was behind the automotive industry was a contributory, if unquantifiable, factor.

Enthusiasm would be too strong a word but, perhaps for the first time in the coalition, I had a sense of being a Lib Dem minister leading a big government initiative which colleagues across government wanted to be associated with. In my more cynical moments, I saw the genius of the Tory party at work; whenever they spotted a good Lib Dem idea, they would try to take it over and establish exclusive ownership as they were already doing with the income tax threshold, apprenticeships and the pupil premium.

The department was in seventh heaven. There was now the prospect of leading and co-ordinating a significant government project. Submissions came in thick and fast. We identified, initially, a series of sectors which would benefit from the kind of collaborative arrangement we already had with the Automobile Council and to a degree in aerospace: digital and creative industries; traded services like professional services and higher education; energy supply chains for wind, nuclear and oil and gas; life sciences; core 'foundation' sectors like construction.

We recognised from the outset that advanced manufacturing would be the 'glamour' bit of the industrial strategy and there was a case to be made for boosting manufacturing's share of the economy for its contribution to productivity and exports and I was to major on that theme.

But the economic reality was that manufacturing was now barely 10 per cent of GDP and we needed to build up traded services also: not just the City. Setting up and servicing the various sectoral bodies became a major part of departmental life and when I spent time with these groups it was clear that, while some businesses were apprehensive about being sucked into a 'talking shop', most saw them as an opportunity to set out their stall.

And there was an opening for the government. When I confronted firms in the wind power sector and oil and gas with the fact that the UK's share of content in their turbines and rigs was derisory, it was clear that they had never been challenged on the issue before and they started to think about local supply chains. When we got the varied bits of the struggling construction sector together, they started to identify some key systemic weaknesses: the failure to develop industrial building techniques and the particular weakness of supply chain finance for small builders.

It soon became clear that there was a major long-term task in driving this process which could keep me productively occupied for the rest of the life of this government.

In another part of the forest, a serious row had built up over the budget. I had been engaged in conversations with Osborne over how to realise his ambition to get the top rate of income tax below 50 per cent. We agreed that any tax cut favouring high earners must be balanced by an increase on valuable property – the so-called 'mansion tax' – in the form of higher council tax bands. He could see the economic and political arguments and the attractions of a tax which couldn't be avoided. But Cameron was adamant that it couldn't happen: the idea was a red rag to a bull amongst wealthy Tory donors. The issue fell to be resolved in the so-called Quad with Nick and Danny Alexander representing the Lib Dems.

What emerged was an agreement to cut the top tax rate and 'in return' there was a modest increase in the personal allowance, which the Tories had no problems with and were already claiming credit for. There was also to be an inquiry into a so-called 'Tycoon Tax', to restrict the scope for high income tax avoidance but which was left very vague. The Lib Dem spring conference followed, in a fractious spirit, with Matthew Oakeshott pouring cold water on the 'Tycoon Tax' in the press, and me failing to offer full-blooded support since I knew nothing about it. The frosty reception when I met the Clegg team suggested that I was seen as having colluded in the public critique of the budget. My new spad, Emily Walch, had a baptism of fire, trying to dampen down the flames.

This episode brought to the fore an issue which was to prove a growing source of friction: the Quad. I hadn't been in the least fussed about it until this point since it hadn't encroached on the economic issues I was involved in. I also had a high regard for Danny who was both likeable and capable. But sooner or later there was going to be a point at which there would be a problem with having the two Lib Dems representing the party, who were seen – fairly or not – as closest to the Tories and to Treasury thinking.

The Gateshead spring conference, which followed immediately after the rows over the forthcoming budget and the leaked letter, was not a happy event. Apart from the ill feeling about the pre-budget rows, there was mounting anxiety amongst our parliamentarians and activists about the NHS Bill in Parliament, which had given Labour a big stick to beat the government with, including the Lib Dems.

Accusations of 'privatising the NHS' may have been unfair, especially after Nick's success in diluting the more controversial bits, but they resonated with the public and Shirley Williams was leading a Lib Dem revolt demanding a rethink. Then, Nick said that the coalition was a 'staging post' to another coalition which the activists took to be a continuation of the present one.

Many of the local government activists had already been defeated in the previous year's council elections and the party now faced another massacre, so the mood was restive.

March 2012: V has been very much in the news over a letter he wrote to Cameron and Clegg about industry policy having been leaked to the press. It has been well timed for the annual Trade and Industry dinner at the Mansion House. V and the Lord Mayor both made long speeches. I was treated like royalty. I wore my glittery Indian top (a charity shop find) together with the 'crown jewels'. And a long black skirt. My hair was freshly done and hands manicured. I felt good and 'in role'.

This Lord Mayor is much more interested in trade than the last one and, as I had sat next to him at the Obama banquet, I sort of knew him. His wife was a former teacher and really delightful. Superb food and drink; I had far too much.

Off to Gateshead for the party's spring conference. There was a lot of press coverage about tax. Cable (or Clegg) had failed to get a Mansion Tax in return for cutting the top rate of income tax. Nick is talking about a 'Tycoon Tax': clearly a fig leaf to cover up the failure. All this had contributed to a big bust-up between Matthew Oakeshott and the leadership which rumbles on. I was snapped by the press walking with Vicky Pryce, making our friendship 'political', which it isn't. It's personal.

Then tried to do my job as conference rep but got into the health debate late and didn't grasp the full significance of the Shirley Williams amendment deleting key lines from the leadership's motion.

March 17 2012: V is off for another two-day visit to Delhi speaking for the government at a big international conference. I am on the farm alone, though there is a visit from V's elder son Paul, his wife Agi and V's grandson Ayrton. Ayrton is to interview me for a film he is making, aged nine, on compassion in farming. He agrees that my cattle enjoy 'compassionate' farming before they go off to the slaughterhouse; and films me driving my little 1964 Dexta tractor.

The March budget was largely empty and a PR disaster. The significant arguments about income and wealth taxation had already been aired publicly. What was left were minor tweaks to VAT which quickly become the "pasty tax" and the "caravan tax" and other changes which were caricatured as a "granny tax" and a "charity tax".

Osborne was left looking foolish, with little good news on the economy and fending off attacks over incompetence in matters of detail. The budget was nicknamed the 'omni-shambles' budget. The coalition was left looking fractious with the arguments over the budget adding to the list of quarrels and frustrations. The press picked up on the unsettled mood which hanged over the coalition until the Queen's Speech on May 9. A shortage of fuel caused by a strike of tanker drivers and a staff shortage at Heathrow causing vast queues didn't help.

Simon Jenkins in the *Guardian* predicted: "This may be the last of the hurrah for the Tory-Lib Dem accord."[90] A sudden post-budget plunge in Conservative support from the 2010 level of 37 per cent, which it had held since, to under 30 per cent, added to the sense of political panic (the

---

[90] *The Guardian*, 21 March 2012.

Lib Dems were stuck at just under 10 per cent). David Cameron had an approval rating in a YouGov opinion poll of minus 31 per cent; a large majority thought George Osborne should resign as chancellor; a two-to-one majority thought the coalition was incompetent.

The *Sunday Times* wrote about "Cameron caught in a perfect storm",[91] and the *Express* complained that: "Clegg is killing the Tory Party" doing "potentially lethal damage to Conservative electoral prospects" through acts of "sabotage".[92]

The next big hurdle was the Leveson Inquiry. I had, I thought, done enough to establish that I was broadly right on the merits of the issue; but the inquiry would probe in detail whether I had acted properly in the decision-making process. I had, but would have to explain the anti-Murdoch outburst. In the event, the cross-questioning, while testing and long, was something of an anti-climax since neither Douglas Jay (for the inquiry) nor the judge seemed very interested in the competition issues. Their focus was on hacking. The Murdoch lawyers remained largely silent which told its own story.

May 31 2012: V appears before the Leveson Enquiry. He has nothing to be concerned about, whilst there have been endless revelations about the Tories' collusion with Murdoch's people. But the department is nervous.

I have been advised not to walk in with him in case it looks as if he needs emotional support, the implication

---

[91] Isobel Oakeshott and Mark Hookham, 29 April 2012.
[92] Patrick O'Flynn, 28 April 2012.

being that he would only need emotional support if he felt threatened by the process. He doesn't but it has been hard not to get a bit wound up about it. There are mountains of papers prepared by the department and piles of statements from other witnesses, all of which V has had to absorb, sitting alongside me in bed reading until very late.

The Royal Courts of Justice are as imposing on the inside as on the outside. But the room itself is relatively modest, though there are about 50 people and 20 computer screens. We had two sessions with a break in the middle. V had a good quote about approaching the matter with an 'independent mind, not a blank mind'.

In Douglas Jay's questioning it was clarified that his advisers had not behaved in the way Jeremy Hunt's had (badly); nor had V been unreasonably prejudiced against NewsCorp. When we got to the 'sting' operation on Dec 3, V admitted to being close to losing his temper and 'war' was in the air because of the big demonstrations outside his office over student fees.

Judge Leveson wanted to know if V thought politicians should be relieved of responsibility for such decisions but he strongly defended the accountability of politicians in these instances. The News Corp lawyer cross-questioned V but not very effectively. And, suddenly, it was all over. We had a canteen lunch at BIS with Jo Crellin and Emily, his spad. Jo insisted we went home, and we headed off to Tate Britain and looked at the Picassos.

The arguments leading up to the Queen's Speech centred on two issues which affected other parts of government. One was the proposal to legislate for gay marriage. Lynne

Featherstone, the Lib Dem minister in the Home Office, was gathering support in the parliamentary party for a political push. I had no problems with the idea but didn't understand the priority and was not as enthusiastic as I should have been. A mistake on my part: not recognising the importance of the symbolism and the public celebration of love over and above the practical aspects of discrimination, which I thought had been covered by civil partnerships.

The public was broadly supportive: 45 for to 36 against, but it was 35 for to 50 against amongst Tory voters. To his credit, Nick ran with the issue and to everyone's surprise, Theresa May came on board in addition to the socially liberal Cameroons. This was to prove a major concrete achievement for the coalition and Lib Dems, in particular, but at this stage, the Queen's speech merely offered a 'consultation'.

The other issue was House of Lords reform, an issue Nick felt strongly about, as did the activist base, frustrated by the absence of any progress on more important constitutional issues like voting reform and party funding. It was a subject on which I maintained a discreet silence since I had voted in Parliament in the past for outright abolition, along with the likes of Labour left-winger Dennis Skinner.

I confess to having felt a twinge of resentment towards the Lords, having got into the Commons at the fifth attempt over 30 years and seeing people ennobled for no more than having done a favour for a prime minister or party leader or donated party funding. Other, very worthy, people sit on the sidelines or are blackballed.

The subject was awkward since there were getting on for

a hundred Lib Dem peers, many of them very good, some of them friends and some of them doing useful work on legislation. I expected to see the new legislation fail and was delighted that Nick had been tactically astute and established a link with the boundary review: if Lords reform legislation was blocked, we blocked the boundary review, which was giving a net gain of a dozen seats to the Tories (a source of great relief since the first draft of the boundary revision divides Twickenham in two, making it much less winnable).

I was more concerned with land legislation implementing the Vickers Report on banks. The issue had lost its salience but was no less important for delivering one of the key achievements of the coalition so far. I also got to introduce legislation for an Enterprise Bill simplifying the respected but very cumbersome mechanisms for competition policy and power for a Green Investment Bank, which BIS would run.

It was a more modest undertaking than Chris Huhne originally fought for but I reckoned that, even without initial borrowing powers, there was quite a lot of leverage which could be achieved with £2bn in government equity. I relished the chance to show the critics that I and the department were delivering something big and concrete, not just talking about it. I had more mixed feelings about the legislation I was introducing in the form of a Bill easing the limits on 'unfair dismissal', but my embarrassment was lessened when the Tory donor, Adrian Beecroft, discovered rather belatedly that I and the Lib Dems had killed off his recommendations for allowing (compensated) 'fire at will' and was apoplectic.

Beecroft's outburst had the remarkable effect of bringing to the surface supporters that I didn't know I had. One of the most sympathetic pieces of the whole coalition era was in the *Daily Telegraph*, no less, by Peter Oborne: 'Leave Cable alone – he's the moral centre of this Coalition.'[93] Quite apart from the flattering headline, he noted important details which other right-wing commentators had missed: that I had accepted all of Beecroft's recommendations bar one and that after consultation. Oborne's overall verdict, as a Tory, was that I was an "important ally of enterprise and, above all, one of the most loyal and supportive members of this government". Others, less well disposed to the Tories, went further in expanding the eulogy into an appeal to replace the chancellor.[99]

A flurry of such speculation led to predictable outrage amongst tribal Tories. The *Sunday Express* responded with "Reel in Cable and lift the Gloom".[94] I had also maintained a line of communication to Ed Miliband, directly and through our spads, and good relations with my opposite number on the Labour front bench – Chuka Umunna. This attempt to establish business-like dealings and to get away from childish name-calling was reported in the press in highly conspiratorial terms and some commentators linked

---

* The *Daily Telegraph* led with "Socialist Cable not fit for office: Business Secretary and fellow Lib Dems are damaging the economy with objections to cutting red tape warns No 10 adviser (23 May 2012). Hilarity ensued including by Owen Jones in the *Guardian*: "How did 'socialist' turn into an insult?". Jones pronounced me "certifiably non-Socialist".

[93] 24 May 2012.

[94] *Sunday Express*, 29 July 2012.

it with the latest coalition public rancour to predict a "Lib-Lab Pact: the Return".[95] Our party high command was not happy either.

June 2–3 2012: Jubilee Weekend. After an hour's cycle ride along the Thames, we attended an amazing event at Hampton Court in V's Twickenham constituency. Up to 7,500 people picnicking by the time we arrived, Union Jacks galore! Sooty and Sweep puppet show, fancy dress (1952) competition etc. The palace staff looked after us very well and their PR lady arranged pics of V with a baby in a Union Jack dress for the local press.

The next day, we did two street parties in Twickenham, a Sikh gymkhana club event in next door Hounslow and an Ahmadi Muslim community centre gathering, all very worthwhile and heartening. It poured with rain on the last street party and we were glad to escape to the farm in the evening. Sank into a stupor in front of TV coverage of the jubilee.

July 2012: While Vince was tied to Parliament until the summer recess, I had a brilliant outing for a few days to Shetland with my friend Jane Puckering, also my art tutor for the last few years. We started with a drive from the airport to the village of Walls via the tombolo at St Ninian's Isle, one of my absolute favourite places in the world. And I noticed that I concentrate better on my sketching with Jane just out of earshot but knowing she will be casting a professional eye over my amateur efforts. She overcame

---

95 Dan Hodges, *Total Politics*, 16 July 2012.

her fear of flying to come with me to Shetland, which is a compliment; and she is so generous with her time and skill as well as fun to be with. As is Bessie Barron, who had us both to stay in her bungalow overlooking the harbour at Walls.

Outside the Westminster bubble, very little of the coalition politics was noticed. The country was in a festive mood with the Jubilee celebrations of the Queen's 60th year on the throne. And then there was the build-up to the Olympics, which contrary to most predictions, including mine, were a brilliant success: well organised, devoid of unpleasant incidents and a great result for British athletes. As the *Guardian* reflected at the close of the year: 'The summer told us a great deal about who we are and what, as a society, we have become, although there are no guarantees that the new understanding will be taken to heart.'[96]

In August, Rachel and I embarked on a proper 18-day holiday in the Balkans – Croatia, Bosnia and Montenegro. Lots of sun, sea, history and mountains and a reminder, in Bosnia, of the ugly, violent, ethnic hatred which seemed light years away from the Britain of Mo Farah and Jessica Ennis. But the umbilical cord of ministerial responsibility wasn't cut as I discovered with daily calls on the financial crisis at Redcar's Thai SSI steel company.

One day, as Rachel and I were walking in Sarajevo from the site of the assassination of the Archduke Ferdinand by a Bosnian Serb (precipitating World War I) past beautiful

---

[96] Richard Williams, "2012: A truly remarkable sporting year to be relished over and over", 28 December 2012.

mosques (with guards preventing us from going in) to the market square which not too long ago had been shelled by Serb rebels from the nearby hills, when a call came through from Bangkok, from the Thai Finance Minister in Bangkok with news of funding for the plant in Redcar. Was this both the 'End of History' and the 'End of Geography'?

Chapter Eight
After the Olympics

The sense of national optimism which had been generated by the Olympics failed to survive the summer. The economy was showing little sign of the expected recovery. But there was enough ambiguity in the data to head off calls for a fundamental rethink. The rapid fall in unemployment, the fall in inflation, and growing numbers of good news stories from the car industry: all contributed to a case that something positive was happening.

In the political world, Osborne was getting a bad press; after the 'omni-shambles' budget, he had been booed at the Olympics. Lord Lawson, amongst other leading Tories, called on him to give up one of his two jobs: as Chancellor or as Cameron's main adviser on strategy. The press made much of my innocuous comment on *Newsnight* that I thought I could do a "good job" as chancellor, while making it clear that I didn't expect the job and wasn't pushing for it.[97]

Matthew Oakeshott raised the political temperature by drawing attention to Osborne's lack of business experience: "He is doing a good job for someone on work experience".[98] A ComRes poll had Osborne and me at level pegging in popular support to be chancellor with one in five Tories

---

[97] *Sunday Times*, 29 July 2012.
[98] *The Independent*, 1 August 2012.

preferring me. But Cameron made it clear that Osborne was to stay until 2015.[99] It was, however, a relief to be linked to Osborne's job rather than Nick Clegg's. Nick was again demonstrating the impossible nature of the job of being Lib Dem leader in the coalition when Tory MPs voted down his carefully crafted Lords' Reform Bill.

It was good to escape the Westminster hothouse on a Lancashire visit. I went to Kirkham Prison to launch a scheme teaching prisoners basic English and maths using a model of learning developed successfully by the army for its recruits. It was a quirk of ministerial dividing lines that this fell to me rather than Justice. But it was genuinely moving to talk to prisoners desperate for basic education which they had missed at school and which they realised that they needed on release to get on the first rung of the occupational ladder.

These were people marked by inadequacy rather than evil. I feared, however, that the cuts to the prison service and the pressure of growing numbers of prisoners would soon overwhelm this worthwhile initiative.

From there to the BAE Systems' high-tech facilities: some of the most advanced engineering work being done in the UK. Here was the physical embodiment of the dilemmas around the arms trade: well-paid, highly skilled manufacturing jobs and frontier technology destined for the Saudis and other 'friendly' countries.

The midsummer gossip and intrigue were a prelude to a ministerial reshuffle in the first week of September. One

---

[99] "Osborne stays at his post, says Cameron", *Daily Mail*, 3 August 2012.

imaginative Tory commentator had me replacing Theresa May as Home Secretary so that she could become Foreign Secretary.[100] In fact, the basis of the coalition was that the two party leaders would operate within the pre-agreed carve-up of departments.

The biggest shift on the Tory side was dropping Ken Clarke from Justice to be replaced by Chris Grayling: an awful move but at least Ken kept his cabinet place which was crucial to ensure a good balance in economic arguments. Largely overlooked at the time was the significance of the replacement of Justine Greening by Patrick McLaughlin at Transport. Patrick was an affable, well-liked ex-miner but his importance at Transport was that he replaced a minister opposed to Heathrow expansion.

For the Lib Dems, the main change was the reintroduction of David Laws. His self-confidence had taken a battering from allegations around his expenses and exposure of a gay partnership, but he was a real asset. Nick Harvey was dropped as Minister of State for Defence which surprised us all as he had done good work halting Trident to get a proper evaluation.[101]

The main change in my department was the introduction of Michael Fallon as Minister of State and Matt Hancock as a junior minister, replacing Mark Prisk and John Hayes. The move was widely interpreted as an upgrade for the department and the introduction of stronger ministers who

---

[100] Paul Goodman, "Be bold PM, make Mr Cable Home Secretary", *Daily Telegraph*, 20 August 2012.
[101] Patrick Wintour, "Nick Who? PM brings decisive end to rosy days of coalition", *The Guardian*, 5 September 2012.

could 'reel me in' on behalf of No 10 and No 11.[102] I took the move as a compliment and adopted the policy: 'leave your weapons at the door and let us see if we can work together'.

Fallon made no secret of his idolisation of Margaret Thatcher whose picture hung on his wall. Whatever his private feelings about me he was always business-like and respectful. Hancock was initially trickier: like an over-enthusiastic puppy, he was clearly looking for mischief. But he settled down to become an effective minister with a good brain and work ethic. I grew to like him and was genuinely pleased to see him climb the ministerial ladder, transferring his allegiance to whoever in the Tory party would advance his career.

For the Lib Dems, Norman Lamb, after a brief interlude at BIS, moved to Health where he made a substantial and lasting contribution on mental health issues. Amongst my colleagues, I rated Norman close to the top: very capable, independent-minded and totally genuine without the sharp elbows and inflated ego which usually went with rising political status. He was replaced by Jo Swinson. Quentin Letts wrote about the 'pink-cheeked earnestness of the pony club novice' and thought that she had been sent by the Clegg office to keep an eye on me.[103] Whether or not that was true, she was a strong addition: a very capable and confident performer and tipped for higher things.

She was also a badly needed woman in our male-dominated ministerial team. She promoted issues like

---

[102] James Kirkup, "Free market Tories arrive to reel in Cable", *The Telegraph*, 5 September 2012.
[103] "Vince looked as if he was under house arrest", *Daily Mail*, 7 September 2012.

shared parental leave which was to become a landmark piece of Lib Dem-led legislation. Her appointment also signalled an attempt to change the public profile of the parliamentary party which was overwhelmingly male albeit with a handful of impressive women: Jo Swinson, Jenny Willott, Tessa Munt, Lynne Featherstone, Lorely Burt and Annette Brooke. Our party had also had more than its share of sexual scandals and complaints from women about wandering hands. We had a 'culture' problem which would only be overcome by getting a better gender balance.

Two of those women played an important part in the latter stages of the Parliament. Jenny Willott stood in as a junior minister when Jo was on maternity leave. The common view of colleagues and civil servants was that she had star quality: highly competent; an excellent communicator; and very nice with it. After she lost her seat in 2015, she had an opportunity to come back but prioritised her young family over a political career. The other was Tessa Munt who became my PPS, an unpaid role linking ministers with backbenchers. She had a rare talent for networking, developing relationships with MPs of all parties through good, diligent, case work, chasing officials and alerting the department to political sensitivities. She also lost her seat but has kept fighting in Somerset. These two women and Jo have been a big loss to Parliament.

I like to think I helped to promote the cause of gender equality within the department at all levels and to advance issues like getting better representation of women on company boards. We made good progress. But I was irked by the almost complete lack of recognition in the civil service – and in the party – of a more glaring inequality: the near absence of ethnic minorities in positions of responsibility. By contrast, David Cameron deserved credit for bringing in high-quality black and Asian MPs into 'safe' and white parliamentary seats. And Boris Johnson's cabinet is impressively diverse too.

Conference season promised to be difficult within and between the coalition parties. But out of the blue came an olive branch: an offer from the Treasury to finance an idea I had been pushing: to set up a purpose-built state bank to provide the kind of financing to small and medium-sized companies which the market was not providing or supplying at great cost. The Treasury was willing to put up £1bn. which we could leverage to generate perhaps £10bn. of new lending: not an enormous sum in relation to the overall credit supply problem but a good start. This was to be the British Business Bank (BBB).

I looked for the catch: 'George wants something in return,' I was told. The catch was an idea floating around, originating with one of the Tory donors, about a new type of company in which workers would have the option to trade in their employment rights for shares in the company.

I was getting used to the idea that one of the Tories' techniques for extracting donations – over and above the sale of peerages and other 'gongs' – was to offer donors the chance to turn their wacky ideas into legislation. After Beecroft: this. But the advice I received was that there would be little business interest and that (unlike the Beecroft 'hire and fire' proposals) the proposal was harmless. It was clear, talking to Osborne, that he didn't really believe in it either; he was probably just going through the motions to accommodate Number 10. So I saw the possibility of getting something for nothing.

I sold it to my colleagues on this basis: they could rubbish the idea to their hearts' content in parliamentary debates provided they held their noses and voted for it. My transactional cynicism appealed to colleagues who were fed up with pretending to agree with bad policies and getting nothing much in return. The upshot was an opportunity to make a positive announcement at conference followed by setting up the BBB, which was soon in action.

An early success was getting peer-to-peer lending off the ground, through Funding Circle, Zopa and Rate Setter followed by innovative forms of supply chain and export finance. A decade later, the BBB had become the vehicle for large-scale business funding through the pandemic. 'Rights for shares' wasn't heard of again.

Conference was all about post-coalition positioning. Some (most?) of us were anxious to make sure that we shouldn't be locked into a continuation of the Tory coalition and should keep alive the option, should electoral arithmetic present it, of working with Labour, notwithstanding the virulent hostility directed at the coalition. Labour was every bit as tribal as the Tories, if not more so, but, if we meant what we said about 'working with other parties in the national interest', we had no choice but to work with people who were publicly rude about us.

I got involved in two episodes which touched this particular raw nerve. I had been exchanging friendly texts with Ed Miliband and had had amicable conversations with him, as with his former boss, Gordon Brown. Someone chose to leak the information which was predictably lapped up by the Tory-leaning press: 'Miliband texts Cable in charm offensive for a 2015 coalition',[104] 'Miliband uses Cable texts to sow discord'[105] and 'Ed texts to Vince are blow to Clegg'.[106]

On the small number of occasions I met Ed, he was very affable and good company, but I was struck by his interest in trying to formulate big, abstract, ideas which made for interesting, if rather unproductive, conversations.

His leadership was not a success. One particular disaster was the rule change he led in the Labour Party which opened the door to the Corbynite left and set back Labour's progress for a decade at least. He never overcame the legacy of his narrow leadership victory over his brother, achieved by mobilising the left which, in turn, used him. But he was genuinely passionate about some important causes, like climate change, which he had successfully pursued as a minister and is now doing again.

I was also 'love-bombed' on television by Ed Balls when he offered to "work together" on a common agenda including a Plan B on the economy and a 'mansion tax'. The episode was mildly embarrassing to me, as it was no doubt intended to be, and produced a predictable crop of headlines: "Tories' anger after Cable cosies up to Labour,"[107] 'Ed our way, Vince'[108] and 'Balls targets Cable to drive a wedge into the coalition,'[109] together with a more thoughtful warning: 'Vince is popular but he should be wary of all the

---

[104] *Daily Mail*, 7 September 2012.

[105] *Daily Telegraph*, 7 September 2012.

[106] *The Sun*, 7 September 2012.

[107] *Daily Express*, 10 September 2012.

[108] *The Sun*, 10 September 2012.

[109] *The Scotsman*, 10 September 2012.

attention.'[110] I didn't begrudge Ed his mischief; he was being pretty transparent. The unsympathetic media portrayed him as a surly political thug. But he was, as the country discovered on *Strictly*, a likeable human being with a nice line in self-deprecating humour. I later discovered, through a shared involvement in adult education through the City Literary Institute, his quiet work helping people master a stammer (as he had).

Conference involved walking the usual fine line between talking up the positives of the coalition; resisting being consumed by the Tory narrative; and giving hope to the increasingly disaffected 'social liberal' 'left' of the party. The fine line was getting thinner as the party struggled. Nick had an entourage of outriders – mostly rather self-important young men with limited party background – sniffing out real or imagined plots and disloyalty and the press gave them plenty of raw material: 'Boris and Vince – fear of rebellion stalks the conference season.'[111] Poll ratings fuelled the paranoia.[112]

I tried to shift the political speculation onto our relations with the Conservatives in the coalition. Simon Hoggart caricatured my take on the government rather well: 'We are the monkey and we want you to know that we have the organ grinder under our thumb.'[113] But the internal strains were becoming very difficult. I felt I was walking on eggshells and breaking quite a few. I was only too relieved

[110] John Kampfner, *The Guardian*, 11 September 2012.
[111] Toby Helm, *The Observer*, 16 September 2012.
[112] *The Guardian*, 25 September 2012.
[113] "Vince Cable comes to praise Clegg, not to bury him", *The Guardian*, 24 September 2012.

to get back to serious work in the department.

September 7 2012: *Am writing in the aftermath of the party conference, on the train from Kings Cross to Inverkeithing, to visit Zoe and family. I think I've now recovered my wits and life support systems and am glad of some "me time"! I had left my mobile in the pocket in the jacket I wore to collect V from surgery on Friday; so bought a cheap replacement in Brighton which took me three days to even begin to get to grips with. On the upside, we found ourselves upgraded to a 'deluxe' suite, where the ghosts of the Brighton bombing still lurk.*

I attended quite a lot of debates and fringe meetings on my own account as Rachel Smith, New Forest conference rep. As usual, the motions are a bit too longwinded but, if they weren't, some smartarse would point out that something had been excluded. The weather (apart from Day 1) was full-on equinoctial gales, so any thought of swimming was abandoned.

V is a bit flat – the great reception of his speech has given way to rather carping articles and all the wagons being placed in a circle around Clegg, including Paddy Ashdown being installed as elections campaign manager. There are cartoons of Vince as the undertaker measuring up Nick for a coffin. In fact, of course, he's the least confrontational of people. But he is ambitious, and he is able, and Clegg's ratings with the electorate (or even with the party faithful) are awful. If they don't change, then next year the pressure will grow, and it is clear that Ed Davey is positioning himself. Or being positioned by an anti-Vince faction? The video which accompanied Nick's speech had pics of Davey in factories talking to apprentices rather than Vince, who was the major architect of the expansion of the apprentice programme.

September 27 2012: Vicky Pryce is at conference and toying with the idea of a political career. I am very sympathetic to her. Having been through a similar scenario of being ditched suddenly back in 1997, I can't imagine what it must be like to have it happen in the full glare of media exposure. In the meantime, she is carving a good niche for herself as a commentator on economics in general and the euro crisis in particular. She has found time to write a book called Greekonomics, which I will buy. But I think re-inventing herself as a politician is a non-starter right now.

September 30 2012: On the train back from Perthshire, where I have been visiting my daughter's household. The fields are now lakes on each side of the tracks and the sky black. The banks of rosebay willow herb are just pinko-grey tassels and remind me of pink-rinse pensioners, but I neither wrote a poem about them nor painted them. I soon got into the wholesome rhythm of Zoe's household, where everyone was engaged in making entries for the local garden show: plaited loaves and sporty spuds included and Stuart standing in for an absent Dad in a father-and-son golf tournament. It's not quite Little House on the Prairie but it is charming and humbling. I'm sure we weren't such good parents. Zoe herself went off to a felting class and came back with a stylish hat; and we had fun making up a ballad for my son/her brother Dylan's 40th *birthday, which comes up in October.*

I was delighted to be able to get out of the political bubble for a trade promotion visit to Nigeria and South Africa. My previous visit to Nigeria had been with Shell in the dark days of the Abacha dictatorship, when I had been sent to present a scenario exercise on the future of Nigeria to Abacha and his team of generals. It was our subtle way of telling Abacha that, if corruption and human rights abuse did not improve, the company would start to withdraw from the country, stopping the flow of revenue on which the regime depended. There was a heart-stopping moment when the civilian finance minister, a notorious crook, told the gathering: 'How dare this white man come here and talk to us about corruption. There is no such thing as corruption in Nigeria'. There was a long silence but then Abacha burst out laughing and everyone followed suit. I got out in one piece.

This time, in democratic Nigeria, the atmosphere was more relaxed. I went to the presidential compound in the middle of the day rather than in the middle of the night. And I began to appreciate the tremendous potential of Nigeria from the entrepreneurial energy of the business class and the intellectual fizz around the media. The biggest treat was a helicopter ride over the delta oilfields and the spillages and gas flares which had caused so much grief for Shell but which I hadn't seen on earlier visits.

In South Africa, the mission was to promote British railway systems, but my main interest was in political conversations with ANC politicians who were feeling the pain of post-apartheid disillusionment. I also met Helen Zille, leader of the opposition Democratic Party which was in power in Cape Province. She was seeking to manage a smooth transition from white liberal to black leadership, and seemingly succeeding. One by-product of the Lib Dems' relationship with Helen was that we inherited her political strategist, Ryan Coetzee, who was to guide us through the next general election. Suffice it to say that his undoubted skills did not translate well.

October 14 2012: *V back from five days in Africa – Nigeria and South Africa – while I have been doing my beef merchant thing, and going to the Museum of Archaeology and Anthropology in Cambridge for the ceremonial opening by the Earl of Wessex. Lots of standing about, but he did his bit well once he actually arrived.*

We went together to watch V's grandson Charlie play football. He is very enthusiastic – and brave – but also good at the histrionics, "writhing in agony" after any contact with the ball or another player!

October 21 2012: *V and I were together at the Cheltenham Literary Festival, V promoting* The Storm *and justifying coalition.*

Seven year old Rosie's vivid description of her Uncle Dylan's 40th Birthday yesterday runs as follows: "I begged my Uncle Max; then I got into his AWESOME open roof car to the bisicall (=bicycle) polo; mum and dad were pirates, but the Scots were winning but then they got disqualified; then after the polo I went swimming with the Cids (= kids); then I saw that the hot tub was open so I went in; it was lovely then I got dressy because there was bola nas (=bolognese); I had some for tea then I watched

Underdog". *Evidently a good time was had by all.*

November 15 2012: *Wagner with the Prince of Wales was a different kettle of fish altogether. It was a sumptuous event, and mercifully Vince was not too tired to enjoy it. Prince Charles was very matey with him. Camilla was not much in evidence, apparently at another event beforehand and almost late at the concert in a splendid purple gown but without jewellery! A logistical glitch? It was an incredibly glitzy event – lots of women with dresses that had a small train, making the movement of the hundreds of people very slow, for fear of standing on the dress in front!*

We were assigned to a table of politicians, all parties, but the Osbornes were very unapproachable. I would have liked to talk to her about her writing, but felt frozen out.

A fleeting visit to Brussels, the scene of future battles. At the ambassador's residence I was introduced to a lobbying group from Amazon who were setting up a chain of warehouses and wanted me, to appreciate their job potential. At that stage, Amazon was largely unknown and their future role in retailing not yet appreciated. I tried to sound positive, but they hadn't appreciated that I was not involved in planning issues.

From there to a meeting with the Commission and a meeting with Vice-President Joaquín Almunia. Britain was very supportive of his strongly pro-competition role, in the tradition of Liberal commissioners (He was succeeded by Marguerite Verstayer who took on the big US tech companies). But the process of state aid clearance was slow and a lot of important interventions, like the Green Investment Bank, were stuck in the queue.

Rumbling in the background was an issue of massive industrial importance: a prospective merger between BAE Systems and EADS, the pan-European parent company of Airbus, which made wings at a factory on the Welsh borders at Broughton. BAE was in some trouble. The company had lived for years on contracts from MOD which allowed them to earn generous profits while allowing serious slippage in cost and delivery. Under the coalition's more competitive defence procurement, overseen by Philip Hammond, commercial disciplines were causing serious pain, leading to job cuts. But BAE was a repository of a vast amount of engineering excellence and technological know-how and was too important to fail.

The issue was sufficiently major to engage Cameron, Osborne, Clegg as well as myself in a series of meetings in Cameron's small office next to the cabinet office. BIS was able to deploy a very knowledgeable and effective team of aerospace officials. But the arguments were not straightforward. Although a merger seemed the best option for the UK, there was nervousness about a French-dominated strategy for the company emerging from the joint HQ in Toulouse. The issue was tricky for me in that I had a quasi-judicial role in approving the merger. An innocuous, general, remark at party conference criticising irrational prejudices about foreign ownership was used to create a story.[114] In the event the merger foundered on German objections.

---

[114] James Moore, *The Independent*, 25 September 2012.

November 26 2012: *Woke up in Twickenham to a cup of tea in bed brought by Vince, looked up and saw a stain on the ceiling not there the day before. Exactly under the water tank, according to Vince, so while he went off to run the country, I contacted a plumber and unscrewed the panel to access the roof. Cleared a pathway along a joist and peered into dirty, dusty loft space. 11.30 am – plumber confirmed the corroded tank, so I have to go back on Thursday to be there first thing Friday morning, though V will be in Hatfield on Lib Dem 'Away Day'.*

His schedule is:

* *Mon: CBI speech am, Brussels by Eurostar pm (and back).*
* *Tues: Breakfast with Danny Alexander. Meetings all day, press dinner.*
* *Wed: Meetings + Birmingham.*
* *Thurs: Cabinet at Hatfield.*
* *Fri: Back from Hatfield. Surgery. Dinner in Newbury after surgery.*
* *Sat: to Exeter SW Regional Conference, then back to Twickenham.*
* *Sun: Thanksgiving Lunch with Deanne Julius and Ian Harvey (Surrey). Evening: Asian Curry Awards.*

A short visit to Paris to meet my opposite number, industry minister Arnaud Montebourg and trade minister Nicole Bricq. Mme Bricq was a new minister learning her brief and she read from officials' notes. In any event, EU trade policy was a largely dormant subject at the time. Montebourg, on the other hand, was expansive, entertaining, handsome and charismatic. He was, at that point, the darling of the French left, a centre of resistance in the socialist government to the European 'austerity' being blamed on Germany. He was stunned to discover from me that Britain had an 'industrial strategy' – like finding polar bears in the desert – and we had an animated discussion which suggested that the gap between French 'dirigisme' and British 'liberalisme' wasn't as vast as initially appeared. He was eventually replaced by Emmanuel Macron and after a failed bid for the Socialist presidential nomination, he went off to become an entrepreneur, making money.

December 19 2012: Went to the Associated Newspapers general shindig at Claridge's, invitation courtesy of Viscountess Rothermere (who she? – "slim Essex woman" according to a naughty Mail *journalist). I have stuck my neck out by taking issue with Peter Hitchens in response to his 'Alien Nation' centre page spread in last weekend's* Mail *on Sunday.*

A week's seasonal ski-ing in the recess with friends and my son, Hugo, who had come to learn. I only learnt to ski a few years ago (in my sixties) and am now more confident but prone to embarrassing falls and crises of confidence. Can now do the easier red runs. We missed the luxury of the Ducs de Savoie Hotel, which was fully booked by Russians, but it was very convivial and lighter on the wallet.

The New Year produced a ministerial resignation in BIS; but more comedy than tragedy or scandal: Lord Marland. He was rich and had charm, but I struggled to find out what he had been appointed to do. Cameron clearly owed him a favour as a former party treasurer and fund-raiser. When I sought to give him a serious role in the ministerial team, using his business expertise, he made it clear he had no wish to do any work beyond travelling. His travels included a trip to Mozambique 'to keep up his suntan'. When I pressed him to do more he resigned in protest at the 'workload'.[115] To the fury of the permanent secretary, he then continued to use the BIS underground car park for his Jaguar until the combined weight of BIS and Number 10 officialdom managed to prise him out.

Cars were a problem. As part of our 'austerity drive' in BIS, I had agreed to dispense with the ministerial car and use a 'pool car' when necessary. I enjoyed the daily normality of commuting from Twickenham with my ministerial red plastic bag and walking from Waterloo for exercise. David Willetts went one better, commuting in by bike in full lycra. But some of the junior ministers, led by Matt Hancock, saw the ministerial car as essential to their lifestyle. The civil servants fed me endless gossip on the battles around who should have the car.

January 10 2013: *On the train to Cambridge. I found I was still obsessing about Hitchens. I started to write an article called 'Spot the Immigrant'; based on the fact that in our immediate families, most of the brown faces were born in the UK whereas many of the white ones, especially on my side, were born in Africa or Asia. Lazily, I never finished it. I am conscious that the ever more intermittent nature of this journal reflects an increasing feeling that I*

---

[115] *Financial Times*, 8 January 2013.

am changing direction or at least emphasis. My limpet-like grip on the farm is giving way to a slightly more cerebral, social self, veering towards Twickenham and Cambridge. Nonetheless, the farm is where I feel truly 'at home' when I'm alone. My Monday Sing4Fun class, Tuesday yoga and Jane W's 5-mile walk, Wednesday grandchild Tallulah after school (sometimes) and Thursday art class with Jane P is a lovely routine that I fall into with joy. Twickenham, when Vince is not there, is still odd, in spite of a handful of real local friends by now.

January 15 2013: When he is there, he is preoccupied: this week with a speech on Europe at Ditchley Park, in which he is trying to set a moderate, pro-European tone before Cameron's much-heralded speech on Friday.

To fill my time more productively, I took on deciphering and typing part of the diary of Von Hügel, founder of the Cambridge Museum of Archaeology and Anthropology (MAA), which had turned up when mountains of paper and artefacts had to be moved for the major refurbishment of the MAA. This covers three months of 1878 in Java at the very end of his two years of travels in the Far East, when he was tired and homesick. The excitement would be if this demonstrated the provenance of any of the artefacts he brought back; but so far he seems mainly interested in butterflies and pretty girls (and, typically of that era, wanting to classify the exact shade of their skin).

This involvement on the Friends of MAA Committee brought me into contact with Professor Dame Carol Black, Principal of Newnham College, Cambridge, where I did my anthropology degree. She is delightful and being very helpful in promoting the refurbished museum, which is how I came to have tea with her at the Athenaeum Club in Mayfair, which is all buttoned leather, polished mahogany, crackling fires and pools of light from the tasteful lamps. The self-service tea lowered the tone a bit, but a genuine waitress in a pinny served us sandwiches from the tea bar. Another new experience for my collection. I described myself to her as an 'anthropologus interruptus'. I don't think the Latin tag has a feminine rendering!

February 6 2013: Steven Hooper, who co-edited Von Hügel's major Fijian diaries many years ago, has made contact and is genuinely thrilled with what I am doing, so V and I had a meal with him at the Archduke restaurant, near Waterloo, and I was presented with a signed copy of his book.

Chapter Nine
Battle lines harden

Serious politics wasn't long in coming. On January 23 2013, David Cameron made a speech on Europe which set the clock running for an event which was to become the defining event of the decade: the Brexit referendum. He pledged to let the people "have their say" at a point – after the next general election – when the government had renegotiated the terms of membership. He would campaign "heart and soul" for British membership.

Another pro-European Tory, Boris Johnson, then Mayor of London, said he was confident Britain would vote to stay if a better deal had been reached. There was minimal controversy over the speech at the time, though it was noted that UKIP was rising in the polls.

I got a chance to respond to Cameron the next day, in Dublin where I had been sent to address a big and welcoming crowd of Irish businessmen at Croke Park Stadium, famous for the massacre during the Irish War of Independence; latterly for less bloody sporting battles. Anglo-Irish relations were at a high following the Queen's visit in 2011 and the sense of our being united in the European project – though Ireland was still reeling from the 2008 banking crisis and the austerity which followed.

A few days later government plans to redraw constituency boundaries for the next general election were thrown out in Parliament: Lib Dems' revenge for the defeat of Lords reform. There was relief in the party not merely over the fact that we could fight the next election on existing boundaries but over a demonstration that we could successfully draw a line in the sand.

Then, in a dramatic turn in the Chris Huhne trial, he pleaded guilty which meant that he had to leave the House of Commons, precipitating a by-election at the end of February. The omens did not look good. The national poll rating was barely ten per cent. The MP, although well regarded locally, had been forced out in disgrace. The formula which had won the seat – originally with David Chidgey and, later, Chris – was based in part on Labour tactical voting which could no longer be relied upon.

But as the campaign got underway, it became clear that the position was by no means hopeless. The Lib Dems had a good reputation locally thanks to an impressive council group led by Keith House, which had established, in control, a good record of delivery (and which retained control until recently). There was a formidable by-election machine which would bury the town in paper and leave no voter uncanvassed. Activists poured in from all over the country and ministers pitched in delivering leaflets and knocking on doors. There was a real sense of comradeship in adversity and morale was sky-high, for the first time since the start of the coalition.

We were fortunate also in splits amongst our opponents. UKIP had not been placated by the Cameron promise of an EU referendum and decided to fight flat out. Disillusioned Tories who were not happy with the coalition had someone else to vote for. UKIP intervention was crucial. They came second and Mike Thornton, our candidate, got in with a majority of 1,771.

What had started out as a local by-election, caused by the personal difficulties of the MP, proved to have huge national implications. It helped to establish UKIP – and its core issues of immigration and Europe – as a major force which, without actually winning elections, was reshaping British politics. Cameron's critics on the right-wing of the party were emboldened: 'Once ministers fawned on Cameron. Not anymore'[116] and 'Tory dinner-table plot to unseat the Coalition.'[117]

By contrast, Nick Clegg's position was considerably strengthened. At midpoint in the coalition, from a Lib Dem standpoint, the world looked much better. The legislation to legalise same-sex marriage, which the party had campaigned for against a lot of Tory misgivings, passed the House of Commons with a big majority: 400-175. Lynne Featherstone had led the campaign, and Nick had thrown his weight behind it. More broadly, the coalition wasn't happy but hadn't broken down. Government functioned pretty well despite the disagreements. We also took comfort from signs of economic improvement: 'Britain's working... as record 30mn. have a job',[118] with the highest-ever proportion of the working age population (71 per cent) in work and unemployment continuing to fall.

February 6 2013: I have been watching the Huhne/Pryce 'speed points' case unfolding with some horror. Yesterday, the prosecution had a field day with the

[116] Steve Richards, *The Independent*, 7 March 2013.
[117] *The Times*, 7 March 2013.
[118] Alison Little, *Daily Express*, 24 January 2013.

case against Vicky, who is pleading a defence of 'marital coercion'. I am texting brief 'chin-up' messages to her. It's a Greek tragedy. She may well have to go to prison too. Anyone who has met Vicky for more than five minutes would conclude she was no pushover if she didn't want to do something, though those who know her best say she is more vulnerable than she appears. Certainly she is brittle, so I fear she may break when she might be better to bend. When she asked two weeks ago if I would visit her in prison, it seemed a very improbable outcome, but now it looks increasingly probable. I said yes, of course I would.

February 9 2013: *We biked to Richmond to join the Lib Dem action day. Nick Clegg came, and he and Vince did a double act for the cameras. Then all the toffs left (including us) while the real workers got on with the leafleting and canvassing. Tomorrow we go to Eastleigh. 12-2.30pm, brought forward a bit to give me "down" time before the BAFTA awards in the evening.*

It was raining heavily when we got back so Vince relented and the BFI sent a car for us, instead of getting the train to Waterloo. So off to the BAFTAs – sopping red carpet and hard to avoid puddles everywhere but we proceeded along it in the wake of Ben Affleck and George Clooney (what an anti-climax for the fans!)

We were guests of Greg Dyke and his wife Sue Howes (an interesting person who started life as a probation officer and then did teaching and educational DVDs). The ceremony was interminable but entertaining, with Stephen Fry as compère. Argo, Les Misérables and Life of Pi were the big winners, with a few others getting the odd look-in. Then we transferred to the Grosvenor Hotel with dinner for hundreds of people (we were table 67). We were due to go at 10.45 pm by which time the prizes had arrived but not most of the food and we left at 11.15 pm, having kept the car waiting...and were home at midnight. I shook hands with Kevin Spacey and we were within touching distance of Judi Dench. The event was an "experience", but one I would not wish to repeat.

February 20 2013: *Vicky's case ended (for the moment) in farce: the jury couldn't agree and there will be a retrial.*

February 23 2013: Question Time *in St Paul's Cathedral. Other participants were Heseltine, Abbott, Hitchens and (Giles) Fraser. Heseltine opined that if people were old enough to enlist in the army, they were old enough to be on a jury. Hitchens said they only fought because they were too young and unwise not to. Heseltine heard it as "too stupid" and they got very heated.*

Then just as Chris and Vicky faded from the news, a new Lib Dem scandal surfaced. Chris Rennard, former chief executive of the party, was accused of touching young women inappropriately in the office. Having been around Chris quite a lot when V was acting leader, I was surprised. I think I've got quite good antennae for this sort of thing and didn't get any whiff of it. Nor, it seemed, had some other women who worked in his office.

March 3 2013: *Victory in Eastleigh. The news came through at 2.30 am on Friday morning – a reduced majority but safe at 1,770. Whew! The newspapers are still* *full of the sex in politics or the politics of sex... But at least Nick Clegg's leadership is secure for the moment.*

March 8 2013: *A new jury found Vicky guilty of perverting the course of justice for taking Chris's speeding points. It is said they will both get custodial sentences.*

Despite the improved employment statistics, the economy wasn't in great shape. While we politicos had been pounding the streets of Eastleigh, Moody's – the rating agency – had downgraded UK bonds from AAA to AA1 ('stable'), the first such downgrade since 1978: 'UK ratings cut turns up the heat on Osborne.'[119]

George Osborne had been in Davos talking up the economic recovery, so the news was particularly embarrassing. The ratings agency had identified the key dilemma; policies designed to reduce deficits and debt also impacted negatively on growth which in turn made the fiscal position worse. Robert Chote of the Office of Budget Responsibility set out the economics: 'tax increases and spending cuts reduce economic growth in the short term.'[120] Osborne had already pushed back the cost-cutting programme to 2018 so that we were now following the timetable of the original Darling Plan – though neither Osborne nor the Labour Party, for their own reasons, wanted to draw attention to this convergence.

The Bank of England had done its best to support demand through ultra-low interest rates and quantitative

---

[119] *Wall St Journal Europe*, 25 September 2013.
[120] Letter to the Treasury, 8 March 2013.

easing. The only option, now, was to find other ways of boosting demand. I thought that this was the time to make the case for "greatly expanded" public investment and published another in my series of articles in the *New Statesman*.[121] I wanted it to be clear that the Lib Dems were not passive spectators in the economic debate and that my department – styled the 'department for growth' – was just that.

I defended the economic policy of the coalition to date and made the case that 'the balance of risk had changed' and called on the reasoning of the IMF in its last country review, arguing that 'losing market confidence as a result of higher borrowing is now outweighed by the risk of public finances deteriorating as a consequence of continued lack of growth'. By contrast, we should not "undermine the central objective of reducing the structural deficit" and may even "assist it by reviving growth".

The prime minister made a speech on the same day saying that there should be no change of course and so, predictably, the headlines were suitably lurid: "Cable launches his biggest challenge to PM's authority";[122] "Cameron to snub Cable's call for more borrowing";[123] "Cable exposes divisions over Coalition cuts";[124] "PM brakes Cable."[125]

More worryingly, my intervention provoked a hostile

---

[121] "When the facts change should I change my mind?", New *Statesman*, 7 March 2013.

[122] Andrew Grice, *The Independent*, 7 March 2013.

[123] *Daily Mail*, 7 March 2013.

[124] *The Guardian*, 9 March 2013.

[125] *The Sun*, 8 March 2013.

private and public response from Nick Clegg which was, sadly, to lead to an increasingly acrimonious rift. He was adamant that we should not diverge from the Tories on economic policy; I was adamant that a policy of suppressing public investment was not what we had signed up to in the coalition agreement and that, in any event, circumstances had changed. He believed that Danny at the Treasury was our voice on economic issues; for my part, I should stay in the government but stick to the useful things I was doing in the department like the BBB, Green Bank, industrial strategy, catapults, etc.

I sensed that his concern was political rather than to do with the policy issue: not wishing to create an irreconcilable rift with the Tories. Also, I always tended to underestimate the force of tribal politics; he believed that we couldn't be seen to endorse a position promoted by the hated Labour Party. The fact that the Labour Party targeted him with sustained vitriol didn't help.

Behind the issue itself, there were obviously deeper factors around the leadership. I explained, and I think he recognised, that I was not lusting after his thankless job; I was not, in any event, very interested in or knowledgeable about most of the issues he was dealing with. But there was an awkward reality that the people in the party and in the press, who were pushing for him to go, agreed with me on the big economic policy issues and the two were easily conflated. In particular, there was a hard core of a dozen or so MPs and more peers and activists in the country who were becoming openly hostile to the leadership and were citing me as an alternative, despite Eastleigh.

The argument spilled over into our spring conference.

The Social Liberal Forum failed to secure an emergency motion around Plan C (for Cable). 'Unflinching Clegg rejects Cable's call for £14bn. extra borrowing',[126] and made an appeal for party unity. The argument detracted from his excellent, liberal, speech on immigration.

The row over economic policy helped to frame the budget two weeks later. My calls for higher borrowing for investment were matched by Tory right-wingers calling for big, unfunded, tax cuts. Neither happened and I think Osborne was grateful for me giving him some political cover. Instead, the Lib Dem policy of raising the income tax threshold was accelerated which enabled Nick Clegg to claim a victory and the Tories to claim that it was really their policy.

In the background, another row was brewing over the next round of public spending allocations to be agreed by the summer. I found myself in an unlikely alliance with Theresa May and Dr Fox: the National Union of Ministers.

March 10 2013: The Spring conference in Brighton opened on International Women's Day. Jo Swinson did a rather 'stagey' performance, defending her actions (on the Rennard issue) back in 2008 when she and Danny Alexander were responsible for staff complaints. Alongside this rumpus was a policy disagreement involving the Social Liberal Forum wanting V's support for a motion supporting economic stimulus, whilst Nick was sticking with Osborne's 'austerity' and saw this as an assault on his leadership.

---

[126] *The Independent*, 11 March 2013.

March 12 2013: *After conference, family. A trip by train to Perth. But first, home for granddaughter Tallulah's 8th birthday party, for which I got her Nail Art as well as a Cave Painting Kit (only to be done under supervision!). Looking forward to seeing Zoe and family. It seems ages since I've seen the three girls and they change so fast. Their lovely golden labrador, Sage, is saggy – expecting puppies in about a week's time.*

(Later). V has joined me for the Scottish Lib Dem conference where the press is having a field day mocking the motion for self-government for Orkney and Shetland! I assume it is designed as a reminder to the SNP that separatism can be invoked at many levels. When I was in Shetland in the 1970s, Scottish policemen (many imported from Caithness, said the locals) were criticised for arresting the drunk and disorderly rather than taking them home, which was the traditional 'Shetland way' or so we were told. And Shetland feels quite different to Scotland.

March 20 2013: *New Forest Villages Housing Association's AGM on 18th (which I still chair) at last brought some good news on that front: the offer of two off-the-shelf houses in Ashurst at cost off a bigger association which had negotiated them as their quota of "affordable housing" but didn't really want the hassle of managing them. All our other more ambitious schemes have hit planning delays or vicious NIMBY resistance for the last five years, so this brace of birds in the hand – as opposed to flocks in the bush – is welcome and my committee has been persuaded to snap them up.*

Margaret Thatcher died on 8 April and I was lined up to go to the ceremonial funeral on the 17th. Most of my friends hadn't a good word to say about her and Rachel reminded me of the many ways she had undermined the better things in British life with her 'no such thing as society' mantra, like the sense of local community and recognition of public service, giving respectability to greed, and playing on people's nationalism.

I had a more sympathetic view. Perhaps it came from my complicated relationship with my very conservative and Conservative father, with whom I had fought over many issues. He had finally embraced my Indian wife, Olympia, and our children at the end of his life. He also found a purpose in his idolisation of Mrs Thatcher as the national saviour. He died after rushing out into the snow and ice after a heart attack delivering leaflets for her and contracted pneumonia. I recognised that the values she represented for him – hard work, thrift, striving, self-reliance, resilience, patriotism – were not virtues to be sneered at.

Shortly after he died, I was adopted to fight my hometown of York for the SDP. There was a brief glimpse of a new type of politics designed to appeal to the best of the Tory and Labour traditions and rejecting the worst. But the bubble of hope was quickly pricked by the Falklands War which generated far more powerful emotions than our social democratic and liberal alliance. It also gave Mrs T the political credibility and support to launch her economic revolution.

The economist in me recognised that there was, indeed, 'no alternative' to some of the difficult measures which followed the hapless end of the Labour government of which

I had been a minor part as a special adviser to John Smith at the, then, Department of Trade.

Most of the Thatcher era I spent working for Sonny Ramphal at the Commonwealth Secretariat and, whilst I lived in London, Thatcher's Britain was merely one of our member states and psychologically a long way away. I was angered, like most of my multi-racial colleagues, by her obstruction over South African apartheid; but seeing her in action at a heads of government and state meetings, I had a sneaking admiration for her bloody-mindedness and refusal to be cowed by overwhelming opposition.

The funeral, however, was dire; the sheer weight of establishment pomposity and self-importance made it overwhelming. It completely misrepresented her real importance as a radical and outsider.

April 21 2013: Vince went to Mrs T's funeral on Wednesday. I declined. I heard him saying to the diary secretaries that I was 'away from London', managing to make it sound as if I was in Vanuatu. The papers filled another thousand column inches with comments on her. And renewed media exposure for the dreadful 'Boy Mark', now a baronet. I want to have a campaign for Carol Thatcher to be a dame! Rather more deserving of honour for minding their frail mama while Mark cavorted on the world stage. At least it's over.

I could feel quite magnanimous about the Thatcher legacy until I was reminded, by all the news clips of her in full rant, how awful she was in so many ways.

In June, there was the much-anticipated public spending review for the next four years. It promised to be a good deal less draconian than that in 2010. Ministers in spending departments had become more adept at defending their departments, and most of the 'low hanging fruit' had already been picked. The Tories were not willing to go after the perks of better off pensioners or raise more tax from controversial proposals like a 'mansion tax' so Lib Dems blocked ever deeper cuts in benefits.

As the more perceptive commentators like Peter Oborne noted, the cuts were far less draconian than the rhetoric (an overall 1.5 per cent cut in government spending).[127] But there were some deep cuts in local government, difficult reforms of public sector pay, and 'efficiency savings' which were scarcely concealed cuts. Osborne achieved his political aim of getting Ed Balls into a position of accepting the spending framework.

I was the last minister to settle having taken the view that, as the department charged with promoting growth, we needed more, not less, funding for scientific research and innovation and the industrial strategy. George Osborne came up with more money and BIS was considered a 'winner' along with Defence (Hammond) and Health (Hunt).[128] The BIS budget survived 'largely intact'[129] and the *Financial Times* noted 'Vince Cable's hard bargaining won a surprisingly moderate cut for his department, a little victory that will incentivise other ministers to test the Treas

---

[127] Peter Oborne, "Soon, we are likely to need a braver chancellor than this one", *Daily Telegraph*, 27 June 2013.
[128] *City AM*, 27 June 2013.
[129] Steve Richards, *The Independent*, 27 June 2013.

The spending tightrope: Morland in the *Times*, 25 June 2013,
(*courtesy of Morland*).

-ury's mettle in future'.[130]

[130] Janan Ganesh, *Financial Times*, 27 June 2013.

Chapter Ten
Privatising the mail

I was conscious of the littleness of the victory and the fact that, with the coalition well into its third year, there was scant chance, now, of a radical change of direction or a change in the party's position. I had a choice between sloping off into disgruntled resignation and opposition or making the best of the scope I had in government to get useful things done and to rattle cages where necessary. Inertia prevailed and I picked up some useful issues to run with.

I worked with the *Daily Mail* on a campaign to get Google proactively to block child porn.[131] I was appalled to encounter lobbyists for Google who thought that censoring paedophilia on the internet was an infringement of free speech and the beginning of a 'slippery slope'. Google already had an unhealthy influence on Number 10 and Eleven – CEO Eric Schmidt was often around – and I was very happy to work with Mr Dacre's rottweilers to rein them in.

My own relationship with the *Mail* was odd. On one level I was an appalling leftie sabotaging a Tory government. But on another I agreed with some of their positions, notably

---

[131] "Now Show You're Not Amoral, Google! Cable leads call for internet giant to proactively block vile child porn", *Daily Mail*, 1 June 2013.

with their admirable business commentator, Alex Brummer, and got an easier ride than Lib Dem colleagues, including Nick Clegg.

Then a controversy arose over a posthumous pardon for Alan Turing, the mathematical genius who was crucial to breaking German codes during the war and had been a key figure at the National Physical Laboratory in my constituency. He had killed himself after a conviction for 'gross indecency' for a consensual gay relationship and a barbaric sentence of chemical castration that would not have been out of place in Saudi Arabia. Bureaucracy intervened at the Department of Justice, then under Chris Grayling, and his deputy, Damian Green, announced that 'now is not the right time'.

I made common cause with Michael Gove to campaign for a reversal.[132] A mechanism existed in the form of a 'Royal Pardon' thanks to an enterprising Lib Dem peer, John Sharkey, and, a few months later, Grayling agreed to recommend a 'Royal Pardon' which was granted. In 2017, a general amnesty for convicted gays was legislated for.

Another campaign had opened up when I met the campaigning group Global Witness, who were pressing for an open register of 'beneficial ownership' to identify the underlying owners of companies, which had made use of opaque structures to hide their identity from tax authorities or regulators or other public scrutiny. Initially, officials were sceptical or hostile, fearing that it would seem 'anti-business or be impractical.

---

[132] "James Forsyth in the corridors of power", *Mail on Sunday*, 14 July 2013.

Yet a G8 summit was coming up in mid-June, to be held in Northern Ireland, and David Cameron was looking for initiatives to give substance to the theme of transparency. Number 10 enthusiastically grasped the idea – and other measures designed to limit tax dodging in mining companies specifically and more generally – and Cameron took the lead in pressing for widespread adoption of registers. I was given a mandate to legislate for a British register and, thanks to advice from Global Witness, was able to circumnavigate conservative Whitehall ruses designed to keep the register as innocuous as possible and in particular, keeping it from being open to public inspection.[133] I was wooed by lobbyists, especially from the Channel Islands and shadier places, desperate to keep their secrecy and fearful that the UK government might force them to adopt an open register.

In the event, Cameron called the British dependencies to a summit in London to demand registers but gave in on 'openness'. Years later, I thought that the British register was a genuine achievement but noted the growing number of 'national interest' exemptions, the lack of checks on honesty and the failure to act on registering property and land.

Sometimes circumstances dictated working with Tory colleagues on a common agenda; sometimes it was necessary to call them out. In late July, there were reports of Home Office vans going around areas with large ethnic minority populations telling (illegal) immigrants to go home or face arrest. The van campaign was incendiary. Nick

---

[133] House of Commons Briefing Paper 8259, 8 February 2012.

Clegg replaced our minister, Jeremy Browne, with the more combative Norman Baker. I was, I thought, appropriately aggressive in calling the van campaign 'stupid and offensive', which added to my long list of unwelcome comments on immigration issues and produced a predictable reaction from the Tory tabloids.[134] One of the more thoughtful Tory commentators credited me with understanding and using 'hit-and-run politics: he is both a friend and a foe of the government of which he is a vital cog'.[135]

My parting shot before departing for a short holiday in France was the most reckless: opening fire on the Bank of England. The operational independence of the bank was a major political achievement (by Gordon Brown) and I made my maiden speech in Parliament in support of it. After the financial crisis, central banks had done a lot of the heavy lifting through monetary policy to keep Western economies afloat. And Britain's (then retiring) Mervyn King was a brilliant economist.

But one of the side effects of post-crisis financial management had been gradually to tighten the requirements on the banks to hold more capital against loans to such an extent that the banks were no longer lending to small business. Of course, there had to be capital buffers and I had supported action to curb bank profligacy. But there was a blind spot around small business loans.

I had tried unsuccessfully to persuade Mervyn King to flex the regulatory requirements or to adopt the idea of the

[134] "Unplug Cable", *The Sun*, 29 July 2013.
[135] Paul Goodman, *Daily Telegraph*, 30 July 2013.

bank's own Adam Posen to buy bundles of SME loans as part of QE. So, out of frustration and irritation at the Bank's conservatism and smugness, I let fly at the 'capital Taliban' in the bank. My outburst earned the distinction of a headline in the *Financial Times* and a telling off in the editorial.[136] My comments provoked a lot tut-tutting and gave Osborne an easy hit defending Gordon Brown's legacy from interfering politicians. But I thought the point hit home and, for a while, I luxuriated in my new reputation as the banks' friend. I later noticed that in the next big crisis (Covid), the regulatory obstacles had gone.

August 2013: For me, the end of an era. The start of life on the farm, without my own animals. My last domestic pet, Aslan the cat, died last year. My Dexter cattle were proving hard to get in calf: both resistant to the charms of visiting bulls and not responding to artificial insemination. I resolved to wrap up an enterprise which had been an important part of my life for 14 years. I was enough of a farmer to send the last two for slaughter, but compassionate enough to make sure they made their last journey together. But I missed them horribly. V and I went off to the Isle of Wight for a couple of nights so that I didn't have to stare at the empty fields. Before long, the same fields would provide grazing for other peoples' horses: a less demanding and more lucrative business.

Our summer break in France was divided between a few days getting to know my younger son's prospective in-

---

[136] "BofE 'capital Taliban' choking fragile recovery, warns Cable", *Financial Times*, 24 July 2013.

laws at their little summer house on the beach at Pornichet, in western France, exploring the salt pans at Guérande by bike with them and going on to Brittany to see the area which includes the astonishing avenues of standing stones at Carnac, which had been on my bucket list for a long time.

We then had a week of 'la France profonde' in the Auvergne. It was as idyllic as expected until rudely interrupted by a call from London for Vince to return immediately to vote on military intervention in Syria following a suspected chemical weapon attack by the Assad regime. He got there in time after several changes of train and reappeared after a couple of days. It was all in vain from the government's point of view. After some Conservatives and most Lib Dems rebelled, the government lost by 13 votes. *

The autumn proved to be, for me, the most difficult period since the 2010 'winter of discontent'. One of the big events of the coalition years and – initially – a very difficult one for me was the privatisation of the Royal Mail. I had been persuaded a decade earlier, when I was shadowing Labour DTI ministers, that this was a necessary step and one which the Lib Dems, unencumbered by ideological baggage, could pursue for pragmatic reasons.

The argument was that mail services faced an existential threat from new technology – email – and from courier

---

* The repercussions were vast, diminishing Cameron's authority and causing Obama to retreat from his planned intervention. Almost a decade later, the civil war continues, and Assad is still there.

competition (being introduced as a result of EU competition policy and deregulation). They could survive – to provide a continued basic service for those needing it – only by modernisation and heavy investment in new machinery and systems to capture new markets like parcels deriving from emerging internet commerce.

Yet as a nationalised industry, the Royal Mail was unable to raise finance for investment through equity or loans, the latter because of Treasury opposition to increasing the public sector borrowing requirement. And arguably, it was difficult for a nationalised industry to compete in an aggressively entrepreneurial way. The basic logic had been accepted by my Labour predecessors – Alan Johnson and Peter Mandelson – but they had been blocked from even partial privatisation by trade union objections.

Margaret Thatcher had also baulked at privatisation, allegedly because it might offend the Queen (whose head was on the stamps); and neither e-mail nor Amazon existed in her day.

There was also a political motive, at least on my part. I was conscious when we were drawing up the coalition agreement, and subsequently, that most of our battles with the Tories would be fought from the left. It was useful to be able to parade a big asset sale to set against my arguments for more public investment and nationalised banks. When I made it clear in the early days of the coalition that we intended to proceed with the sale there was a blast of hostility from Labour-leaning papers.[137] [138]

But we set out a distinctive Lib Dem approach which guaranteed a ten per cent shareholding to be set aside for the workforce; and provided strong, legal guarantees of the 'universal service obligation' – delivery of mail at a uniform price nationwide, six days a week (which Ed Davey steered through Parliament with some skill); and split off a publicly owned post office network with substantial additional funding (£1.3 billion) to expand, modernise and offer a wider range of services, including financial services.

We also got the Treasury to take on the pension fund, plugging a £9 billion hole and safeguarding employees' pensions.

There remained the sale itself. I made the mistake of thinking this was a largely mechanical exercise, the difficult politics having already been accomplished. I agreed to Business and Enterprise Minister Michael Fallon's request to manage the process in the ministerial team. The first decision – to make a public share offering, including a 'Sid' (Scheme Information Document) offer to small investors rather than a 'trade sale' – wasn't difficult: we could envisage the outrage if the successful bidder was Deutsche Post or an asset-stripping operation. Our overall approach was well received.[139]

Over the summer, as we prepared for the IPO, problems started to emerge. The first was the Communication

---

[137] "Post Waste: Cable Blasted for 'Devastating' Royal Mail Sell-Off", *Daily Record*, 11 September 2010.
[138] "Con Dems Mail Fight", *Daily Mirror*, 11 September 2010.
[139] "Cable's Right Call on Royal Mail", *Financial Times*, 11 July 2013.

Workers Union (CWU). Ed Davey, in particular, had developed good relations with Dave Ward and his team and, aside from the occasional grumbling, we admired the way they had buckled down to the modernisation agenda of Royal Mail management, delivered good results and helped deliver a profit for the first time in years.

But they were implacably opposed to privatisation and threatened strike action. We suspected that they were bluffing, but the effect was to dampen investor interest. The mood was further soured by finding that, with only weeks to go before the flotation, it emerged that CEO Moya Greene had agreed with chairman Donald Bryden to have the company buy her a house. I vetoed it in a very acrimonious meeting and she had to hand back the money made from the property. This was a minor episode, but it fed the narrative of fat cats against workers and the public.

The team at BIS and the advisers – Lazards – had carried out a detailed study of investors' assessments of the value of Royal Mail and also of comparable businesses in Europe. But it became clear that they were erring on the side of caution since they were judging success by 'getting the sale away', particularly after some spectacular flops earlier in the year, notably by Facebook. I stressed that my aim was to get the maximum for the taxpayer and to push the price to the limits. The price range was moved up after I had pushed for it. But my bullish approach was not helped by the threat of a strike.

The final advice we got from those handling the sale was to sell at £3.30 a share (valuing the company at £3.3 billion). In the internal arguments, when I was pushing the team to be more ambitious, I was faced with the unanimous opinion – including from Fallon – that I was putting the sale at risk. One key influence was the permanent secretary, Martin Donnelly, an unassuming but genuine and clever man, who persuaded me to listen to the professional advice, on the basis that, as the BIS accounting officer, it was his neck which would be on the block if a bad judgement was made involving taxpayers' money.

The immediate impact of launching the sale to the 'Sids' – the private investors – was that it was massively oversubscribed. As a rationing device, I adopted a proposal to exclude all large investors and senior managers at Royal Mail seeking over £10,000 of shares. This provoked a furious response from some rich individuals who got to David Cameron to protest. He in turn rang me while I was laying the foundation stone for a sweet factory on an industrial estate near Pontefract. He accepted that it was important that the flotation should be seen as fair as well as commercially successful and the decision stood. A total of 700,000 people got shares; 36,000 big investors were excluded.

Then came the actual flotation which would see institutional investors acquiring the bulk of the shares. We had one final, bad-tempered meeting when I threatened to pull the sale or restrict the number of shares sold and to reopen the initial allocation. Contrary to what I had been told – that there was an exclusive group of committed, long-term investors (pension funds and sovereign wealth funds) – the list to be allocated shares included a leading hedge fund. But with hours to go, rewriting the rules would have caused chaos and endless litigation. The IPO went ahead, was massively oversubscribed and the price shot up by 36 per cent on the first day and then in the weeks that followed, to over £5 a share. I was left arguing that this was speculative froth – as much of it was – and that the market would in time come to reflect real value. It did, but a long time later. Needless to say, critics of the sale went to town on the taxpayers being short-changed.[140]

I was partly reassured that the *Times*, the *Financial Times* (Lex) and others thought that I – or we – would be vindicated.[141] For the next few weeks, however, there was continued criticism and inquisition in Parliament and the press. It was a very uncomfortable time and the vindication (even apologies from some critics) came many months later after the market adjusted to the reality of the Royal Mail's position and I had commissioned a full independent inquiry into the IPO by respected Labour peer Lord Myners. By then, however, the media circus had moved on.

---

[140] Jonathan Ford, "The taxpayer has been sold short by the Royal Mail flotation", *Financial Times*, 12 October, 2013; Jim Armitage, "There's no Froth on the Royal Mail Skies – taxpayers have been shortchanged", *The Independent*, 24 October 2013; "Ministers Accused of shortchanging taxpayers as Royal Mail shares soar", *The Guardian*, 12 October 2013; and "The Royal Fail", *The Sun*, 11 October 2013
[141] "First Class Mail", *The Times*, 12 October 2013; Terry Murden, "Why the price is right for Royal Mail Sell-off", *Scotland on Sunday*, 13 October 2013; and Anthony Wilton, "MPs posturing about 'underpriced' Royal Mail share sale is all a bit rich", *The Independent*, 19 October 2013.

Chapter Eleven
Hit-and-run politics

Meanwhile, there were serious tensions within the Lib Dem team. I became aware of them at a summer Lib Dem 'Away Day' for MPs. Nick had appointed Paddy Ashdown to be the next general election 'supremo' and we were given key performance indicators to work on like military cadets. Then the new South African strategic planner, Ryan Coetzee, introduced us to our new party slogan – *Stronger Economy. Fairer Society.* – to be repeated in all media interviews. But the centrepiece of the event was a 'debate' on economic policy in which Danny and his advisors explained the official line with the help of Treasury overheads.

I tried to point out some of the areas of disagreement and was supported by a few like-minded colleagues like Norman Lamb, John Pugh and Tessa Munt. Then, a succession of 'loyalists' had been primed to endorse the line and the meeting concluded with a 'consensus' that we should not question the Treasury view including spending (and investment) limits.

Beyond mild irritation, I thought little of the incident until I saw an article in the *Sun* based on comments from sources close to Nick Clegg, explaining that I had been humiliated as my leadership plot was scuppered by colleagues endorsing government spending limits.

I realised that I had underestimated the extent to which

expressions of dissent at spring conference, and my advocacy of more public investment, had been interpreted as a threat to the leadership. It was clear that autumn conference would be difficult, with the leadership on full coup alert and myself under constant observation for signs that I might be 'on manoeuvres'.

I wasn't. But a lot of my friends were determined to have a confrontation with the leadership, come what may. They believed – probably rightly – that the leadership strategy was to cling to the coalition with the Tories until the election and then, hopefully, to join another afterwards. That meant going along with a lot of Tory policy they didn't agree with and which wasn't in the coalition agreement. Attaching ourselves to the Tories could ultimately lead to the irrelevance of the pre-war National Liberals.

There was, however, no appetite in the party for a wider rebellion against the leadership. There was a recognition that we had to hang together as there was no future for a small break-away rump; the sad history of the far bigger and better organised SDP was a salutary warning. The underlying problem was that the British electoral system barely accommodated a third party, let alone variations within a third party. In Holland, traditional Liberals like Mark Rutte (who was, I think, Nick's role model) were in a different party from, but worked with, social liberals. In Britain that was not possible.

My conclusion wasn't very inspiring or courageous but, I believed, realistic: that the best option was to avoid open confrontation and to stick with the leadership; to continue with the coalition while keeping all our options open after the election; and to maintain our party identity with 'hit and run' raids attacking the Tories aggressively on particular issues. Patience.

But my logic didn't fit with the reality of conference proceedings. The leadership had put up a rather innocuous motion on economic policy which side-stepped the main areas of contention. The Social Liberal Forum put up a cleverly worded amendment which identified the key points of difference which I had been arguing for months. The leadership made it clear, however, that voting for the official motion was a vote of confidence in Nick.

For reasons which I never understood in retrospect, my political brain froze. Decades in politics should have taught me that, in such situations, you speak one way and vote the other. I had done so many times, in Parliament, making the necessary points in debate but voting the official line. Some of my more radical colleagues, like Steve Webb, did just that, to great effect, praising the amendment while urging a vote for the leadership.

Despite the urgings of my special advisers, I had decided to sit out the debate and work on my conference speech which followed. This was the worst option to have chosen. It advertised the rift[142] [143]. But I disappointed my friends since I had remained silent and finished up having to turn up to vote against their amendment. The leadership was not slow to claim victory for its version of the economic orthodoxy.

I tried to retrieve the situation with a forceful speech

[142] "Cable risks rift with Clegg by missing economy vote", *The Times*, 16 September 2013.
[143] "Clegg and Cable at odds over the economy", *The Guardian*, 16 September 2013.

which, perhaps reflecting the emotional upheaval at the time, came out as something of a caricature. The press seized on a few choice phrases: "Cable strikes at hated Tories"[144] and "Ugly, nasty and blinkered: Vince Cable's verdict on his Tory colleagues".[145] The Tory press retaliated in kind with "Shameless Treachery: Mr Cable is the most disloyal and devious politician of our times".[146]

The publicity wasn't all bad.[147] But the colourful phraseology had the unfortunate effect of detracting attention from my central messages: that we needed to maintain 'equidistance' in any forthcoming election and keep open the option of walking away; and that we shouldn't allow ourselves to be tarnished by the right-wing 'dog-whistle' politics we were hearing more and more from the Conservatives directed at immigrants and people on benefit. I also had some useful proposals to regulate 'zero hours contracts' which mostly got lost in the noise.[148]

What I hadn't bargained for was that some of the language had hurt. I had rather assumed that, as Paul Goodman had put it: 'His Tory colleagues have got used to the business secretary's carefully calculated detonations, rather in the manner of the inhabitants of Beirut getting on with their lives amid the chaos.'[149] But, on return to London,

---

[144] *The Guardian*, 16 September 2013.

[145] Jason Beattie, *Daily Mirror*, 17 September 2013.

[146] Stephen Glover, *Daily Mail*, 17 September 2013.

[147] Chris Blackhurst, "Foolish to dismiss the prophet Vince", *Evening Standard*, 18 September 2013.

[148] "Cable to vow crackdown on zero-hours contract abuse", *The Scotsman*, 16 September 2013.

[149] Paul Goodman, *Daily Telegraph*, 30 July 2013.

Matt Hancock came to my office visibly upset and asked: 'Do you really hate me?'. The answer obviously was 'no' and after a frank conversation, our relationship improved considerably.

September 2013: *Glasgow. Our hols seem a long time ago. There is a lot of tension around conference because the leadership feels it is on trial – and our friend, Matthew [Oakeshott], has added fuel to the flames by publishing an analysis of the prospects of the Lib Dems under Nick Clegg compared with A N Other (who could that be?). The leadership picked a fight over a Social Liberal Forum amendment on the economy which V wanted to support but couldn't. There is a lot in the press the next day about V being yesterday's man and not destined to be leader: a post he isn't seeking anyway (in spite of opinion polls).*

We are due to leave for Shetland, but V is told firmly by Emily that he must stay behind for Nick's speech, otherwise it will look like 'sulking' after the shenanigans earlier in the week. So I have to go ahead and he follows a couple of days behind.

Blissful break with old friends on the main island. And a stunning walk on the west side on a sunny day. We are told that this is where the windmills will go: an issue which is bitterly dividing the islanders, including our best friends.

Then a sail around Bressay to see the astonishing birdlife on the cliffs at Noss. Rather cold, but V is happy to be allowed to steer the boat. He also gets in some politics with a fundraising dinner for Alistair Carmichael, the local MP, now in the cabinet as Scottish Secretary, and a memorial dinner for Jo Grimond (with V as the main speaker) surrounded by the Grimond family and Tavish Scott, the MSP (a distant relative of mine by marriage). V reports back on a dinner with Alistair, who is reassuring about V's 'rock solid' position, despite the conference dramas. But Emily, on the phone, warns that there will be retaliation for the 'insubordination' in the form of making life difficult in the upcoming spending review.

There was no shortage of issues which lent themselves to constructive policy action or to 'hit and run' raids attacking bad things coming from the other side of the coalition. One of the latter was housing policy. Virtually no social housing was being built which was one of the main candidates for the public investment I was arguing for (and the existing stock was being sold off at more generous discounts). Any MP who was reasonably conscientious with their case work would be aware of the growing desperation of low-income families without secure accommodation.

To make matters worse, owner occupation was more difficult than ever because prices were so high in many parts of the country. In the USA, the 'bubble' of house prices leading up to the financial crisis had burst; but not in Britain, where production had fallen more than demand and now prices were rising again.

Osborne's response to the housing crisis was Help to Buy: announced in July and due to come into effect in January, the government would guarantee 20 per cent of loans for house purchase. The effect would be (and was) to push up prices, pushing people off the housing ladder while subsidising others to get on. The scheme was attacked from the *Financial Times* to the *Daily Mail*. And I pitched in warning of the dangers of a new 'bubble' and the dangers of pumping in demand rather than boosting supply.[150]

But, for the Tories, the scheme was a stroke of genius. As several Tory colleagues disarmingly conceded in cabinet, rising house prices were very popular with the (mainly elderly) owner occupiers who were their political base while a plan appearing to help people to buy homes was a no-brainer. Osborne was also smart enough to see the attractions of a scheme which fitted the model of developer-led housing. Rising prices created bigger margins and made building more profitable while also inflating bonuses and profits in the industry (and grateful donations to the Tory party).

He had also managed to get onside the new governor of the Bank of England, Mark Carney, who, in our first private meeting, argued strongly, to my surprise, that rising house prices are good for the economy. He was clearly a very bright man, but I felt it could be difficult to respect a governor so obviously taking a line to please his political masters. Osborne would be pleased; but I doubt that Mervyn King would have made the same judgment.

There was the predictable rash of dismissive comment that I was interfering in matters which didn't concern me. But, as it happened, one of the most valuable bits of the industrial strategy was in the construction industry where we brought together people from the sector to co-ordinate better skills training and to promote industrial building techniques and also got the Treasury to back a small builders' credit scheme. So I persisted with what were

---

[150] The *i* newspaper, 29 July 2013.

regarded as unhelpful criticisms of 'Help to Buy'.

Unfortunately, my public attacks on 'Help to Buy' caused another unpleasant argument with Nick and Danny, who thought my interventions were just making trouble, though I was pleased to see that Nick came round to recognising the problems.[151]

September 2013: *Back home I was so glad to see that housing policy was getting some attention at last. Chairing New Forest Villages Housing Association is hard work, our development programme – or rather lack of it – increasingly frustrating. The government's Help to Buy Scheme is socially right-wing and economically illiterate, and I am glad V is making an issue of it. On a practical level, the retirement of our extremely efficient (and only) employee at the end of the year, means we have to recruit a replacement, which is worrying and time-consuming.*

The department was always anxious to send me off doing some trade promotion in the 'dead' period of the other conferences. This year: Sweden and Finland. I was a great fan of the Scandinavian social and economic model and enjoyed the easy conversations with people who talk frankly and to the point (and fluently in English). I was able to spend time with Carl Hamilton, the leading Swedish Liberal and Europe Minister, with whom I had written articles for the World Bank forty years earlier on international trade policy.

---

[151] "Clegg feels disquiet over Help to Buy", *Financial Times*, 17 September 2013.

I discovered only recently that this utterly unpretentious academic and politician was a count: Swedish aristocracy. Much like the leading members of the fabulously wealthy and influential Wallenberg family, with whom the delegation had dinner, there was totally genuine personal modesty. The politician who made the biggest impression was Annie Lööf, leader of the Centre Party with whom I shared an open meeting. But despite her highly articulate explanation, I totally failed to understand how her party differed from the other Liberal parties. Indeed, all the Swedish parties, except the communists and the populist, anti-immigrant, democrats could have fitted comfortably within the Lib Dems.

September 2013: In Scandinavia with V on a quick visit to Stockholm and Helsinki: city tours for me, factories and ministers' offices for him. Concludes with embassy dinner in Finland. The Finns seem very dependable and have consensual politics, though even they seem to find a coalition of six parties a struggle. I was told that the consensus is possible because the communists are not very communist and the right wing not very right wing. The Finns also have a highly educated population and, like the Dutch, appear to be good at languages and often fluent in several. I warmed to them. I suspect that Alex Salmond would cite them as a model for Scotland: also five million people.

And on from Scandinavia to Russia, my second visit there to promote trade though the immediate priority was to help secure the release of some Greenpeace protestors (they *were* released). British exports were rising more rapidly than to any other significant emerging market since, unlike in India, China and Brazil, there was no strong protectionist lobby against Western imports.

My interlocutor was Igor Shuvalov, who was deputy prime minister to Medvedev in President Putin's government. Shuvalov was the suave, business-friendly face of the regime, though his reputation had recently taken a hit with the emergence of papers showing that he and his wife had amassed a fortune of several hundred million dollars, some in London property (including part of Whitehall Place). Our meetings were brief and business-like.

I also arranged to see another of Putin's inner circle of technocrat-businessmen, Anatoly Chubais, whom I had first encountered visiting Russia with Shell in the Yeltsin period. He had then masterminded the privatisation plan which created the generation of Russian oligarchs. He explained the plan then: 'Let them steal and steal. When they are finished with stealing, they will become respectable law-abiding Russian capitalists defending their property rights.' He had now become an oligarch himself and was devoting his considerable talents to nurturing innovation through a nanotechnology company, Rusnano. He was fascinated by our 'Catapult programme' and its technology and innovation network but I suspected that there were easier ways to get rich in Russia than innovating.

I am not sure if Alexander Lebedev (Evgeny's father) was a Putin man or not. The relationship was ambiguous. He treated me to a meal in a vast restaurant where we were the only guests (apart from guards at the entrances). He ate raw meat and fish and took me through an incomprehensible series of conspiracy theories which had lost me long before the end, but hinted at his powerful connections and KGB past.

The gloomy British embassy immediately opposite the Kremlin was the source of endless stories of life in the Cold War and before. But, while there, I was introduced to members of a 'human rights' group: young people who were building up a protest movement around Alexander Navalny. And I got a chance to renew my acquaintance with the leader of the Russian 'social liberals' (Yabloko), Grigory Yavlinsky. This brave man had seen many liberal friends and colleagues assassinated and it was said that his son, a concert pianist, had had a finger amputated by gangsters to intimidate his father.

Back in London, the main issue was RBS. The Treasury was trying to get it ready for sale but that required a complex process of separating the 'toxic debt' into a 'bad' bank and isolating a 'good bank' which could operate commercially and retrieve most of the taxpayers' money. I had no problem with the approach in principle but could not understand why a publicly owned bank could not contribute (as Lloyds now was) to financing British small and medium sized business or why it dragged its feet on hiving off the Williams and Glyn subsidiary to provide more competition. There was also a bigger, legacy, problem: the many angry businesses that had been dragged down during the financial crisis by the Global Restructuring Group. I was sitting on a report assembling the evidence.

The report had been prepared by Yorkshire businessman, Laurence Tomlinson. I had met him on a regional tour (and been given a hair-raising ride around country roads in the Ginetta sports car he was manufacturing). I suspected that he was a pretty right-wing Tory, but we hit it off. I found his story of dealing with RBS very compelling and I put him forward to be an Entrepreneur in Residence, a scheme I had started with Michael Fallon. Civil servants, especially the women, didn't warm to him, but he did what he undertook to do and assembled a damning dossier of RBS case studies.

The department wanted to bury it, but I wanted to publish it, as well as to send it to the bank and the Financial Conduct Authority. Its publication caused yet more cases to emerge. The FCA behaved as if it had been handed nitro-glycerine and six years later it was still dragging its feet on releasing to Parliament its own damning conclusions. Mr Tomlinson went from strength to strength and was last reported as being worth approaching $1 billion, having successfully sold the care home business which RBS had tried to close down as unviable.

The other bit of RBS legacy which hung around was the inquiry into the activities of Fred 'the Shred' Goodwin and the RBS directors, pre-crisis. The matter had ended up in the Scottish government and seemed destined to sit there. I wrote a rather provocative, chasing letter made more provocative by being mistakenly sent to the (Lib Dem) Advocate General rather than the (nationalist) Lord Advocate whose responsibility it was. The incendiary response helped prepare me for the big debate of 2014 around Scottish independence.

December 10 2013: *Vince is in India for four to five days, after our early Christmas lunch for the Cable family, this* *time also including my younger son Max and his fiancée, which was nice for me. V's younger son, Hugo, is looking online for flats in Bristol and left soon after to go and wrap up his life in Singapore and sign off with their tax authorities.*

Another visit to India. I loved these trips, albeit intense business visits which never gave time to visit old friends and hardly ever my late wife's family in Goa and Mumbai. My official task was to make progress on trade policy and investment issues; but progress was difficult since India had a largely protectionist approach in activities that the British were keen to promote (banking and other legal and financial services; whisky and other spirits) and had a set of demands around Indian IT workers which the Home Office would not countenance.

My meetings with my opposite number, Anand Sharma, a Congress Party stalwart and Gandhi family loyalist – who I had got to know through his frequent visits to London on family matters (an autistic child) – were friendly but unproductive. They were largely concerned with the tribulations of British companies – Vodafone, Westland, Cairns Energy – which had been caught in one of the many traps laid by Indian bureaucracy.

India was booming economically – with growth rates almost in double digits: faster than China – due in part to the reforms brought in 20 years earlier by Prime (at that time Finance) Minister Manmohan Singh. India's economic success, however, meant that there was even less appetite than before for concessions to the former colonial power. I tried to cultivate ministers who might buy goods and services from Britain. One was a minister whose reputation for corruption was legendary. His main interest in the UK was developing the potential of the Duck Boat on the Thames, whose amphibious technology could – he thought – be the answer to India's transport problems.

Our trade-promotion staff – including several British Indians who had risen through the diplomatic service – wanted to take me to the rapidly growing and well-developed southern cities like Chennai and Coimbatore, which offered big opportunities to the (few) British companies trying to do business there. Amongst the visits was one to the Chennai plant making buses for the Optare business of Ashok Leyland owned by the Hindujas (Optare buses are also made in Yorkshire). I had a good, business-like, relationship with the Hinduja brothers – who have topped the British rich list at times – but was careful not to get too close, all too aware of their reputation and the damage familiarity did to my predecessor, Peter Mandelson.

December 13 2013: Vince got back from India in good shape, though short of sleep – and overfed – he said. In the evenings, we have been doing personal Christmas cards till our eyes close: V's spad Emily has added another 70 for journalists and 50 for politicians, on top of the several hundred we've already done.

December 24 2013: Christmas Eve. Vince was on Andrew Marr *last Sunday morning and made headlines in almost all the Monday papers for having said there were tensions in the cabinet over immigration policy and the*

EU. It all seems a long time ago, now that we are with Zoe's family for Christmas in Scotland. So it is particularly good to be here, right away from the media world in London. Unlike the arctic weather of 2010, it was very wet and windy for our two-hour walk up a hill with three other families: heavy going through the thick wet grass interspersed with heather and bog myrtle. Rosie has written to Santa to ask him not to forget her dogs. Vince read her the Carol Ann Duffy poem about Santa Claus and she is clearly in two minds about whether he really exists. Her big sisters have been sworn to secrecy.

Chapter Twelve
Hanging together

January 1 2014: *My New Year's resolution, formulated on the long train journey back from Scotland, diverted via a night in Carlisle because of floods, is to write something more consequential than this journal. Or paint a picture that is really worth looking at. "Meantime, I shall fritter away the time on the FT crossword or quiz". The road to hell, paved with good intentions?*

January 6 2014: *Back at the farm, a large oak has fallen over the drive between me and the house beyond me on the edge of the farm and taken our telephone line with it. Luckily, not the electric cable on the same poles. As I write, the telephone engineers are busy, one in the house and another up a pole; and (later) have reconnected me, the only house so far, which I put down to the cups of tea I gave them.*

It has been nearly a week since I wrote that. Vince, in the same week, has written about 17,000 words of his book Storm 2 *(or* After the Storm*). I have merely typed it. He is determined, despite all the other pressures, to have on record his version of the economic arguments in government and the party.*

The New Year began with a repeat of the earlier row about house prices. I had warned of a new housing 'bubble' based on the fact that house prices had risen 15 per cent in London and nationally by 8.4 per cent in the previous year. My suggestion that the coalition's good work on the economy was in danger of being undone by a housing bubble, repeating the mistakes of Gordon Brown, was contradicted by the prime minister, creating more headlines of a 'coalition split on the economy' and he and Osborne pushed ahead with the Help to Buy scheme.[152] [153]

A separate row broke out over the minimum wage. I was due to announce an increase based on the consensus recommendation of the Low Pay Commission (LPC). The commission had been established 15 years earlier by Gordon Brown to provide an independent assessment and recommendation, insulating the process of setting the minimum wage from political pressure. I had followed the tradition of ministers accepting its findings but challenging it privately. But the minimum wage had been falling for some years in real terms and there was a growing feeling amongst economists and other analysts that the labour market no longer worked as it did and there was no longer a simple trade-off between wages and jobs.

I asked the Low Pay Commission to look at the possibility of a substantial increase, above inflation. There then emerged press stories that the Tories wanted a big increase to be announced in the budget as a way of

---

[152] "House price rises must stop", *Daily Telegraph*, 4 January 2014.
[153] '"Housing boom could kill the recovery", Cable warns', *The Times*, 28 January 2014.

dissipating the 'nasty party' image.[154] [155] This led to an unseemly row about who got the credit for any increase, which infuriated the LPC whose attempts to prevent the minimum wage becoming a political football were at risk.

These two squabbles set the tone for the remainder of the Parliament. The long run-in to the next general election had started and party politics would trump 'policy'.

January 14 2014: We've been canvassing in Hampton for a council by-election. My hip is playing up: too much biking or too little? V set off at 7ish this morning clutching his DJ to wear at a dinner this evening. I am on the train to Cambridge for a Friends of MAA (the Museum of Archaeology and Anthropology) meeting.

January 16 2014: Went shopping in Kingston and bought two coats and two swimsuits – an odd combination! Then spent over two hours at the hairdresser going 'ash blonde' for the Westminster correspondents' dinner. A car was on offer as Vince's dinner jacket needed to get there too. Hooray! It was quite an entertaining evening, nice meal and a jokey speech by the PM, before we were whisked off by V's spad Emily to do Newsnight.

Off to the Gulf, my main task being to open a new centre to help British exporters in Dubai and to persuade the airlines in Dubai and Abu Dhabi to buy British (the Airbus: British

---

[154] "Tories 'nicking' Lib Dem policy on low wages", *The Guardian*, 8 January 2014.
[155] "The Nice Party? Tories support above inflation rise in minimum wage", *Independent*, 8 January 2014.

in part).

We had been persuaded that the Germans had a good model, as part of their overall success in export promotion. In major centres there was a 'chamber of commerce' facility where exporters could come for practical support and to compare notes. The idea wasn't very complex or controversial, but somehow Britain had never got round to it. Now we were adopting this model in major centres like Singapore and the Gulf.

The Burj Khalifa was amazing; but why here? The highlight of the trip was a visit to Sheikh Mohammed's stables where I somehow managed to get bitten by a horse which was annoyed by too much ministerial attention; and a visit to the Sheikh's uncle who, we were told, called the shots. I didn't sell any aircraft.

January 18 2014: V left for Abu Dhabi at 7 am. I stood in for him to make a short speech at the goodbye party for constituents Upali and Cherrie Wickrama Sekera, who had enlisted our help to raise money for a project in Sri Lanka and who are going back to Sri Lanka to find "better health care". He was the force behind an impressive fundraising scheme to build a village after the catastrophic tsunami of 2004. A dynamic but controversial man. I said his legacy was a new word in the English language: to be "upalied" was to be gently squeezed for slightly more than one initially intended to give to a charity – at which he was very effective.

The papers are still full of the Rennard scandal. Nick is between a rock and a hard place; nothing is <u>proven</u> against Chris, yet the witnesses are said by the internal disciplinary enquiry by a QC to be "credible". My thoughts on this are:

1. Should Rennard be crucified when none of it can be proved?

2. Being told to apologise is not the same as apologising. Without the voluntary element, it loses most of its force.

3. If you are on your own and the man (or woman) has the power to promote you or otherwise, it's bullying.

4. I wish Chris hadn't said he looked forward to resuming his roles in the party. House of Lords is one thing, training sessions are another.

January 30 2014: Lorely Burt lost out to Malcolm Bruce in the deputy leader election by 25 votes to 28. A shame, as it would have cheered up the ambitious women in the party.

February 8 2014: Joined the gym under the rugby stadium and started swimming in London, expensive but "I'm worth it".

And I gave a speech – "On Being Mrs Vince". Public speaking was not in my marriage contract, as I mention to my audience of Twickenham Lib Dems. It was not a disaster, but it was hard work as there were no doors between the "private room" and the rest of the pub, which was heaving.

I got a laugh for my tale of googling 'Cable Wife' about four years into our marriage, to find about 20 photos, none of them of me. There were two or three of Vince's late wife, Olympia. Quite right. But Annette Brooke MP? Tessa Munt,

Wannabe MP at the time? And even some blokes? So I asked his kind researcher Pippa Morgan what to do. Was I being unduly sensitive? She thought not. She would 'googlebomb' it.

Several months later, I looked again. This time there was no subsection 'Wife'. Instead, 'Vince Cable Women'. What Women? Some battles are best avoided, I told myself, they only make matters worse. With some trepidation, I opened it up. It turned out to be about his campaigns on women's issues, like screening for cervical cancer. Phew!

I ended with Shenagh Pugh's poem Sometimes, which I find inspirational. She said she wrote it for a recovering addict, hence the reference to 'snow': but it is generally not understood in that way.

February 14–21 2014: Skiing was fun when we managed to get away for our annual week in the French Alps. The Oakeshotts and Strasburgers were good company. We play bridge, pool and scrabble in the evenings. We even visited Aida and family at the next-door resort.

March 6 2014: I am interviewed by Christina Odone for the Telegraph before getting ready for the annual Lord Mayor's Trade and Industry Dinner. There is the usual long wait at BIS, in my finery, until Vince and Emily can join me. I am an old hand at this by now, less intimidated by the gilded surroundings and processing into hundreds of people handclapping and so forth. The Lord Mayor is a rather elegant and impressive woman, a lawyer called Fiona Woolf.

My annual outing at the Mansion House Trade and Industry dinner. I had never felt comfortable with the formality and fancy dress, but the guests were usually down to earth business people and I felt I was (mostly) among friends and am certainly not seen as the anti-Business Secretary any more, if I ever was.

I decided to take aim at the Home Office immigration policy in support of what the British Chambers of Commerce, the Institute of Directors, the CBI and others were saying about the damaging impact of attempts to enforce the net migration target. I was able to release a report prepared jointly with the BIS and the Home Office, which the Home Office had been trying to suppress, and which directly contradicted claims by immigration ministers that immigrants were depressing wages and destroying British jobs.[156]

Then, off to spring conference, majoring on the folly of the Tories' 'UKIP-induced funk' over Europe. My line of attack was somewhat ahead of its time but has proved to be prescient – how do you expect the Scots to ignore the siren voices of nationalism and separatism when you indulge British nationalism and Euro separatism?[157]

March 7 2014: Train to York, requiring 8 am start from Twickenham. Lots of publicity around Vince's pro-immigration stance and lots of tension around Vince's speech for the rally. This business of letting everyone

---

[156] "Firms lash out at government over migration", *City AM*, 7 March 2014.
[157] "Cable blows fuse: the EU referendum is bad for growth", *Independent*, 7 March 2014.

comment on his speech till the last moment is bad for everyone's nerves. I got a lecture from Dee Doocey over breakfast about putting V's conference speech to bed earlier, a case of preaching to the converted.

March 10 2014: *Christina Odone asked me a supplementary question about the conference. I spoke in glowing terms (sincerely) about Nick's speech on Sunday – facing the future with hope, not fear, whilst relishing all the idiosyncrasies of being British – none of which appeared in print, as far as I know.*

New Forest Housing Villages Association AGM today. I am lying awake at 2.30 am, fretting about our only really problematic tenants, who allow the property to deteriorate whilst piling up horse paraphernalia and rusting vehicles outside, thereby incurring the wrath of their neighbours and parish council alike.

March 11 2014: *The* Daily Telegraph *article came out, referring to me as Sarah Smith! And a bit of a disaster, making a meal of the lost invitation to George Osborne and family to visit the farm; and appearing to be approving of the antics of Sally Bercow and disapproving of Vicky Pryce, neither true.*

It also claimed that Dirk left me with three young children to run the dairy farm alone: tosh, as you only have to 'do the math' to see that, after a 31-year marriage, the children would be grown up and to listen more carefully to know that we produced beef, not milk. Even Odone was cross: it had clearly been in the hands of a political editor. So I am in the doghouse all round. Mercifully, Vince is supremely relaxed about it.

Amidst the high-profile coalition rows in the press and the occasional surfacing of tensions in the party around leadership and our electoral strategy, ministerial life was largely about quietly getting things done. One example was a lot of time put in with FTSE CEOs and chairs and women's groups on getting more women in the boardroom. Since 2011, the proportion of women in board roles had gone up from 12 per cent to over 20 per cent and was on track to meet the 30 per cent target. I launched a code of conduct for head hunters and we sought the help of the Equalities Commission to get around the legal worries about 'all women short-lists'.[158]

I went to Glasgow to launch the latest of the Catapults – for offshore renewable technology. The programme, which we had launched in 2011, now had 1,400 scientists and engineers in seven advanced manufacturing hubs together with another six centres whose focus ranged from cell therapies to satellite applications. I asked tech investor Hermann Hauser, whose ideas we had built on originally, to see how best we could expand the network.[159]

Another intervention was to try to recast the HS2 project to make it more attractive to the north of England. The cabinet had approved HS2, but the economics were doubtful and the political appeal already fading outside of those enthused by a faster commuter route from

---

[158] "Top firms face all-women hiring rule", *Daily Telegraph*, 4 March 2014.

[159] "Catapult centres face entrepreneurial scrutiny", *Financial Times*, 13 March 2014.

Birmingham to London. I argued for starting with the northern city links, reflecting the views of northern council leaders, and Sir David Higgins' review of HS2 endorsed a northern prioritisation.[160]

I also managed to overturn a decision to locate an HS2 training academy solely in Birmingham and to get a large slice of the work for Doncaster. These controversies were small, early warnings of the larger post-Brexit battles to come over 'left behind' England.

It was pointed out to me that I had now been in the job longer than any of my predecessors for 60 years, surpassing Heseltine, Tebbit, Mandelson, Harold Wilson and numerous shorter-stay occupants.[161] Apart from personal satisfaction, my experience taught me about the folly of rapid rotation of ministers. Getting to understand a big, complex, department took years. I now knew the issues better than many of the officials and could challenge their advice and push them to do things in a way that was impossible two years ago.

Though I was perhaps not conscious of it at the time, the satisfaction of being able to get past the brickbats, navigate the department, and achieve a tangible legacy was beginning to exert a powerful counterforce to the strong voices wanting to call time on the coalition. 'Hit and run' guerrilla raids from a secure base inside the government seemed preferable to set piece battles outside it.

---

[160] "Cable demands high-speed rail rethink to ease north-south split", *Observer*, 16 March 2014.
[161] "Cable brings rare longevity to the business of work in government", *The Times*, 12 April 2014.

Chapter Thirteen
Hanging separately

March 18 2014: *Vince is busy working on his response to the budget. The news is full of western indignation about Russia annexing the Crimea, and claiming that 97 per cent of its residents were in favour. The other news is of the MH 370 flight from Kuala Lumpur to Beijing, still missing without trace after ten days – a hijack gone wrong?*

These random disasters are upsetting, whether or not one has any personal connection with the people involved. And of course, we know about them almost immediately. Only news-averse people like my sister-in-law, Helen, simply avoid all news channels. I fear I am addicted to the Today *programme for at least half an hour in the mornings and* Channel 4 News *at night, which sometimes results in insomnia.*

There's been a full moon for a few days, and I can meander out into the walled garden in the middle of the night to admire it – an upside of being alone here! And the wrens are very active in the early mornings, collecting moss for their nests.

March 24 2014: *My faithful farm-helper-cum-handyman Paul Rawlinson and I are busy assembling a new bed in the spare room in anticipation of hosting Max's French in-laws this summer. It puts me in mind of what Susan Kramer's late husband, John, described as the most* dreaded words in the English language: "Some Self Assembly Needed". It took us two hours.

March 31 2014: *Hugo is gradually moving his stuff up to the attic, prior to his move to Bristol, which means his bedroom is like the Sargasso Sea, a whirlpool of objects going round and round for the last fortnight.*

April 1 2014: *There is a lot of backwash around the Royal Mail sale. And last night the much-heralded Clegg v. Farage debate took place. I thought blows were fairly evenly traded but the audience came out nearly 70 per cent on the Farage side of the argument.*

April 17 2014: *Vince was on Jeremy Vine's Radio 2 programme yesterday, called 'What makes us human' – in V's case "love of dance". We had written down some thoughts together ten days ago and I was pleased that he described our relationship as "rock solid". I was visiting our housing association tenants, so missed a bit, but we got the Louis Armstrong song loud and clear on the car radio. V has a sexy voice with a reassuring mild Yorkshire accent. And on that note, I might get to sleep.*

April 29 2014: *Birdsong. Vince is preoccupied with the day job, though* After the Storm *is now 30,000 words and growing – six chapters done, more to come.*

Matthew Oakeshott has had some market research done and the national outlook for the Lib Dems is dire, though V's prospects are still good. Our fundraiser for the local and Euro elections with Shirley Williams as main speaker made £6,000. She's always good, though a friend used to say that she had such a mellifluous voice that it didn't matter what she actually said.

May 3 2014: *Vince arrives this pm after two events in the constituency. He's had a rough week: Royal Mail chickens coming home to roost and threat of AstraZeneca merging with Pfizer, with possible loss of jobs to the USA.*

The month of May brought one of the biggest challenges yet to a more coherent approach to British industry. Pfizer told the stock market on April 28 that it had made a bid for Astra Zeneca which, if successful, would create the world's largest drug company and mark the biggest foreign takeover of a British company. An earlier approach had been rebuffed by AZ, but Pfizer weren't giving up and its boss, Ian Read, came to London the following day to win over the shareholders and the government.[162]

He rang me on landing and set out the case for his bid. We got off to a bad start; I didn't think he had been briefed on the UK political scene. He openly admitted that a primary reason for the bid was to take advantage of US tax inversion rules, saving the company a billion pounds in tax. He was very positive about the research campus at Cambridge, but unwilling to make long-term commitments. I told him that on the basis of what I had heard I thought that the government would be unlikely to welcome the bid, whatever shareholders decided.

---

[162] "Five days that shook a British drugs giant", *The Times*, 3 May 2014.

When my department alerted the Whitehall machine to the potential problems with the takeover, the first reactions were not encouraging. There was no obvious 'public interest test' which could be invoked under the takeover legislation; there was no national security, financial stability or media issue. There was the takeover panel, whose powers had been strengthened post-Cadbury, but they were not sufficient to stop a bid if shareholders accepted it and the bidder followed the rules. The first reactions from the Chancellor's office and Number 10 were that we should not fight the takeover; Britain must not be seen to be hostile to foreign investors and we should concentrate on extracting promises to retain R & D in the UK (Osborne had a particular interest, having seen AZ pull out of his constituency and relocate to Cambridge).

It soon became clear that the takeover would not go smoothly. AZ management intended to fight it. Scientists deluged Whitehall with demands to stop it. A key AZ investor, Neil Woodford, rejected an improved offer on the basis that the company was still being seriously undervalued.

The Whitehall machine was now whirring with activity and a BIS official, Bernadette Kelly, coordinated the key players to make sure that government could use its limited powers to extract the best possible deal from Pfizer. I decided to make public my opposition to the takeover.[163][164] This was written up as a coalition split story or to illustrate

[163] "Cable Hints at Halting Pfizer", *The Sun*, 7 May 2014.
[164] "Britain's future is not a tax haven, warns Cable", *The Independent*, 7 May 2014.

the government's lack of powers.[165] [166] I sensed, however, that Pfizer valued goodwill and would be put off by a public display of hostility, as it was.[167] And if we didn't fight, the whole idea of an industrial strategy and the promotion of 'long-termism' would be toast. With the Labour opposition and most of the press in full cry, we had to lead from the front.

In the event, the government pulled together. Nick Clegg gave me strong support and the two sides of the coalition converged on a hard line in demanding stronger guarantees than the company was willing to concede.[168] I was fortunate to have a 'mole' on the board of AZ who was able to advise on the mood inside the company and to recommend tactics. Within a week of the Pfizer bid becoming public knowledge, there was a full-scale national campaign to stop it. Parliament had summoned the key business participants to select committee hearings; and I trailed the possibility of legal intervention (though I was skating on thin ice).[169] Pfizer made a fourth and final offer to AZ and, when that was rejected, they gave up.

The threat to AZ had been seen off. The company's faith

[165] "Coalition Rift Over £63bn Offer For UK Drugs Group", *The Guardian*, 5 May 2014.

[166] "Osborne Ignores Cable's Crocodile Tears", *Sunday Telegraph*, 4 May 2014.

[167] "Pfizer 'could abandon bid if it fails to get UK blessing'", *The Independent*, 8 May 2014.

[168] "Cameron seeks more pledges from Pfizer", *Daily Telegraph*, 8 May 2014.

[169] Alex Brummer, "Elements move against Pfizer as takeover bid for AstraZeneca looks increasingly shaky", *Daily Mail*, 14 May 2014.

in the long-term approach of its CEO, Pascal Soriot, and the board, and – I liked to think – the government's support through the industrial strategy and political intervention were vindicated years later. AZ strengthened commercially and its share price moved well above what Pfizer had been willing to pay. Crucially, the company would later play a central role, with Oxford academics, in developing an easily usable, safe and effective, vaccine to fight Covid, delivered at cost.

What had been exposed was the weakness of the 'public interest' test for takeovers which took no account of the public interest in a strong science base, much of which the taxpayer had subsidised. But there were serious obstacles to making a legislative change.

Colleagues in government were reluctant to see measures which would be construed as hostile to foreign investors (and I agreed that economic nationalism should not be the motive) or would weaken the commercial discipline of the takeover market (about which I was less convinced, given the fees and other vested interests in takeover situations).

There was also European framework legislation which precluded new restrictions. I established a bond with my new French opposite number, Emmanuel Macron, who had followed the AZ story closely and was intrigued by our pragmatic and 'light touch' industrial strategy. We agreed to work together to build up support for a wider EU change.

May 5 2014: Investigating poems by Gerard Manley Hopkins, prompted by my friend, Vanessa, quoting from him on our Tuesday walk through bluebells. From The May

Magnificat *I found:*

> *And azuring-over greybell makes*
> *Wood banks and brakes wash wet like lakes*
> *And magic cuckoo-call*
> *Caps, clears and clinches all". It's such a magical season.*

May 14 2014: *Preparation for Vince's big trip to China under way: my part is to try to address the wardrobe issues, so I go shopping in Kingston. We are required to restrict ourselves to hand baggage to speed up the flight transfers on these major travels but still have to 'dress to impress' at intervals. My mother and grandmother, who travelled extensively and much less comfortably during Britain's late colonial era, were dab hands at the quick change after long journeys but had hat boxes and porters in their day. I bless the trouser suit option, which they didn't have!*

No sooner had the AZ takeover been successfully seen off than a political crisis erupted around the leadership of the Lib Dems and our party's increasingly desperate prospects as the general election approached. It was now less than a year away. I had seen the scale of the problem from constituency opinion surveys carried out to help our local preparations. Matthew Oakeshott had offered to fund and organise mine and several others around the country.

The Twickenham survey showed that, on a party basis, the seat was a lost cause. But I drew some reassurance from the favourable personal rating suggesting that the personal brand was sufficiently strong locally that the seat could be held. Dee Doocey, who had undertaken to manage my campaign again, was less sanguine. If her focus group of dog walkers was any guide, I was in deep trouble.

She followed up with some carefully targeted canvassing by experienced party colleagues. The results were clear: whatever their assessment of the local MP, previous Lib Dem voters could no longer be relied on. The personal brand was positive but had been damaged during the coalition and was unlikely to withstand a strong Tory campaign. She was up for the fight but pessimistic locally and predicted a national wipe-out.

The mood amongst colleagues varied from gloom to despair. Gallows humour was much in evidence. The line from the leadership and Paddy's campaign team, that we could retrieve the situation in most seats by delivering our KPIs and staying on message, was regarded with incredulity. Various constituency surveys and national polling showed that the 'Nick' brand was negative and there was a mutinous mood around. The consensus was that if, as seemed possible, the Lib Dems lost all their (11) seats in the European elections on May 25, Nick's position would become untenable.

I was sounded out by colleagues, including those I regarded as hard-core loyalists. I think my distinct lack of enthusiasm for taking over a sinking ship may have come across as false modesty. And I undoubtedly made a mistake in not stamping more firmly on leadership speculation and agitation.

When I reviewed my thoughts in retrospect, I believed I could make a positive difference to the future campaign, but

I could also see that there was little attraction in presiding over a limited – rather than a 'mega' – disaster. In any event, I was committed to a visit to China and wasn't in a position to respond to any political emergency in the wake of the Euro elections.

May 25 2014: *My 69th birthday, sitting with our bags in the first-floor cafe of the Excelsior Hotel, Hong Kong, having had a proper birthday treat; Vince all to myself and lobster for lunch at the Peak Lookout Hotel. We walked back down, thinking the taxi driver who said it would take 1½ hours was exaggerating, but it was true and my sandals without socks (pure vanity!) gave me blisters.*

China: Shenzhen, Guangzhou, Beijing, Qingdao, Chongqing and back via Hong Kong in as many days as places. It was a story of its own, masterminded by Emily and helped by Saskia from BIS.

The China visit got off to a great start. The Chinese had rolled out the red carpet and I got to see top officials in each of the provincial centres. I had a long debate with the party secretary in Guangdong, Hu Chunhua, who was regarded as a rising star (and later a member of the politburo), about labour rights: why nominally 'communist' China appeared to be tolerating exploitative wages and conditions imposed by a capitalist market-place while I, in a Western, capitalist economy, was legislating to deal with 'zero-hours contracts', upholding the right to strike and enforcement of minimum wages. There was a good deal of give and take and I noticed that if it was clear that someone like myself was not trying to score points in public debate and 'humiliate' them,

Chinese officials were perfectly capable of intelligent and open-minded debate (his answers had to do with relative levels of development).

Thanks to the British consul in Guangzhou, I also managed to see a group of human rights activists involved in campaigning for LGBT rights, compensation for victims of a blood contamination scandal and against abusive employers. Several were nervous that they had been followed to the consulate, but they were uninhibited in their criticisms.

In Shenzhen, there was a visit to the global HQ of Huawei, which was then seen just as a good, uncontroversial investor in the UK. Chongqing was memorable for its spectacular cityscapes and the confluence of the Yangtse river – then much depleted after the Three Gorges Dam completion) and a tributary.

I also wanted to understand the local politics, since it was at the centre of the national power struggle from which President Xi had emerged victorious at the expense of his main rival: the local party chief, Bo Xilai, now in prison. I got to see Bo Xilai's successor, Sun Zhengcai, in a very grand hall where he regaled me with the president's new idea of the 'Road and Belt': what was to become the new Silk Road initiative. He wasn't up for debate. I subsequently followed his glittering career which ended up in a life prison sentence after he had been accused of taking 'massive bribes'.

The main purpose of the visit was to promote British creative industries and had, as its centrepiece a display in various provincial capitals of the mechanical horse from the stage version of Michael Morpurgo's *War Horse*.

We spent time in Qingdao, formerly a German

concession and now a nine million city of beaches, parks and high-rise flats. I likened it to Bournemouth x 50. The highlight was a performance of Chinese popular music including from the winner of the Chinese version of *Britain's Got Talent*. That year's winner, a very talented young singer of Chinese pop, turned out to be a British student from Nottingham in her gap year. When we met her, she was nice, unassuming and seemingly unfazed by winning the world's biggest talent show.

We then went to the HQ of an extravagant entrepreneur, Wang Jianlin, the head of Dalian Wanda who wanted to harness British media expertise as part of his vision of creating a Chinese Hollywood and Bollywood. He had already made ambitious acquisitions in the west and showed us his plans to create the biggest film campus on earth. He has since been reeled in and told by the authorities to curb his overseas expansion, like other eager Chinese billionaires.

As we flitted from one Chinese city to another on a packed itinerary, news arrived of events in London. First came news of the disastrous European election results. One MEP (Catherine Bearder) had survived by a handful of votes. That was enough, and Nick reaffirmed his commitment to soldier on.

But then came news from the following morning's *Guardian* of Matthew's polling data showing how unpopular Nick was and by implication that someone else (me) would do better.[170]

---

[170] "Clegg taking Lib Dems to wipe-out", *The Guardian*, 27 May 2014.

This was not new; these polls had been used before to make a similar point. I had had a very useful poll in my constituency. But, this time, there was also negative polling data from Nick and Danny's constituencies. Worse, Nick's press office had decided that I was at the centre of a big conspiracy; and Emily, on a mobile phone to London, was desperately trying to make sense of the situation to give a media response. Her advice was to make a clear factual statement of what I knew and didn't know about the polls. But the press team in London ignored it and put out instead a version which raised more questions than it answered and wrongly claimed that I knew nothing about the polling exercise.

Conspiracy theories had run riot in London without our being there to deal with them. A British camera followed me round my remaining events from a Buddhist temple up a mountain to meetings with Chinese dignitaries, who were no doubt impressed that my every move was of such close interest to British television.

One outcome was a day of appalling headlines in the UK newspapers.[171] Another consequence was that Matthew was humiliated by the collapse of the story. He had nothing personal to gain from trying to promote a change in the leadership and responded by withdrawing from active political life beyond helping individual Lib Dem, Green and

---

[171] "Cable ally's botched coup against Clegg", *Independent*, 28 May 2014.

* There is an alternative scenario described in *What If?*, a 2021 book of counterfactual history by Duncan Brack and Iain Dale. Nick Clegg stands down after the European election disaster and I take over, leading to a smaller disaster for the

Labour candidates and MPs, which he continues to do. Nick could never understand or forgive the fact that I had one of his most outspoken critics as a friend.

There was a wall of hostility and suspicion on return followed by a meeting of MPs assembled like a Maoist self-criticism session to pledge undying loyalty to the leadership and the official strategy for the forthcoming campaign. Those who were not totally convinced, prepared for local campaigns to hold their seats, or prepared to look for other jobs, while others lobbied for peerages after retirement at the end of the Parliament.

I tried humour, which I think was better received than rancour. I then took the view that I should spend the next year consolidating the many unfinished pieces of policy in the department and to shore up defences in Twickenham as far as was possible.*

June 1 2014: *Apart from a few petals still falling off the red roses the hotel gave us for our tenth wedding anniversary in Chongqing (in a private room to evade the press interest in the 'coup' story'), China is a fading dream. The weekend was spent at the farm, looking after Max's prospective in-laws, who were very nice guests. We took them to the D-Day Remembrance event at Newtown Park, a quintessentially British event, with people, dogs and aeroplanes intermingling in a seemingly haphazard way.*

There was plenty to do. I had a visit to Scotland as part of

---

* Lib Dems in 2015, and another minority government with enough MPs to stop the Brexit referendum. Maybe.

the growing referendum campaign and some tricky interviews with sharp Scottish journalists who had dug out my contribution to Gordon Brown's *Red Papers on Scotland* from 30 years earlier. I had been a strong advocate of devolution – home rule – which was interpreted as betraying a secret sympathy for the Scot Nats; not so, but a dangerous thing to be accused of. And my references to the potential of new oil wealth for Scottish development were an uncomfortable reminder of the way it had since been squandered: a major nationalist complaint.

I was invited to give a lecture at my old stamping ground of Glasgow University on the (negative) economics of independence, but was rather taken aback by the nervousness of the principal and vice-chancellor, Anton Muscatelli, an impressive economist by trade. His colleagues explained that universities were more directly under the thumb of government than in England because of the funding arrangements (no tuition fees). It was important not to antagonise Mr Salmond. But on the other hand, there was freedom of speech and I was a distinguished visitor and alumnus (staff and doctorate).

I had unwittingly created a diplomatic problem. But the university was a really impressive place with world-class research in bioscience amongst other specialities and it gave me a lot of pleasure to revisit my former home and workplace.

As one of the few people in the cabinet with any experience of Scottish politics, albeit decades earlier, I was co-opted into the group preparing for the referendum. This was one area of government, where Lib Dems dominated: Michael Moore, the very solid and dependable secretary of state who did much of the heavy lifting (before being replaced by the more combative Alistair Carmichael); (Lord) Jim Wallace, who had led the Lib Dems in the first Scottish government, a coalition with Labour; and Danny Alexander. But it was Osborne who called the shots.

In any event, the dynamics had changed from the rather flattering 2010 general election which had given the Lib Dems 11 MPs to only six for the SNP and one for the Conservatives (with 41 Labour). It had since suffered a dramatic loss of public support.

The SNP, by contrast, were the new Scottish government. And they behaved accordingly. When ministers visited Alex Salmond, we were welcomed and photographed next to the saltire flag, as if we were visiting the President of Uruguay.

June 20 2014: *A trip to Scotland was very welcome and included my eldest grandchild Elsa's 14th birthday there, in gorgeous weather.*

June 22 2014: *A big and beautiful bouquet arrived from Hugo, thanking me for food, presents etc, while he orchestrated his move to Bristol. I was very touched as I had been less than patient while this was going on for months. I also spent some time trying to help Max finalise his LSE dissertation, as haymaking was in full swing on the farm. I have caught a bad summer cold.*

June 29 2014: *I hosted a canvassing party for Vince's campaign: tea and sandwiches for 10-12 people before they set off on their mission. Dee is quite wound up already* *and very worried about the election which has to be held within the next year. Vince is overtired. And he wants five more years of this?!*

July 12 2014: *We are back from a BBQ at Chevening, courtesy of Nick and Miriam, for Lib Dem MPs and their families. There were lots of children and we met baby Swinson as well as Ed and Emily Davey's baby girl, a sister for John, now aged six. Ed was working elsewhere so we joined Emily to lend a hand with John, who is disabled and needs a lot of help.*

A couple of days ago, I was showing off my garden to my son Dylan and granddaughter Tallulah, when their terrier found a large grass snake entangled in the strawberry netting. I was proud of T who helped without squeaking while D held the snake and I cut off the netting. I think the snake was in search of the mice who have been gorging on my strawberries in spite of the netting, which I've now discarded.

July 25 2014: *The Israelis have launched an offensive in Gaza, so far killing about 700 Palestinians (and 30 Israelis). We'd attended Vince's case worker Sandra's 60th birthday party last week. She is lovely and very good at her job but was a keen member of Zionist Youth; and very quick to defend Israeli actions and prickly about any fraternising with the Palestinian cause, so I had to button my mouth tightly.*

In general, when pressed, I stick to the line that Israel has a right to exist but not to expand, nor to confiscate Palestinian property to make way for Jewish settlements;

and that it is not anti-Semitic to want a better outcome for Palestinians than they currently suffer.

The other recent news is the shooting down of a Malaysian airliner (en route from Amsterdam) over Ukraine by Russian separatists – by mistake, it seems – killing almost 300 people. Distressing.

August 2014: *The first week of our holiday was dominated by the festivities around Max's wedding to Héloïse in Nantes; the second was spent in a characterful village in Languedoc called Graissessac, formerly a coal mining centre, in a house belonging to a fellow Lib Dem, auctioned in aid of Jo Swinson's election campaign, where I finally did some sketching.*

The Gaza situation is still awful. Hammond, now Foreign Secretary, is more pro-Israeli than his predecessor and Baroness Warsi seems to have resigned her ministerial post because of it. The office needs to talk to Vince about export licences and suchlike.

Anthropology field note: I have discovered that notices reading 'Pas de Pub' do not mean Not a Pub, but No Publications, in other words, no junk mail, only occasionally followed by svp (s'il vous plait).

I was spending much of the holiday on the phone to London, keeping abreast of the fighting in Gaza and what this meant in terms of our arms export licensing policy. The Arab-Israeli dispute was a vipers' nest and I had always tried to stay well clear of it. 'The politics of the last atrocity' someone once called it; also, as a 'conflict between right and right'. I had sympathy for the basic position of both sides and believed that as far as possible we should avoid pouring paraffin on the flames as the protagonists of both sides in the UK were inclined to do.

The rather cynical irony was that British firms were making a small fortune selling weapons to Israel's Arab neighbours and a sizeable amount (around £200 million in five years) by selling arms to Israel also.

The latest wave of fighting had been triggered by Palestinian rockets, which were no doubt alarming but not very effective. The retaliation, in the form of airstrikes, was by contrast highly effective and was causing large casualties in the Gaza strip. Arguably the strikes were greatly disproportionate, however justified. On that basis, I had instructed officials before leaving London to suspend arms export licenses. There was, however, strong resistance from the Tories in the coalition, in particular from Number 10 and from Philip Hammond, the Defence Secretary. While the fighting went on, decision-making was paralysed. Around 2,000 Palestinians had died and around 70 Israeli soldiers.

As for the coalition, Nick Clegg weighed in strongly on my side and the press picked up on the fact that there was a coalition disagreement.[172] The issue was resolved by Hammond ringing me while I was visiting Roman ruins in the Languedoc. He had a long list of items I had cancelled which he wanted to discuss in detail in terms of their military potential. We settled for a list of 12 licenses for military radar, combat aircraft and tanks.

---

[172] "Coalition split over arms sales to Israel", *Financial Times*, 11 August 2014.

But by now the fighting had stopped and the ban applied in the case of a resumption of fighting. Both sides were angry. On one side, 'Warsi attacks Cable over arms exports to Israel,'[173] and there was a legal challenge from pro-Palestinian lawyers. There were also ominous attacks on the Lib Dems in the *Jewish Chronicle*.

August 15 2021: We visited my university friend Ann at Lacoste in south eastern France on the way back; and then did the long drive to Limoges over the Millau Bridge. We biked around the city and next day visited Oradour-sur-Glane, the village where the German SS rounded up the entire population of 642 in 1944, shot the men and set fire to the church with all the women and children inside. There was one survivor. The charred remains of the whole village are intact, and a superb underground museum illustrates the atrocity.

Back to Scotland for last-minute campaigning on the referendum. I spent time in Jo Swinson's constituency in the prosperous Glasgow suburbs, where there was strong anti-independence sentiment, in contrast to the nationalist mood in the city as in my old ward of Maryhill down the road. The campaign had been difficult. The economic 'fear' arguments, put by George Osborne in particular, focusing on the lack of clarity around the currency of an independent Scotland, had undoubtedly cut through. But the Tory contribution to the campaign had also antagonised a lot of

---

[173] "Warsi attacks Cable over arms exports to Israel", *Daily Mail*, 13 August 2014.

Scots and it been left to Gordon Brown to appeal to hearts as well as minds, as well as the Lib Dem Secretary of State (Alistair Carmichael).

In the event, independence was rejected by a comfortable 55:45 margin. But the nationalists were far from beaten, as we were to discover in the coming general election and after, since the wave of national feeling stirred by the campaign was to lead to Labour being wiped out, leading in turn to a Conservative government and to Brexit and its aftermath.

The October conference was back in Glasgow but without the pyrotechnics of the previous year. The disagreements about our post-coalition destination and the underlying economic strategy remained but there was a general understanding that we needed to pull together as best we could to face what Nick Cleg called 'the fight of our lives'.

After the dramas of recent months, I was very relieved that my major speech went down well in the hall and in the press. The real problems happened off-stage. In a private meeting with Paddy Ashdown and Dee Doocey to discuss our campaign preparations, Paddy launched into a personal attack on Dee, unprovoked and very unpleasant, stemming from disagreements many years earlier including her having helped me secure the party nomination in Twickenham when he was promoting one of his protégés. She agreed to stay to manage the Twickenham campaign, but we were conscious that we weren't going to get much help from the national campaign.

October 7 2014: *The conference has been very busy and* *fairly fraught. Easier now that Vince's big day with speech is over (yesterday).*

We have been picking up pieces of Dee, who was pulled up by Paddy Ashdown (at a private meeting with Ashley, a new spad, Vince, and Paddy on Sunday). Paddy is requiring targets on pamphlet delivery and she got a very unfair bollocking. She is deeply mortified. It appears Paddy has dredged up old quarrels going back decades. We are worried she may resign though she is gradually regaining her usual composure. Vince is "waiting for the dust to settle" which may be the same as "sweeping it under the carpet".

On October 9, I was off to India for my fifth official visit in five years. No one could say we were not doing our bit to develop a special relationship with India. Some routines in Delhi; very friendly meetings with ministers, this time the 'Indian People's Party', Bharatiya Janata Party (BJP); but no give on the issues affecting British firms. My Indian friends were mostly full of foreboding about a BJP government, fearing a revival of religious nationalism and more authoritarian rule. But some liked the idea of the smack of firm government and the pro-business rhetoric.

It was difficult not to be impressed by my interlocutors; Nirmala Sitharaman, the softly spoken but formidable commerce minister (later to become defence and then finance minister – the most powerful woman in India); and Arun Jaitley, who somehow combined being finance and defence minister, very much the economic brains behind the government.

In Mumbai, I was hosted by the UK consul-general,

another of the very bright British Indians who now occupied key roles in the diplomatic service. His apartment was distinguished by being located opposite the utterly gross and overbearing multi-storey building which was the home of the Ambanis: the richest and most powerful business family in India. The Ambanis provided the inspiration for the lead characters in my novel, *Open Arms*, which I started the following year. Wandering around Mumbai reminded me of the sights and smells of the city which later provided the background texture for my book.

The highlight of the visit (for me) was to be the first British minister to make an official visit to Goa. The local chamber of commerce organised a very grand reception and, as my Goan brother-in-law and nephew were present, I received an exceptionally warm welcome, not just as a 'bigwig' but as an 'in-law from the UK'. I was showered with honorary awards at the state university and generally made a fuss of.

As it happened, the BJP chief minister, Parrikar, had just left for Delhi to serve in the cabinet, so I was hosted by his deputy, a Christian, who – I gathered from the family gossip – had a terrible reputation for corruption even by the standards of the state (The previous chief minister had been a smuggler, a profession which had helped rather than hindered his political career, it was said). I left Goa with real sadness, wondering when, or even if, I would return.

We approached the end of the year with another coalition economic row, this time over how the budget would be financed for the three years after the election. The issue, on one level, was somewhat academic since it related to the future when neither party would necessarily be in government. But Osborne had been trying to position the Tories as favouring continuing spending cuts rather than tax rises, to finance further deficit reduction, and to promise tax cuts. I hit out strongly in cabinet and in public against the new round of proposed cuts[174] [175] and he retaliated in kind.[176]

October 2014: *I escaped from all the tensions with a fortnight's visit to Tanzania, my birthplace, a long-planned trip with my girlfriend Gill from our days at Mbeya School there. Our rendezvous in Dubai from her home in British Columbia and mine in England, in order to travel on together, was a miracle: there she was, on a lounger in the vast corridors on the way to the correct departure gate! We found each other easy company – "like a pair of old socks" – Gill with her enormous camera and lens cases slung around her neck and me with my notebook.*

We began with a visit to our boarding school, now a technical college for boys and young men, which is what the Germans originally intended it to be, before it became the whites-only co-ed prep school that we attended in the British colonial period. We also got involved with a charity helping the many HIV orphans in Mbeya, now a city of several hundred thousand, not the scruffy little 1950s

[174] "Osborne's plan for £7bn. of tax cuts is 'total fantasy' warns Cable", *The Guardian*, 23 November 2014.
[175] "Cable turns on Osborne to denounce 'brutal' cuts", *Daily Mail*, 4 December 2014.
[176] "Chancellor declares war on Lib Dems", *Sunday Times*, 7 December 2014.

stopover town on the Great North Road. We shared rooms and marvelled at the African night sky in Ruaha National Park by a campfire; and enjoyed amazing hospitality at a lodge on the shores of Lake Tanganyika, before boarding a bumpy little plane back to Dar es Salaam, where we looked at the beaches we'd frequented during our school holidays and reminisced about our colonial childhood. In retrospect, we led a charmed life, privileged and with undeserved deference from the locals.

The year ended with a comforting piece of analysis of the Royal Mail flotation a year and a half earlier. By now, the share price had fallen from its peak of over £6 to £4. I had asked a Labour peer, Lord Myners, a respected figure in the City and no apologist for the government, to do a thorough review of the IPO. The department had been very unhappy over my decision to commission an outsider to review its performance, but I was not willing to carry the can for the activities of City advisers and believed we should be open to constructive criticism by someone with no axe to grind.

Myners was critical of some of the technical aspects of the valuation but, on the sensitive issue of price, he thought if there was under-valuation it was very little. A press assessment was that 'Business secretary Vince Cable has taken a political beating over Royal Mail. He is entitled to revel in the finding that the sale was "a complex exercise executed with considerable professionalism"'.[177]

December 2014: *As the year drew to an end, Vince's*

---

[177] *The Guardian*, 19 December 2014.

constituency office became the hub for the election effort and I spent more time there, doing a regular slot, and navigating between the agent (Dee), the constituency organiser (Dan), and the staff (Joan and Shona). All of this only intensified, plus canvassing insisted upon by Vince, resulting in us both succumbing to coughs and colds. Just what we needed to take ski-ing between Xmas 2014 and New Year 2015, this time with Paul and Eve Strasburger in Tignes in the French Alps. Deep snow and arctic temperatures!

Chapter Fourteen
Countdown to the election

I was getting used to the idea that 'holiday' usually meant sitting in a hotel room with a mobile phone responding to a crisis back in London. This time, *après-ski* meant responding to the collapse of the delivery company City Link leaving 2,500 workers redundant in the middle of Christmas. The company was technically insolvent on December 22, with an administrator called in, leaving the workforce none the wiser and contractors left high and dry.

The Department had oversight of the insolvency process but operated within strict legal parameters, so trying to get the administrator to manage the process in a way which recognised the workers' pay situation without interfering with his legal duties was tricky, and I had unions in one ear and departmental officials in the other trying to sort out the mess. On return, there was a clamour for a full enquiry such as the one I had launched for the Comet collapse in Christmas 2012, though in this case there was less obvious misconduct by the directors.

Back to the office with an election to fight in my spare time!

January 11 2015: I am tired after three consecutive days in the office. Yesterday I kept the folding and stuffing machine going: we are halfway through the next delivery at 30,000 copies. Dee and I worked well together from 10 am till 5 pm, helped by just three volunteers – but good ones. Tomorrow, I start a whole week of volunteering there. Denise Carr, who once chaired the local Lib Dems, has joined the core team and is very good news.

January 15 2015: *I've just glanced at my email: Dee to Joan at 8.20 am saying she expects surgery to be upstairs and the waiting room for it to be in the kitchen, so that the rest of the premises can be used for election activities. And Dee has told me she wants the whole wall of filing cabinets to be moved out before the General Election. So, I am expecting World War III tomorrow (which duly broke out when Joan failed to "export" V's weekly surgery). And the envelope stuffing machine broke down.*

I have a week at the farm to include an injection for bursitis and examination of the wrist I broke before Christmas.

Departmental work didn't stop because there was an election in sight. And one of the blessings of the Fixed-Term Parliaments Act was that the date was pre-arranged, enabling us to plan ahead in a rational way. I was also reminded that being secretary of state was a real privilege, enabling me to work on a wide range of fascinating topics and make a difference.

I had been invited to give the annual Schumann lecture in Brussels. The subject was the creation of a digital single market. I was there to remind the audience of Eurocrats, think-tankers and journalists that the single market was a British contribution to the European Project – thanks to Mrs T – and we now wanted to push the boundaries further in the digital sphere.

I was struggling to get my head around some of the issues, not helped by difficulties understanding the Estonian commissioner, whose country has set the pace in Europe for e-government. But the discussions helped in shaping the outline of what would become the GDPR in two years' time. The lecture itself was very well received in Brussels, but totally ignored in the UK.

Back in London, some old chestnuts were reappearing: banks, banks and more banks. Now they were closing down large numbers of bank branches. The reason was technological; internet banking was replacing footfall. But villages and isolated communities were losing their banking facilities essential for local traders and for non-digitised older people (I was one!).

I had to negotiate a stronger but voluntary 'last bank in town' protocol to stop the collapse of the network to get banks to own joint branches and to mobilise the Post Office to deliver financial services instead which, after our financial rescue operation and the 'transformation programme,' they were in a position to do. I also had to pick a fight with the Scottish government, which had now been sitting on the report into Fred Goodwin and the RBS directors for three years, and remind them of angry taxpayers.[178]

One of the many small and unrecognised achievements of the Lib Dems in the coalition had been to introduce anti-monopoly powers to regulate dominant purchasers

---

[178] "Cable: why have RBS bankers not been prosecuted?", *Daily Mail*, 31 January 2015.

(monopsony in economic jargon). Despite lack of support from the competition authorities – who seemed not to understand monopsony – and strong resistance from the supermarkets, we had managed to establish a supermarket ombudsman (the 'grocery code adjudicator' – GCA). Although the Tories had weakened its powers it was potentially a useful protection for, *inter alia*, dairy farmers. I was pleased to see that the GCA decided to take on Tesco.

I was also keen to see the same model used to protect pubs from the so-called 'pubcos' who used tie arrangements to squeeze pubs' rents and beer prices, driving many out of business. The department was initially very reluctant to fight the pubcos who also had powerful Tory friends. But thanks to a very persistent and forceful Lib Dem MP, Greg Mulholland, the issue was kept alive and he persuaded me to introduce legislation which was going through Parliament, albeit in the face of guerrilla warfare from Tory backbenchers. Matthew Hancock was a particular help in steering through the Bill.

For light relief, I got to try out self-drive autonomous vehicles at the motor research centre – MIRA – in the Midlands and in a pilot scheme in London. It was possible to imagine the future of motorised transport in these vehicles, though I might not be around to see it.

February 5 2015: Vince is nursing a painful knee injury from falling on astroturf during a frosty game of rugby in Twickenham with Nick Clegg and a bunch of 12-year-olds. Nick is here promoting school sport in one of V's local schools. It is good to see that they are bonding again over the coming campaign.

I am finding I still can't deliver leaflets for long and have worked out that there is still a total of 125 to 150 hours of the current delivery to do before the next one starts clogging up the office.

February 14 2015: *I get back from the countryside where I have been transplanting snowdrops from Gail's paddock to my lawn, to find a big bouquet of 12 red roses from Vince. Yay!*

February 27 2015: *Brit Awards, necessitating a visit to the hairdresser. Much more entertaining than we had expected. Jed Docherty, our host, currently the producer of* Breaking Bad, *was delightful; and we had Sporty Spice at our table, aka Mel, and later on, Baby Spice. Mel was charming. Meeting 'legends' can be fun. Thanks due to Emily for setting it up; she has an eye for these events which also generate good publicity for BIS.*

There was little sweetness and light in the coalition. There was an element of 'professional wrestling': stressing differences to differentiate ourselves. But some of the argument was heartfelt. I got into an argument with Osborne when, in a cabinet meeting, I pointed out that the socialist government in France now had lower long-term interest rates than the UK.

This infuriated the Tories who had a go at me in the press for undermining one of the Chancellor's achieve-ments.[179] I

---

[179] "Cable taunts Osborne in Cabinet: You're doing no better than the French", *Mail on Sunday*, 1 February 2015.

then added insult to injury by referring to the 'economic illiteracy' of failing to distinguish current and capital spending and attacking the net immigration target again: this in my last outing at the Mansion House for the trade and industry dinner.[180] I suspected that this would be my swansong for this audience and merited honesty rather than sweet-talking tact.

Another row erupted over Tory plans to curb public sector strikes. This had long been a bone of contention. The Tories had put forward 15 proposals for weakening trade unions further at the beginning of the coalition and I had blocked all of them mainly on grounds of practicality, though I had developed a growing conviction that the shift of power from employees to employers had gone too far.

It didn't soften the union hardliners towards the coalition or me, but it did help build a strong working relationship with Frances O'Grady at the TUC. Ever since the Beecroft row with the Tories and Ellesmere Port, she had seen me as more ally than adversary and I had developed a great respect for her principled but practical and eminently reasonable approach. Had I returned to office, we were working on ideas for revitalising and democratising unions using online voting.[181] I regarded it as one of the successes of my period in office that I had really excellent relations, not just with Frances, but with John Cridland at the CBI and Terry Scoular at the Engineering Employers' Federation.

---

[180] "Cable attacks Treasury's economic illiterates", *The Times*, 6 March 2015.
[181] "Coalition at war over 'brutal' Tory attempt to curb strike action", *Mail on Sunday*, 11 January 2015.

Another bone of contention was the issue of how to curb 'radicalisation'. The Home Office backed by Cameron wanted to ban radical speakers even if they were non-violent and hostile to terrorism. I became involved since it involved banning such people from university campuses: a direct assault on freedom of speech in universities and the mirror image of the no-platform policy of student unions directed at right-wing speakers like Nigel Farage: what was later to be called the 'cancel culture'.[182] I got strong support from Greg Clark, the new Tory universities minister, whose quiet, unassuming style could lead to his being underestimated.

I was realising that in these 'cultural wars' with the Tories there were interesting differences: the Home Office/Number 10 axis was very solid and instinctively authoritarian; but Osborne was instinctively liberal on these issues, as – to my surprise – was Pickles (who had been a very fierce ally in earlier battles over giving landlords responsibility for immigration control).

There was a heart-warming – partial – success story with women on boards. We were now close to the 25 per cent level and there was a really upbeat dinner at Lancaster House with 100 women from FTSE boards, organised by Denise Wilson and the team who had led the campaign. There was a genuine appreciation of the role that the department and I, personally, had played.[183]

It was easy to pick holes in the programme: not enough

---

[182] "Coalition split over ban on hate preachers", *The Guardian*, 2 March 2015.

[183] "FTSE 100 women dine with Cable", *City AM*, 11 March 2015.

chairs; not enough executive directors. But overall, the programme was definitely headed in the right direction. I was grateful to Emily, who had encouraged me to get deeply involved and not just do the usual ministerial thing of saying a few nice words popping up for photo opportunities.

But there was a more difficult glass ceiling; the one blocking black and other minority aspirants. I was determined to move on to these more complex and difficult issues and I was delighted to be asked to get behind the 20/20 campaign of Lenny Henry and Trevor Phillips (20 per cent by 2020)[184]; Lenny, in particular, was great company: a mixture of very serious conviction politics and hilarity.

As the election approached, there were some positive obituaries for the coalition. The *FT* hadn't always been positive about my contribution but concluded that the Lib Dems had helped make "a successful coalition" and "had provided the government with some of its best personnel. Ministers such as Danny Alexander, Steve Webb and Vince Cable will depart from government having left an impressive mark".[185] The approach of the *Times* was reflected by one of its columnists: "Ah, the coalition – we'll miss it when it's gone", "It has been great for Britain."[186]

There was, however, seemingly no appetite for a coalition going forward and a deep hunger in both major – and minor – parties to get back to tribal politics as normal.

---

[184] "Lenny Henry's celebrity has allowed us to be heard", *The Independent*, 2 February 2015.

[185] "The curtain falls on a successful coalition", *Financial Times*, 30 March 2015.

[186] Alice Thomson, *The Times*, 18 March 2015.

The Lib Dems were in danger of getting into a ridiculous position: of promoting as our main USP being the party that was in favour of working with other parties in coalition, but ruling out working with any party in particular (and despite the widely held belief that Nick wanted a new coalition with the Tories, while the Tories made it clear they wanted to be rid of us).

I fell foul of this tribalism on a campaigning visit to Scotland for the spring conference just before the election campaign, when my comments suggested that I hadn't ruled out working with the nationalists under all circumstances. Nick, Danny and Alistair were apoplectic, and I escaped immediate excommunication by achieving headlines denouncing the SNP in terms I would normally have reserved for Al Qaeda or the Khmer Rouge.[187]

It became clear that most of our held seats would be fought as local by-elections albeit without the manpower and money required and relying heavily on the local reputation of the Lib Dems and the sitting MP. I was reconciled to a defensive campaign of this kind in Twickenham, but I was struck by the number of colleagues – or at least those that had decided to stand and fight – who wanted nothing to do with the national campaign.

I had been dropped as our economic spokesman which was seen by the press as a snub – and probably was – but which I regarded with relief as an escape and an opportunity to concentrate on Twickenham and helping MP colleagues, like Tessa Munt, my invaluable PPS, who had transformed

[187] "Cable turns on SNP wreckers", *The Guardian*, 14 March 2015.

my relationship with backbenchers of all parties. The official narrative was that we would get back with 30-35 MPs; privately, we realised that half that number would be a miraculous escape.

At first, the local canvassing felt really encouraging and the – less experienced – canvassers reported very positive feedback on the doorstops. Tales came back of hundreds of examples of residents delighted with casework on their behalf and clamouring for window posters. There was much less aggro about 'tuition fees', the 'mansion tax' and the Royal Mail than I had feared. There was the anger of Labour supporters who had voted for me before but hadn't realised that 'they were voting for a Tory government'; I had already discounted them, and my majority could absorb them.

Then I began to notice amongst what we called 'soft Tories' who voted for me before that the gushing tributes to my work as local MP and member of the coalition cabinet were usually followed by a 'but'. The 'but' referred to anxiety about the fearful prospect of 'Red Miliband' and 'that dreadful Scottish woman' getting into power. And though they liked my target letters, they were incredibly impressed to have received a personal letter from the prime minister from Number 10 Downing Street, advising them that, while it was good to have a hard-working, talented, local Lib Dem MP, it was more important to avoid 'chaos' nationally by having a Tory MP.

Nonetheless, I had been reassured by polls which suggested that I would be amongst the few to survive the coming disaster.[188] And by experiences like canvassing in St

---

[188] *The Times* report of YouGov poll, 25 February 2015.

Margarets with an initially sceptical, then incredulous, journalist and finding support in every house. So, to Dee's great, and justified, annoyance I went off to help with fundraising and local publicity in Somerset, Lancashire and other London seats which felt more vulnerable.

My sense of unreality was reinforced by being immersed in a major controversy in the department. I had been following in the national press the escalating violence in the civil war in Yemen and the role of Saudi Arabia using British planes and bombs. I was struck by a report from Médecins Sans Frontières on a bombed hospital. I was still responsible for the department until after the election and questioned officials on the licensing position. It turned out that vast amounts of ordnance had already been shipped out without ministerial approval. The BIS officials reluctantly conceded that I could legitimately call a halt to the continued supply of bombs to Saudi Arabia and I instructed them to refuse future license requests.

There was a furious response from the Ministry of Defence. Michael Fallon, who had been promoted to be the secretary of state, rang me to express concern that I was putting at peril the whole of the UK's relationship with the Saudis, which rested on trust that the UK would honour its commitments. The dispute escalated and Cameron was brought in to support Fallon; there seemed an almost palpable irritation that I was still around making a nuisance of myself. But Nick Clegg became involved and backed me up.

Temperatures rose and I was told that planes were sitting on the runway unable to take off because I was refusing authorisation. There were several days of fraught negotiation, involving ministers and permanent secretaries and our ambassador in Riyadh. Eventually, a compromise was reached whereby British military personnel would be embedded in the Saudi air-force control centre to monitor the use of British equipment (as the Americans apparently did) and make sure that we were not assisting the bombing of civilian targets.

Letters were exchanged with Fallon confirming the conditions attached to the licenses, but I realised at the time that the agreement would only stick if I or another Lib Dem minister were around to check. And, sure enough, a few months later, when another atrocity occurred and I was no longer in government, the MOD denied all knowledge of restrictions on the use of British bombs.

April 3 2015: Good Friday. Having a 'quiet day' at the farm before V comes late tonight having done Any Questions. I arrived on Wednesday and wore myself out gardening with Paul yesterday – but to good effect. Two veronicas moved and camellia that never flowers on its way to London, the dung heap in the corner of the paddock spread on the borders and all the plants I brought back from London on Wednesday planted out to fill gaps.

From now on, I really have to be in London but found time to walk with Jane P. Annoyingly, was in real pain with the hip a lot of the night, despite a hot bath and Ibuprofen. Watched two hours of the seven-way election debate – fascinating. The three women – Green, SNP and Plaid Cymru – were all rather good.

I cannot help a nagging feeling that the Lib Dems have served their main purpose: the mould is broken; multi-

party politics is here.* But how do the nationalist parties (except UKIP) sound so reasonable?! Poor Nick is like the sacrificial anode on the keel of a yacht. History will judge him (and us) more kindly than the electorate does just now. But this "splitting the difference" between reds and blues is not good. I long for my old SDP friend Steve Bene's image of a three-pointed Mercedes star with equidistant spokes. We so miss what Vince's book is saying... but it won't see the light of day for months – currently being vetted by Sue Gray in the Cabinet Office for ethical concerns and confidentiality.

April 8 2015: *Sitting in the car. 'They also serve who only stand and wait', to quote Milton. Nearly 7 pm, Vince canvassing, pursued by* Sunday Times *reporters and only Emily between them and their scurrilous objectives! I've done a bit of delivering leaflets yesterday and today but find canvassing, with all its standing about, very difficult.*

The diary is still a problem. Dee issues a "Candidate's Diary"; and Shona does a combination of BIS and constituency – then Piers Allen gives details of canvassing – and still things fall through the cracks in these paving stones. I have been appointed the candidate's aide and instituted an "Aide's Diary" with columns reading WHEN/WHAT/WHERE/WHO/HOW to keep myself straight. And will reissue it every few days...

Much of Easter and the days since have been taken up with a very tricky BIS issue. The Saudis are busy bombing Yemen, where rebels have ousted the (just about legit)

---

* (or so it seemed at the time)

president who is now in exile. V is holding up an export licence for 40 bombs (part of an order for 300) and is under pressure to release it. Fallon and Cameron are on his case. In the correspondence, it is revealed that 1,200 of these things were approved last summer – without his department having passed it for approval at all. He is livid. The permanent secretary thinks there should be an enquiry. Very awkward. He thought there were two pretty clear criteria not being met, but they turn out to be full of weasel words; and today he had a conversation with the national security advisor, who is very worried about Yemen disintegrating and becoming another haven for ISIL or whoever.

April 9 2015: *Vince finally penned his long letter to Michael Fallon, after steadfastly refusing to be hurried by his private secretary. He was weary after all the media interviews and four hours of canvassing last night.*

As the campaign progressed, I was seeing more of my Tory opponent, Tania Matthias. She was quite unlike many Tory politicians, especially locally in Twickenham, where there were some seriously nasty individuals. She was unassuming, quietly spoken, personally friendly and eager to establish a good relationship.

She had an impressive back-story as an eye doctor working with Palestinian refugees and now in the NHS. At public meetings she spoke up for Palestinians, the United Nations, foreign aid, Europe, immigration and progressive social causes of all kinds. Tory policy was hard to discern.

My supporters thought that this was part of a cunning

Tory plot to steal the Lib Dem vote. But I was very relieved to get way from the usual bile and bluster and treated it as a compliment that the opposition thought the best way to beat me was with a candidate like her.

One of the more surreal experiences of the campaign was lunch with one of my billionaire constituents, Evgeny (now Lord) Lebedev in the grounds of his palatial abode in the middle of Home Park at Hampton Court. I had got to know him a little – he had been our houseguest for a night in the New Forest – but mainly through his father Alexander. Alexander had come several times to see me in my room in Parliament and entertained me once in Moscow. He had a background as head of the KGB in London during the Cold War; had made a fortune in the chaos of the collapsing USSR; and was now posing as a critical friend of Putin.

His son had been entrusted with a share of his fortune and now owned the *Evening Standard*. At this point, Evgeny was inclined to back the Liberal Democrats but wanted also to be on the winning side. The fact that I turned up for lunch on my bicycle rather than in an armed motorcade had, I suspect, rather diminished my status. I gave him a plausible but rather inflated estimate of our likely result which helped secure his – rather equivocal – backing, at least until election day.

April 21 2015: Vince has had his bike stolen at Richmond Adult Community College. He had just cycled to Hampton Court for a posh lunch with Lebedev and from there to Richmond for Nick Clegg's visit, associated with much aggro since the 'team' had decided V should lead on Lib Dem policy on trades union reform: compulsory arbitration in the public sector before strike action – a policy espoused by David Owen in 1987, according to V. Nobody had consulted or informed him before last night... Ashley (a new policy spad) is said to have known about it. So V had a sleepless night and a row with Nick this morning. When I got to Richmond car park to collect him, the battle bus was in the car park with Richmond Lib Dems out in force.

April 25 2015: *The national picture gets even more flaky with the blues and reds promising anything and everything. Nick is just about getting himself heard amidst the sound and fury. UKIP flagging, the Greens buoyant, but the nationalist parties seem to be making the political weather, especially the SNP. Nicola Sturgeon is a very smart operator. I thought so during the Scottish referendum campaign and now Vince is starting to agree.*

Nick has come out strongly against any arrangement with them. Is this a shrewd move to flush out Cameron for not doing so? Labour is of course anguished about its loss of votes to the SNP, popping up to the left of them like the Loch Ness Monster.

I still believed we could win in Twickenham. I was reassured by having a dedicated and loyal local team: people like Malinda McLean and Denise Carr, who had supported me in half a dozen campaigns. As election day approached, however, the omens were looking gloomier. Our canvassers reported that some of our 'definite' and 'probable' postal voters had voted Conservative when they went back to check.

There were reports of big Tory canvassing teams massing in the constituency, one under the leadership of Boris Johnson. Residents reported a barrage of phone calls from people 'calling on behalf of the prime minister': that, and the skilfully drafted and carefully targeted mail, was cutting through to wavering voters. There was absolutely nothing coming from our national campaign that made the slightest impression and we were very dependent on our local volunteers augmented by outsiders I had begged to come, the national targeting having excluded Twickenham.

What, in hindsight, was the final nail in the coffin was an announcement on the national news that Cameron had held his pre-election rally in a garden nursery in Twickenham. I was taken aback as I knew the owner and believed him to be a supporter. On election day, there was still a belief that I would scrape back by a thousand votes or so and I gathered with my family in the evening for a long night of waiting. The tone of the evening was set by the exit poll which had the Lib Dems below our lowest expectations and likely to get nine seats (thought to include Twickenham). Paddy Ashdown had made a fool of himself by talking up our campaign and then threatening to 'eat his hat' when the exit poll arrived. There was then a six-hour wait until the Twickenham result was available. It was a clear defeat.

The announcement was made bearable by the warmth of friends and supporters and also by Tania Mathias, who, apart from being genuinely surprised, was gracious and generous in her comments as were the other candidates. In order to avoid endless painful interviews and recriminations after a sleepless night, we decided to make a quick exit for the farm.

May 7 2015: *Election Day. Have done my stints of delivery but feel semi-detached from the core team at Lion Road. There was a sudden visitation from Nick Clegg on Tuesday morning, which provoked a frenzy of activity: first cleaning and then decorating the office with suitable posters and campaign literature. In the event, he didn't go into the office at all. I bundled leaflets for the day, having felt slightly dizzy outside and been rescued by kind Mike Butlin.*

V has escaped to his dancing lesson on his (new) bike. I am taking time out for a siesta and writing this. We've been around the committee rooms but not the polling stations, increasingly preoccupied with what happens after the election. As is everyone else.

All was optimism until the exit poll appeared at 10 pm and was absolutely dire, predicting ten seats for Lib Dems, losing 47. Ashdown was on the telly saying he would eat his hat on their programme if it was right (he added if it was marzipan...) but in the event, we were down to eight. It was clear by about 2.30 am that we really were in trouble and this time I did believe Dee.

Vince's son Paul had come to spend the early part of the evening with us and Aida came later and stayed through. She drove us to the polling station and most of our gang was outside and clustered around us as we went in. Spad Emily led from the front. Joan and Shona scooped me up and each took an arm, and we followed the posse: so nice of them as I couldn't get anywhere near Vince. Then the result came about 15 minutes later and was worse than Dee had predicted (she had thought approx. 500). He lost by 2,000 votes on a huge turnout (77 per cent). I did get near enough to her to say, "You couldn't have done more," and she said "Thank you".

V's speech was used on Channel 4 News and subsequently. He talked of a well organised campaign by the Tories to promote fear of Labour plus the SNP. Tania Mathias was very gracious in her winner's remarks about Vince, and genuinely emotional about winning, just about getting through her speech without weeping. Even Nick Grant (Labour) said nice things and so did Tanya Williams for the Greens. The Christian bloke said a prayer for the winner (and the country); Magna Carta Man ("all tax is theft") was not to be seen (26 votes). The Labour vote was up by about the margin V lost by.

The news of the wider disaster percolated through as we drove down to the New Forest. Some of the 'awkward squad' had survived on the back of independent constituency-based campaigns (John Pugh in Southport; Greg Mulholland in Leeds; Tim Farron in Cumbria; Mark Williams in Ceredigion). I was delighted to see that Tom Brake had survived in Carshalton, the only London MP to do so and it was a just reward for his dogged loyalty and hard work. The same could be said of Norman Lamb in Norfolk and Alistair Carmichael in the Lib Dem redoubt of Orkney and Shetland.

Nick Clegg had also won in Sheffield Hallam with the help of a lot of Tory tactical voting against a very aggressive Labour challenge. When I reflected, I actually felt sorry for him: the ship's captain who had crashed the ship into an iceberg and hadn't gone down with the crew; and was now left in the lifeboat with a group of mostly hostile survivors.

There would be weeks of clearing up; thank-yous for the people who had worked hard for me; and the sad and difficult business of making my long-serving and loyal team redundant.

But May 8 was a glorious day. Rachel and I went out for a long walk in the forest, lay down in the sun in a secluded glade and were reminded of the joys of living. We walked back feeling refreshed and positive and prepared to make the best of a new life outside politics.

Martin Rowson's picture used for the cover of the *New Statesman*,
September 2012 (*courtesy of Martin Rowson*).

Part II

Things fall apart

After addressing the Lib Dem conference as party leader, September 2017 (picture: courtesy of Getty Images).

Chapter Fifteen
Living with defeat

Everyone who has lost a seat in an election at any level will be familiar with the mixture of emotions which follows: disappointment, anger, recrimination, humiliation, relief, introspection and a sense of responsibility for the people who follow you into political battle, especially those whose livelihoods are at stake.

I was one of the lucky ones. I had a grown and supportive family and no need to service a mortgage or provide for children. I had the emotional support of a loving wife. I had no reason to single myself out for blame after seeing colleagues, also conscientious local MPs and from different positions in the party, targeted by the Tories in the same way and with the same result.

This was a case of survivors envying the dead with the devastation of the parliamentary party and, for Nick Clegg, being exposed to daily mockery and blame and the likelihood of being replaced by Tim Farron, who had been a consistent critic of his leadership and the coalition. My agent, Dee, had never been under any illusion about the election and the national campaign and she organised the tidying up operation, making sure that I thanked the hundreds of helpers. I also sent out a thank you leaflet to constituents, remembering the experience of bad losers and aware of the need to keep the good reputation of the party locally, if not nationally.

Morale was helped by a deluge of local fan mail, a lot of it signalling 'buyers' remorse' along the lines of 'we didn't think you needed our vote'. I even had a few letters from leading Conservatives. One was genuinely warm – from Matt Hancock. I also had a hand-written note from Boris Johnson, whom I hardly knew – we had clashed over transport strikes and 'mansion tax' but were allied over Heathrow; it occurred to me that he was much shrewder, better organised or more generous than his image suggested. I was touched by the gesture.

The Lib Dem disaster, let alone my own, wasn't even the main story of the night. The SNP swept Scotland, wiping out all but one seat from Labour (who lost 40), one Conservative and one Lib Dem. The SNP had a sweet revenge for the referendum and Scottish independence was back in play. More fundamentally, the issue had opened up a deep division within the UK and not just in Scotland. I had been shocked by the visceral, English nationalist, attitude to Scotland which I had encountered on the doorsteps in Twickenham, one of the most educated and middle-class constituencies in the country.

When I wrote an article for the *New Statesman* with my analysis of the election, the editor quoted back at me a pamphlet I had written for the Demos think-tank two decades earlier on the 'politics of identity': 'Our politics could be moving from the old certainties of class and left-right debate to new divisions based on national identity, race, religion and language'.[189]

May 10 2015: V had emailed Georgina Capel even before we left London to check whether Atlantic Books would still want After the Storm *and by the time we arrived at the farm there was an enthusiastic YES. This cheered him up no end and he biked to the village to buy more copy paper. Predictably, I ran out of printer ink while getting him a clean copy as he mowed the lawn for me. We then walked to the pub in Sway and lingered on the way back by the "bonsai'd oaks", the former badger sett on the edge of the farm. The silver lining in this big black cloud becomes more and more apparent.*

Dee and other friends are pressing V to go to the Lords. I am against, mostly because he has so many talents that he can make a future outside it, but also because I so disagree with the whole bloated institution as currently

---

[189] *New Statesman*, 22-28 May 2015.

configured. As he, too, is on record for wanting to abolish it, it would look hypocritical.

A few weeks later the news came through of the death of Charles Kennedy, who had been defeated in the Scottish highlands after over 30 years in Parliament. He was a very talented but troubled man and had fought a long battle against alcoholism. Nonetheless, it was difficult not to believe that a particularly nasty election preceded by a coalition he had warned against – for its impact on the party in Scotland – had taken its toll. Those of us who had worked with him when he was the party leader had some appreciation of his great qualities and also of the demons he struggled with.

Nick Clegg rang me, putting the finishing touches to his list of peerages. To his evident relief, I made it clear I wasn't interested. I could tell that his list of staffers and ex-colleagues wanting peerages was longer than the number Cameron had offered him.

Dee, amongst others, was telling me not to be so cavalier. But I thought it was a bad idea and I was on record saying the Lords should be blown up or words to that effect. I am not against the honours system as such: just that people should not be making laws if they haven't been elected. Being a 'Sir' on the other hand would be a real honour.

I was fortunate to have a project. *After the Storm* was finished. It was a better book than *The Storm*, which had been a best-seller during the financial crisis but would be of less interest to the wider public except as a, by now, rather dated commentary on the economic controversies underlying the coalition. The Conservative narrative had already prevailed but there was a job to do correcting the story for those still inclined to listen.

Before I could become too obsessed by re-fighting old battles, Rachel made the very wise decision to whisk me off for an idyllic holiday in Corsica: warm Mediterranean seas; the smell of pine in the mountain forests; unspoilt scenery well away from tourist haunts. I sketched out my novel and started writing and worked out how best to use my time henceforth.

May 15 2015: *I have cleared my art out of the "garden escape", which is now his "writing shed". V is outwardly calm but inwardly churning. I am in that classic bind of getting what I wished for: more time with V and fewer external pressures, but realising I will now have to carve out a space for my own pursuits.*

May 21 2015: *V's* New Statesman *article has attracted quite a bit of attention, whilst I am merely trying to write an article called "the end of apartheid", a light-hearted piece about the breakdown of our laundry arrangements for at least the last decade, whereby his is done in London whilst mine stays at the farm.*

May 25 2015: *My 70th birthday. We had a big party yesterday next door, courtesy of son, Dylan, and daughter-in-law, Janette, for 70 people: about half family and half friends. Zoe and family turned my house into a cake-baking factory and produced a tower of 70 cupcakes, all beautifully iced. Janette had found school caterers to produce colonial-style curry for the multitude. Max* presented the traditional Kalis-composed poem to me as the birthday girl. Vince made the thank you speech I'd helped to prepare and it was well received! My much loved and only remaining aunt (Margaret) died only days ago, the last of her generation, so now we are truly 'The Oldies'.

May 27 2015: *In London since Monday. Lots of sweeping up after the election is under way. We need to organise a thank you party for all the helpers. Vince's constituency staff Joan and Shona say they are now underemployed and willing to help type V's book revisions, which is immensely helpful. We went to Holborn to talk to Atlantic Books, who have a publication date – September 17 – and a proposed cover.*

On the way back we saw the serried ranks of diplomatic cars emptying their ambassadors into the state opening of Parliament as we "walked the other way", both literally and metaphorically.

June 2 2015: *V has just brought me tea and the news that Charles Kennedy has died at his Fort William flat. "No suspicious circumstances", which is a small mercy. So sad, and so hard for Sarah and their son Donald, now ten years old. The phones are ringing every few minutes from people wanting V's comments and he is collecting his thoughts before going public: "shocked and saddened", which is both safe and true.*

June 18 2015: *We gave V's Twickenham office staff lunch at Arthur's on the Green and exchanged presents: Vince's included* Applemac for Dummies *as he is now the proud* owner of an Applemac laptop for the first time – and a paper shredding machine, now surplus to office requirements!

End of June 2015: V says he is "writing a novel in his head", which is wonderful, though I can tell that he is missing the mental stimulation of the last five years in his big job.

Our holiday in Corsica was the perfect place to start getting it from his head onto paper: self-catering accommodation, a week each at opposite ends of the island, with a long, spectacular drive between and an opportunity to visit our friends Peter and Joan Chapman. They lent me Dorothy Carrington's classic book on Corsica, which kept me company for the rest of the holiday. As always, Vince set an ambitious programme of mountain walks and I retaliated with swimming lessons for him.

I finally settled down to painting in week two, one of the paintings becoming our Christmas card. "The famous aroma of the maquis, dominated by the curry plant (known as 'eternelle' here) but blended with cistus, arbutus, tea tree and honey" competed with the less glorious scent of V's disintegrating trainers, finally consigned to a bin while I got our hire car washed, ready for its surrender in Calvi.

Apart from writing books and articles and occasional speeches, there was a spate of proposals to sit on various boards and undertake 'consultancy' which I believed was par for the course for ex-ministers. I didn't like the sound of most of them: mostly involving helping companies navigate

Whitehall or passing on the names of contacts. Rachel and I had a comfortable but modest lifestyle; parliamentary and ministerial pensions are generous, and I didn't feel the necessity for more money by teaming up with rather tacky outfits.

What I did feel was the urge to make a contribution in an area of BIS work that I felt was especially valuable. FE and adult colleges had taken a big financial hit which I felt guilty about; but I knew, and the main mission groups in the sector knew, that it would have been a lot worse if I hadn't been there. I had partly succeeded in shielding the sector from the bright young things in the Treasury and other graduates in government, who couldn't see the point of spending money on the half of the population who did not have academic qualifications and aptitudes. I was touched when the Association of Colleges organised a 'thank you' dinner.

My first step after the election was to join the governors of the local adult college which had done some really innovative work with those who had learning difficulties and was also making good use of a programme I had started in government to help the mentally ill recover through adult education as my mother had 60 years earlier. And I based myself at the City Literary Institute in central London, a remarkable institution providing lifelong learning for thousands of Londoners.

I also found opportunities to do some serious work in the university sector. I had a visiting professorship at Nottingham and developed with them an online Massive Open Online Course to supplement undergraduate teaching, another at St Mary's working with the admirable

Francis Campbell who had been a key figure in the Northern Ireland peace process and his deputy, Ruth Kelly, a Secretary of State under Tony Blair. The LSE offered a visiting professorship to do some serious economic research. Through Nat Puri, a Nottingham-based Indian entrepreneur who brought me onto the board of his German car component company, I found myself involved in the creation of a new technological university in India.

July 2015: Drinks with the Bottomleys in Smith Square. They plied us with peach champagne and Virginia, now a head hunter, lectured V, her main message being that he should not think he could mix Biz (directorships) with Show Biz (media appearances) while Peter (still MP for Worthing West) and I reminisced about meeting up in Malaysia where both our fathers worked in the 1960s.

I began writing My Life in Less than 100 Objects, *the title being a nod to Neil MacGregor's classic* History of the World in 100 Objects; *but still typing "End Notes" of* After the Storm *for Vince; and enjoying an increasingly manic circuit of social life and my committees. Then on July 28 was poleaxed by a message from my younger son, Max, that his wife, Héloïse, had left him, barely a year after their wedding.*

August 9 2015: My Classic FM *radio programme told me that Cable and Alexander are to get knighthoods. Diana Boulter (of events company DBA Speakers) and I agree that one should learn this by letter from the Queen. But I warmed to the idea of adding Lady Cable to my portfolio of names.*

One of the downsides of being a senior minister was that, for five years, I had not been able to maintain a close involvement with local charities and neighbourhood groups. I was a name on the notepaper: a patron. Twickenham had a deep stock of what is called 'social capital': voluntary groups who, alongside the council and the state, gave real substance to the ideas of 'society' and 'community'. Liberated from red boxes, I was able to re-engage with a dementia day care centre which I had helped to get off the ground with a local vicar; help fundraise for a teenage mental-health charity; and promote the cause of children's hospices whose local home I had helped from its inception and which had established a sensory garden in the name of Olympia. It had achieved some prominence caring for David Cameron's disabled son Ivan and was now struggling to survive.

My defeated colleagues had varied experiences. Some landed good jobs utilising their talents. Steve Webb, who had been Minister of State for Pensions, went to a senior job in the pensions industry; Paul Burstow, who had been health spokesman, to a university chair specialising in social care; Treasury secretary Danny Alexander to a top position in Beijing with the newly established Asian Infrastructure Bank; schools minister David Laws to head up an education think tank.

Others went back into local government: Adrian Sanders in Torbay; John Pugh in Sefton; Tessa Munt, Vince's former parliamentary private secretary, in Somerset. Others had a bigger challenge: both Jo Swinson and her husband Duncan Hames had lost their seats – and had two very young children – but had the resilience to get through. Others were struggling, years later, to adapt to the cruel reality of rejection by the electorate.

__August 9 2015:__ V is getting more involved again in some of the local community activities he supported before becoming a minister. I get drawn into that world and am encouraged to become a trustee of a Twickenham homeless charity, SPEAR, which is expanding rapidly. It starts from the sensible point that homelessness is not mainly an issue of bricks and mortar, but of helping people who often have complex, deep-seated problems around difficult childhoods, mental illness or drug or alcohol abuse, and helps them to learn to support themselves in a tenancy.

But the boards of charitable organisations can be very time-consuming and frustrating, as I know from chairing New Forest Villages Housing Association. Small may be beautiful – and effective – but it is also very hard work.

__August 24 2015:__ In Perthshire with Zoe, both of us distressed about Max's marital situation, which looks terminal. Vince's knighthood finally formalised but people up here neither know nor care about honours, which is refreshing. We did a bit of the Edinburgh Festival and climbed West Lomond. And to cap it all, dear son-in-law Stuart fixed for me to drive a combine harvester, my 70th birthday present from the Robertson family!

__August 31 2015:__ On the train southwards. I've had my fill of bleached fields and armies of magenta willowherb, big skies and scudding clouds (and aching legs).

August Again (from the train)

Big skies and scudding clouds
Hookers green and honey harvest
As we journey south again.
And on the banks each side
Magenta rose-bay willowherb,
Intermittently escorting us.

Now on the last day of August,
Trailing silver petticoats:
Not so much a tartan army
As a Gay Parade
Of pointy pink helmets
And stickleback seedpods
In rich maroon.

It gets scruffier as we head south
There's more thistle and bramble
And less discipline in the ranks:
Burnt umber docks and yellow ragwort
Harass the gentle drifts
Of purplish pink.

Straw bales like giant cotton reels
Are tossed haphazardly,
As balers race to beat the weather,
And fields are already ploughed;
Looking like dandruff on a dark jacket
Are white birds.
Sheep and cows give way to horsiculture

With all its kindergarten coloured toys.
There are giant Lego-stacks of straw
And dykes of shiny silage sacks.
But still the faithful fuschia army
(though paler and more threadbare)
Cheers us on.

Yesterday I drove a combine harvester,
One of those green and yellow monsters:
Its rear view mirrors like deformed antennae
Of some mutated insect.
And for an hour I was a happy, power-crazy,
Harvest Queen.

Vince is beside me, piling on with his novel.

September 15 2015: *Launch of* After the Storm *at Hatchards, Piccadilly. Have we joined the 'glitterati'?*

September 19 2015: *Vince and his grandson Charlie recorded* 'Big Star, Little Star', *with Aida and me in attendance. Charlie was up against two pretty but very precocious little girls, and the question-master's style veered towards titillation, which A and I thought inappropriate. Charlie, aged eight, did really well to just smile and get on with it. Vince flunked the "closeness" test by not guessing that 'ski-ing' was the shared activity done in special clothing and in a big space. Apparently, my grandchildren in Scotland, keen skiers, were yelling the answer at their telly!*

The launch of *After the Storm* in Hatchards was a success. Atlantic had pulled out the stops to turn the book around quickly. The book launch was a preliminary to a tour of British book fairs. In the next few weeks, Rachel and I managed to get around Wigtown in Galloway, Appledore in Devon, Durham, Ilkley, Shrewsbury, Chester and Bath with more to come later. It sounds a chore but I loved these events. We got to see new parts of the country at leisure. And as literary ex-MPs, like Chris Mullin and Alan Johnson will confirm, they are a delight to speak to: often several hundred people who pay to come, listen hard and ask searching, intelligent questions.

The book itself got some flattering reviews, notably from Anthony Hilton in the *Standard*: "Some people can write fast, a few people can write well. Cable shows a remarkable talent for both and had produced a book that made a serious contribution to the continuing debate about banking, housing, China, executive pay, short-termism...".[190] Chris Mullin picked it out as a 'book of the year'[191] and Chris Blackhurst judged it "thoughtful and heading in the right direction". He was kind enough to add "Cable will be missed".[192]

Unfortunately, I was competing with reviews of books on Cameron's premiership: not flattering but compelling reads, like *Cameron at 10* by Anthony Seldon and Peter Snowdon. The most substantial bit of promotion was a long

---

[190] "Cable was a true friend of British business", *Evening Standard*, 14 October 2015.

[191] *Observer*, 29 November 2015.

[192] "How business will find Cable was a pussycat when they deal with Eagle", *Evening Standard*, 16 September 2015.

personal interview in the *Guardian* and analysis which focused on my return to my hobby of ballroom dancing and what the author saw as a rather apolitical, academic animal who had been adrift in real politics.[193]

The party conference in September in Bournemouth was a new experience. Under new management – Tim Farron – the party was coming to terms with defeat and plotting a new direction. I was closer to Norman Lamb whom Tim had defeated for the leadership but it was very understandable that the membership would choose someone who wasn't going to be constantly confronted with questions around the unpopular bits of coalition policy. He also related well to the grassroots campaigning which was the party's strength and was an excellent, uplifting, speaker. And with a referendum on Europe coming, it was sensible to have an unambiguous Europhile at the helm.

I was – rightly – confined to the fringe and spoke about the threats and opportunities presented by the choice of Jeremy Corbyn to lead the Labour Party. I had seen quite a lot of Jeremy Corbyn in the division lobbies where he had often voted, with his friends, against the Blair government. He seemed an eminently decent man but utterly unsuited to lead the main opposition party. It seemed to me that his leadership was bound to end in schism and disaster and that the Lib Dems should be preparing for a civil war in the Labour Party with a possible SDP mark 2.[194] My piece for the *Mail on Sunday* contrasted ideological 'priests' and

---

[193] "It takes two to tango", *The Guardian*, 5 September 2015.
[194] "Defection is never easy... but we may need a NEW party to combat Corbyn", *Mail on Sunday*, September 2015.

practical 'plumbers' in politics. Priests were back in fashion but wouldn't last long.

With hindsight, I should have realised that talking of SDP 'Mark-2's wasn't very helpful to Tim. When I later became leader, I realised that talk of 'new parties' was very destabilising. He had to denounce my talk of possible new ones.[195] Unfortunately, his insistence that any defections had to be to the greatly diminished Lib Dems became an embarrassment when the promised defectors never arrived. None of us appreciated it at the time but the unresolved arguments about the future of the 'centre-left' were still reverberating years later, when the leadership of Labour had passed to Keir Starmer and of the Lib Dems to Ed Davey.

I was reminded of the good things about the coalition period when I was invited to a 'thank you' dinner by the Engineering Employers' Federation (later, Make UK). They had drawn great encouragement from the 'industrial strategy' and practical benefit from a government employing a long-term perspective for manufacturing. At the same time, it was clear that the new Secretary of State, Sajid Javid, wasn't all that interested. He had asked to meet me for a coffee and was perfectly friendly, but as a former – and successful – City banker, with Deutsche Bank, his

---

[195] "Lib Dem grandees at war over call for 'new SDP'", *Daily Mail*, 21 September 2015; "Work with Labour? Maybe says Farron, no way, says Cable", *The Guardian*, 21 September 2015; "Farron dismisses Cable's talk of a new party", *Daily Telegraph*, 21 September 2015; "Farron rules out Cable's proposal for new party on the centre-left", *The Independent*, 21 September 2015.

instincts were very much those of the Thatcher era.

He informed me that, since 'industrial strategy' was associated with my name and the government was trying to rid itself of 'Lib Demmery', he would be dropping it in favour of something less 'interventionist'. He had already dropped one of the most useful programmes – the Accelerator – which I had launched, with John Cridland of the CBI, to give mentoring support to medium-sized firms committed to expansion.

I could see that we were entering a new cycle of the very British disease of the 'not invented here' syndrome; and then, after a delay, reinventing the wheel. I wrote a joint piece with Chuka Umunna (still inside the Labour tent) making the case for a cross-party consensus and elsewhere arguing that manufacturing matters. I also teamed up with Chuka to attack George Osborne's fiscal policy and to restate the arguments for public investment.

September 28 2015: *We arrived in Wigtown for the book fair, pretty weary after a day of travelling, having spent the previous evening going to Grimsdyke, the former home of Gilbert (of Gilbert and Sullivan) to see a 'semi-staged' production of the* Mikado *at the invitation of Nat Puri, the delightfully eccentric and generous chief executive of Purico, international manufacturer of specialised parts for cars. The accompanying festivities included decapitating champagne bottles with a ceremonial sword!*

I took my mind off it by visiting my brother Hugh that afternoon, in St Thomas Hospital, with lung inflammation and congestion and on strong antibiotics and steroids but very weak. My sister-in-law, Gay, had negotiated a bed by the window for him with fabulous river views. She is a good person to have batting for you when the chips are really down.

September 30 2015: Turn around and out again to a concert at the Wigmore Hall with Paul and Eve Strasburger, who have lent their valuable Tononi violin to the amazing Ben Baker, accompanied by a Russian pianist called Petr Livonov. Home at 1 am.

October 3 2015: I have been frazzled by the government's proposed extension of Right to Buy to housing associations and the National Housing Federation's inadequate response; and a bad-tempered exchange with our housing manager at NFVHA (the New Forest Villages Housing Association), now more demanding than ever, culminating in my asking a fellow board member to take over her in-line management from me, while I find cover for her impending maternity leave.

October 10 2015: Appledore was enchanting. We walked to Westward Ho, encountering the Pebbleridge on the way. It is an extraordinary dyke of enormous smooth grey boulders, some with lines of quartz through them, creating white "spectacles" when the curves are right. Brenda Daly is the 'queen' of this book event, which brings to life this characterful North Devon village, once a serious shipbuilding town, now with a very sad empty dry dock and a list on the wall of all the ships built there since 1780, including an icebreaker.

The event itself (in the church) was well attended and it

was good to have former Lib Dem Devon MP Nick Harvey introducing Vince and fielding questions.

On to Durham and Ilkley for more book events.

October 18 2015: And thence to Thame, Shrewsbury and Chester. I needed to get to Cambridge afterwards and Vince to Twickenham before he set off for an appointment in central London at 3 pm, a meeting with the High Pay Commission at 6 pm and Newsnight at 10.30 pm. He really begins to need a club or somewhere to put his head down in central London between appointments.

October 27 2015: We got our long weekend at the farm. It was lovely to potter in the garden together (he is now the bonfire 'expert'), bike to the village and walk out across the heathland from the farm... The autumn colours are brilliant. Sky TV came and did a film clip on Sunday, after a lie-in as the clocks went back.

The hip is very tiresome. A new X-ray reveals large 'spurs' on the 'knuckle' of the joint, whilst the ball and socket are relatively okay. V seems to be having trouble with his back again but determined to go ahead with his dancing competition in Blackpool next weekend.

November 1 2015: Blackpool. You get nostalgic for the famous illuminations when the alternative is fog, a beach with the tide right out and the Soviet-style sculpting of the sandstone 'cliff' below the promenade. But the tram still operates, with a ticket collector (himself a collector's item), to whom you pay real money. We went to the 'social' the night before the contest and got to do a waltz, cha-cha and *quickstep before watching the floor show by the reigning Russian champions – predictably gorgeous. Hip now protesting hard. Vince did creditably but not brilliantly, ballroom better than Latin, and I got some nice photos of him dancing with his teacher Cheyenne.*

November 12 2015: *Bath. A memorable book event in a city church. I am still in love with Vince's voice! And the book has been reprinted.*

November 19 2015: *Dublin. Vince had an audience of 1,000 for his talk to the Association of Auditors jamboree, while I went shopping for a suitable outfit for a Buckingham Palace investiture, now scheduled for December 18. We found time for some lovely walks along the Liffey and admired Dublin's modern architecture, harp bridge etc as well as making a visit to Trinity College's wonderful library and the unmissable* Book of Kells. *Trinity was my maternal grandfather's university, although he was an Ulsterman from Ballymoney. He was a student there at the beginning of the 20th century, so well before the Easter Uprising.*

November 26 2015: *I have been proofreading V's novel, which I think is rather good. He is incorporating my tiny amendments before sending it to Georgina Capel, his literary agent, who will say whether it's worth pursuing with publishers.*

December 1 2015: *Cambridge weekend. V doing a dancing competition qualifier and staying in Balsham with his old friends, Jim and Hilary Potter. They have a* *wonderful old garden, including a maze in the shape of a treble clef planted by them and now mature, alongside a very well-designed modern house. I bought an expensive coat (to go over the dress from Dublin) for the upcoming investiture.*

December 10 2015: *Vince doing* QT *and is grumpy – a mixture of exhaustion and anxiety – following a week which included a book fair in Lewes, a fundraiser for Salisbury Lib Dems and a Chinese 'Icebreaker' award ceremony with the Chinese ambassador. V has joined a distinguished-sounding list of people who have supposedly advanced Sino-British relations.*

December 13 2015: *We host the Cable family pre-Christmas lunch for 12, which includes Hugo's lovely girlfriend Laura for the first time.*

It was good to be away from the political frontline to be able to reflect on what was happening and also to take psychological refuge in escapist pursuits: pressing on with my novel; dancing in a tournament in Blackpool (badly); ski-ing for a week. Buckingham Palace for the investiture was a full stop in my political career, bar the occasional fundraiser for a local party or an increasingly infrequent media interview. And lots of book fairs: commenting on politics from a safe distance.

In March 2016, I was asked to work with another ex-MP, Oona King, in a campaign to head off the privatisation of Channel 4. We succeeded (or at least until the Tories came back five years later).[196] That apart, six months on from the election, I had largely left the world of politics behind. Very little was heard of the party, but that was inevitable given our small parliamentary representation. What I loosely call the 'centre-left' – the big space between Cameron/Osborne and Corbyn – was largely silent, seemingly with nothing much to say and no one to say it. Hopefully Tim would grow into it with like-minded Labour people who seem as collectively shell-shocked by events as the Lib Dems. I started to prepare for another dance competition, this time in Gillingham, Kent. And more book fairs are scheduled to punctuate the next few months: Scarborough, Hexham, Fowey, Hay-on-Wye.

My immediate priority was to help Rachel through a hip operation at a hospital in Southampton. I had unhappy memories of hospitals with Olympia, in and out of the Royal Marsden, with constant worries about her deteriorating health and disability mixed up with anxiety about parking meters outside and the numerous standing committees and other parliamentary events where my many absences were being noted and criticised. This time, I could give my wife undivided attention, even if it was for a shorter time and more curable condition.

February 22 2016: *Choice of reading is V's novel or Mary Beard's SPQR, escapist projects compared with newspapers which are full of Trump on the other side of the Atlantic and Boris this side, both amongst my least*

---

[196] "Selling off C4 would be a dogmatic act of vandalism", *Observer*, 10 January 2016.

favourite people in the whole world.

March 7-11 2016: *Hospital. Vince visited assiduously throughout my stay at the clinic in Southampton (where I had a wretched few days fainting and puking) but was required in York for a Lib Dem event on the day I came out, (so much for "undivided attention"!), so my kind friend Jo Lowis spent the night here at the farm. I was reminded of the story my mother-in-law used to tell about her husband being late to retrieve her and her first baby out of hospital because he had been buying a boat!*

March 13 2016: *Rings and earrings back on! Housing Association meeting tomorrow at my house to review the service level agreement with English Rural HA, now up and running. It's a relief to have New Forest Villages HA under their wing.*

March 29 2016: *Back in the matrimonial bed, which is rather low, so challenging to get up from.*

April 6 2016: *My memoir* My Life in Less than 100 Objects *is almost complete. I am full of doubt about the whole thing but determined to get to the finishing post of 30 objects. Apart from one rather philosophical entry on my marriage of 31 years to Dirk, represented by the box made by him from the 1987 storm oak (which he gave me when he left) I have not dwelt much on my innermost thoughts. I am so content with Vince that the past seems less and less important. Or does it "lie too deep for words"? Certainly, the memoir is supposed to celebrate and* *entertain rather than become a confessional.*

May 9 2016: *I am buoyed up by my friend Jackie Rowley's approval, having plucked up the courage to show it to her.*

I was flown out to Nigeria to speak at a conference on China in Africa. I had a growing interest in China and its increasing importance and had spent a few weeks researching the African dimension. Their trade and investment already swamped the western contribution: a far cry from my involvement with them in East Africa fifty years earlier, when they were blue-suited revolutionaries: and merely an exotic alternative to the dominant western presence. Overall, the African delegates welcomed the Chinese, but there was some unhappiness from Nigerian businesses losing out to competition.

Chapter Sixteen
The dawning of Brexit

June 1 2016: For the first time, baby frogs are to be seen jumping out of my rill, where the pump has failed, making the waterfalls cease and the stagnant water more attractive to them for breeding. I heard their loud croaking in February and saw the clouds of spawn in March. We are about to go on holiday, so I have to stop worrying about the predatory water boatmen, who appear to be able to grab the frogs as they grow their back legs in an aquatic war of the worlds.

The EU referendum campaign was gathering momentum. I felt pretty detached from it all. Cameron and Osborne were leading for Remain and seem confident. Nick Clegg had been rehabilitated. Some Labour pro-Europeans were in evidence – Mandelson, Adonis, Alan Johnson – but Corbyn had gone to ground. With both business and the trades unions and with the Nats on board in Scotland, there shouldn't be a problem.

I got involved in a very sober and civilised debate with former Conservative chancellor and leading Brexiter Norman Lamont at the National Institute for Economic and Social Affairs. Norman was good and, as always, calm and reasonable. But I sensed that, for as long as the debate was about economics, Remain would win comfortably.

I was invited to various local debates in the New Forest

– Minstead, New Milton – at the local sixth form college and some surrounding areas with local MPs or outside celebrities like Tory MEP and Brexiteer Daniel Hannan. I began to get an uncomfortable feeling. The meetings were polite but the voice of Tory southern England was not that of the metropolitan leadership. There was also a palpable generation divide; the elderly were seemingly obsessed by immigration – though there were hardly any immigrants in this part of the world – and appeals to the past: the war and the Commonwealth (meaning the white bit). At the local college, the students laughed at the Brexiteer, and very right-wing, Tory MP Julian Lewis, but at other events the oldies loved him. And likewise in New Milton: they disliked immigrants and loved Tory MP Desmond Swayne.

I also had abiding memories of a debate in the village of Heytesbury with 'leave' campaigner MP Bernard Jenkin. It was a beautiful Wiltshire village; the local church was packed to the rafters; not a single non-white face in the audience of several hundred; and the talk was all about immigrants and the problems they were causing. One very agitated, elderly lady wanted to know where we were going to put 60 million Turks. She intended her question very literally and the audience was clearly on her side. Bernard articulated the prejudices of the audience in very reasonable terms and he clearly reflected the public mood.

As the national campaign developed, the emergence of a credible Brexit team around Boris Johnson and Michael Gove changed the dynamic. Leave was no longer dependent on Nigel Farage, a brilliant debater but seen as extreme and not a Tory.

I was now getting more involved in the national

campaign. There was an event with George Osborne and Ed Balls at Stansted with Ryanair.[197] Conversation with George and Ed was pleasant but a bit forced and was, in any event, dominated by Michael O'Leary, who could talk for Britain (and Ireland) non-stop. Then there was a press launch inside a GKN factory in Bristol, where I spoke alongside Amber Rudd (and Chukka).

Fitzwilliam College, Cambridge, staged a debate for college alumni in the City with me, Norman Lamont, Andy Burnham and Marina Wheeler. It was good to be included in these events but I was no longer in the first division and Rachel and I could slip away for a planned holiday in Puglia without leaving a hole in the campaign. There were a lot of big egos and competing Remain voices; but the dominant one was George, who was trying to repeat the trick he used in the Scottish referendum: scaring the public with the economic uncertainty.

June 16 2016: In San Polignano, we caught up with the horrible news that Jo Cox, a Labour MP in West Yorkshire has been killed ("stabbed and shot") by a fanatic in her constituency, apparently yelling 'Britain First!'. I am really shocked and upset. And it reminds me that seriously disturbed people go to MPs' surgeries. I cannot help being relieved that Vince is no longer doing this stuff.

June 23 2016: Referendum Day and raining. Back in London, V was part of a dreadful telly programme on

---

[197] "Osborne ridicules Leave camp claim of 'global stitch-up' over EU debate", the *I* newspaper, 17 May 2016.

Channel 4 with Jeremy Paxman: about a million celebs competing for space. Paxman looked as if he had overdosed on Valium but maybe it was just that his autocue was too low or he was too vain to wear specs to see it! V was good and the 'undecideds' swung towards Remain by the end...

I spent an hour being an IN presence at the polling station in Twickenham. The borough voted overwhelmingly to stay (69 per cent), but the country has voted by a narrow margin – 51.9 per cent for OUT, 48.1 per cent for IN – to leave the EU.

So now the PM has announced he will resign.

I spent referendum eve on Westminster's College Green, helping the channels to fill the space before the results. It was like old times being a fully integrated part of the Westminster bubble. I feared for the result, however. The latest polls were not looking good. My limited experience in the prosperous southern seats where I had been active suggested that the traditional Tory vote was heavily 'Leave', and the economic stuff hadn't cut through (partly because pensioners had no reason to worry about jobs). Meanwhile, Labour had been conspicuously absent, bar a few active Europhiles.

When the result was known I was standing with Conservative MP David Davis, who had urged David Cameron in a speech in 2012 to hold a referendum on Britain's membership of the EU. He was suitably euphoric and saw the end of Cameron in sight: a personal vindication. When I was interviewed, I identified the key driver in the result as age: intergenerational differences and nostalgia amongst pensioners for "how things used to be". The evidence subsequently confirmed that analysis, but it was not a popular one and the main narrative was all about the disenchanted working class and the failure of the metropolitan elite to understand their genuine concerns over immigration. It did not look that way in the prosperous Brexit bits of the south.

30 June 2016: *What a week in politics! The nomination for the party leader to replace Cameron closed yesterday and it turned out that Gove had shafted Johnson, so Boris announced that he wasn't running for leader. This gives May a better chance of winning. I am mighty relieved not to have our very own "Boriscolini" as PM, but Gove is almost equally awful, which leaves me with Theresa May. The other hopefuls are Crabbe and Liam Fox. Meanwhile, in the Labour Party Corbyn hangs on, with 80 per cent of his parliamentary party against him.*

July 14 2016: *Politics is crazy. Last weekend there was a Conservative leadership contest, down to two women, but on Monday Angela Leadsom withdrew after stupid remarks about being a better candidate because she has children (in contrast to the childless May). On Wednesday, Cameron moved out and May moved into Number 10.*

The Labour Party is arguing about the rules. They have decided that Corbyn, as the sitting leader, doesn't need to be nominated to be on the ballot paper and now there is a third candidate – Owen Smith as well as Angela Eagle. Clearly, unless one or the other stands aside, they may get stuck with Corbyn.

It wasn't a surprise to see the exit of Cameron and the arrival of Theresa May. I had no reason to lament Cameron who, behind a charming veneer, had comprehensively shafted the Lib Dems, and me, and had now, through incompetence and complacency, trashed the legacy of forty years of European co-operation by his Tory and Labour predecessors. He had, however, been an effective leader of the coalition: a brilliant chair of meetings and a relaxed ringmaster who let ministers get on with their jobs.

His departure was marked by a particularly cynical round of cronyism – packing the Lords with friends and supporters – which I was invited to criticise in the press.[198]

I had mixed feelings about Theresa May. We had clashed constantly about immigration policy in the coalition, but she was an honourable person, a conscientious minister and very much the best of the bad bunch, who competed for the leadership. To my pleasant surprise, she adopted industrial strategy as one of her key priorities and my former special advisor, Giles Wilkes, went off to work for her with my encouragement to maintain continuity. She challenged one of the coalition's policies – encouraging Chinese investment in the Hinckley Point nuclear power project – but, to be fair, had worried about the issue earlier.

The 'No' vote in the referendum had given the Lib Dems an injection of life and purpose as the party of 'Remain'. Tim Farron demanded a second referendum and this proved to be a powerful rallying cry for those who felt that the

---

[198] "Dave's cronyism stinks... I thank the Lord I said no to my peerage", *Mail on Sunday*, 7 August 2016.

referendum was distorted by lies and Russian interference. But I was now a free agent and able to say what I thought. When I spoke at conference at fringe meetings, I tried to make the case that we should not be disputing the result of the referendum, however dishonest and wrong the arguments for 'Leave'; it would be better to ally with those who wanted the softest of Brexits, keeping the economic structures like the customs union and the Single Market but with an emergency brake on migration.

This line of argument did not endear me to the hardline 'Remainers' in the party and was to prove awkward when events took an unexpected turn, bringing me back into politics. But I thought it was the right line to take – knowing what we then did – as well as my honest reaction as a retired politician. It was helpful later in providing some distance from the extreme fringe of the 'Remain' movement.

November 9 2016: *Donald J Trump will be the next President of the USA. Acceptance speech mercifully gentler and more conciliatory than the tone of his campaign, but who knows what will happen next. He talks about infrastructure renewal but you need to levy taxes for that – and pay them!*

My political retirement was further deferred by a by-election in nextdoor Richmond Park when Zac Goldsmith resigned his seat in protest at the decision of his government to press ahead with Heathrow expansion. It was an honourable, if quixotic, thing for him to have done. I think he expected that the Lib Dems would give him a free pass since we were equally opposed to the airport policy.

But the Conservatives decided not to put up a pro-Heathrow candidate against him, which changed our calculation, and we decided to fight the election around Brexit.

At this stage, the distinction between opposition to a 'hard' Brexit and opposition to Brexit as such was not seen as important and we were the anti-Brexit party. The issue was deeply damaging to Goldsmith who was pro-Brexit in a 'Remain' constituency. Sarah Olney, the Lib Dem candidate, was a 'newbie' who had been drawn into politics by this issue alone and saw the Lib Dems as the rallying point for those who wanted to fight Brexit. As the former MP for the next-door seat – and, as I realised, still the candidate – I was given a central role in the campaign and I began to realise the passion the issue generated and the energy which it was injecting into the party.

Sarah won and I was quick to seize on the result as a vindication of our opposition to a 'hard Brexit'.[199] The 'hard v soft' issue was given clearer definition a few weeks later when Theresa May gave her Lancaster House speech, in which she said that the negotiating brief would include withdrawal from the Single Market and customs union. For me at least, this clarified the battle lines and justified the demand for a second vote to confirm that the public really wanted the 'hard Brexit' which hadn't been at all clear during the referendum campaign.

But the real action was overseas. France and Belgium were hit by Muslim extremist terrorist atrocities. Trump was elected in the USA, offering a toxic brew of economic

---

[199] Vince Cable, "The march of Hard Brexit can be stopped", *Mail on Sunday*, 4 December 2016.

nationalism and rejection of anything to do with international cooperation mixed in with crude prejudices about women, Muslims and immigrants. There was something deeply unsettling seeing the 'Leader of the Free World' repudiating all the things I had believed in throughout my professional and political life. So far, touchwood, Britain was still some way from that kind of politics.

December 1 2016: *Richmond by-election. I did my stint of vote telling in Ham for two hours after dark in the freezing cold, came back and went to bed to get warm but had to be up for 6 am for V to go to Paris, so I turned on the radio and we had won! V rang me from the train to say there was a celebration at 10 am on Richmond Green, so I went along – and it was very jolly, with all the main political journalists there).*

I was able to introduce Sarah's mother to Tim Farron. She wanted to thank him for the way the party had looked after Sarah. So nice to hear after all the complaints which had been flying around. She will be the only female Lib Dem MP. It is also such a tonic for 'Remainers'.

I was also drawn back into the political world by my old nemesis, Rupert Murdoch. Five years earlier, Murdoch's bid for full ownership of BskyB had collapsed in the face of publicity about the 'hacking scandal' while the bid was being considered by the Competition Commission, where I had referred it. Undeterred, the Murdochs had come back for another bid through 21st Century Fox, which they now owned. the arguments around media plurality were, if anything, stronger: the Murdoch press had a one-third share of the newspaper market; 20 per cent of TV if they owned Sky; and 45 per cent of radio through Sky's control of news content.

Ed Miliband, now freed of leadership responsibilities, wanted to organise resistance to the takeover and approached me to join a cross-party initiative to block the bid. I wrote a piece with Ed setting out the arguments.[200] Scandals at Fox news made the potential new owners even less palatable.[201] I then went to a hearing of competition specialists in the new Competition and Markets Authority with Ed, Ken Clarke and Lord Falconer to argue the plurality case.

Our intervention and the delay it created in the approval process gave time for the US media company Comcast to organise a counter-bid which was ultimately successful. The Murdochs finally gave up and sold their share in Fox to Disney. It was now a long time since my first unhappy encounter with the Murdoch family, but it was gratifying to have finally been on the winning side in the take-over battle.

I was also reminded of another unhappy episode, but in a good way. I was approached by the National Union of Students to work on a joint project: the future of FE and students in that sector. The invite came from the new NUS President, Shakira Martin: a black, single mum who had graduated through the FE route, at Lewisham College. She had seen off a far left opponent who had campaigned on

[200] "No to the Sky deal. The Murdochs can't be trusted", *The Observer*, 18 December 2016.
[201] "Politicians blast Sky bid after sex scandal at Fox", *Mail on Sunday*, 23 April 2017.

Palestine as her big issue. Shakira highlighted and benefited from the fact that the largest number of NUS members were in the FE sector, not universities and, far from being preoccupied with 'tuition fees' and debt created by the fee-loan system, they were unable even to access the student loan scheme.

We were a somewhat improbable double act, but we did a very successful tour of FE colleges from Dudley to Oldham to Harrow. She was an absolute star who had a remarkable connection with teenage audiences and she made skilful use of her back-story. The joint report we produced was, I thought, a creditable piece of work and may have helped her to get re-elected.

The FE exercise also helped me reconnect with my brother, Keith, who taught in an FE College (Farnborough) and represented the staff through their trade union. He had followed in my father's footsteps in FE and also in trades union work (though my father's union, the NAS, was set up to keep women out of the teaching profession, a piece of labour history now conveniently forgotten). Keith had had to manage the tricky position of having a famous brother who was also ultimately responsible for some of the unpopular cuts in the sector. He was a dedicated and successful lecturer who had found a role teaching economics to sixth formers and young adults trying to graduate through a non-university route. I was greatly relieved to find that, when I went to his college, I was shown off with pride rather than with awkward embarrassment.

Another blast from the past came when the government announced its decision to sell the Green Investment Bank to the Australian bank, Macquarie. The government would retain a golden share, but I feared that its mission would be lost.[202] A rival group with a much stronger commitment to continue the GIB's work was dropped for reasons that weren't clear. I went to see Business Secretary Greg Clark to make my concerns felt but I met a very straight legal bat. He dropped enough hints to make it clear that the gods in the Treasury had had to be appeased.

But my future was defined in a meeting in my garden in the spring of 2017, when I was asked to clarify whether I wanted finally to stand down as Prospective Parliamentary Candidate (PPC) and let the local party choose a successor. I said I would stand down as a candidate in June. I expected that to be a formality and we booked our summer holiday on the basis that, in retirement, I had no parliamentary timetable to worry about.

Although the Tories had a big lead in the polls, Theresa May had only had a year in office and there seemed little risk of an early election, given her natural caution and aversion to risk. Then, returning from her walking holiday, to wide consternation, including mine, she announced a general election. I was back in action again.

April 18 2017: *Morning: We are in bed, having tea – another bright cold morning. Vince is working on the next book – non-fiction.**

Evening: May announced a general election for 8 June. All our May and June plans now in disarray!

---

[202] "Selling off the bank I founded could be the final nail for green Conservatism", *The Guardian*, 10 January 2017.
* This became *Money & Power*.

Chapter Seventeen
From retirement and into leadership

Coming out of retirement to fight an unexpected general election proved to be a shock to the system. When I was last in harness for an election, I had a Rolls Royce professional team in my constituency office, a headquarters to use as a base for planning the campaign and a highly effective campaign organiser, Dee, who had managed five of my six previous campaigns in Twickenham. This time Dee's husband Jim was unwell and she needed to focus on his needs, so we started from scratch with volunteers operating under Rachel's supervision out of my garage, with little money and no organisation.

But I soon began to feel life surging back into the local party. The leader of the Lib Dem group on the council, Gareth Roberts, took on the organiser/agent role and provided strong leadership. A derelict shop was quickly found in Whitton High Street. The local activists were highly motivated and keen to help.

Help also poured in from elsewhere and the national party decided to target the seat, judging that I was the best prospect in the region, together with Ed Davey in next door Kingston. Candidates from 'hopeless' seats came to help, notably my former researcher Pippa Morgan, a candidate in Enfield, who was my excellent aide.

Once I got out onto the doorsteps it was clear that this

was going to be one of the more comfortable elections. There was a vast amount of goodwill, partly personal, partly in recognition of the Lib Dems' opposition to Brexit. As the campaign went on, however, there was some confusion, reflected in the national literature, as to whether we were for a 'soft' Brexit or for reversing it in a second referendum (I was later to discover that Tim Farron and Norman Lamb hadn't been able to agree and the confusion in messaging reflected that disagreement). The national campaign was also not going to plan. Tim was not coming across well and our overall national support was stuck under ten per cent. A lot of young people were excited by Corbyn. Most older people were alarmed by his socialism and tempted to return to the safety of the Tories; and as the polls narrowed, this became more of an anxiety for us.

As I travelled around on my bike, canvassing almost every night, I was conscious that this was almost certainly my last election and I was determined to leave on a high note, reversing the defeat of two years earlier. I realised how much wounded pride had been stored up and had a sense of wanting revenge. The latter was not directed at Tania Matthias who had been an independent-minded, strongly 'Remain' MP, voting against the Tory line on key issues, notably the rights of EU nationals. As at the previous election, we had developed a certain rapport, but this time she was the one having a hard time at public meetings and on the doorsteps, trying to defend a government she only half believed in from angry 'Remainers'.

Brexit had also created a strange new demographic, quite different from the voting patterns I had got used to over 25 years of knocking on doors in Twickenham when class had been a big determinant of voting intentions. I and the Lib Dem councillors had tended to give the big, valuable, detached houses a wide berth knowing that we would invariably get a Tory 'no', however politely expressed. But in the dense terrace houses of Teddington and Hampton and modest semis, populated by teachers, science researchers, hospital registrars and middle managers, we weighed our vote; and also, when they could be encouraged to vote at all, the former council estates where Tory was a swear word.

This time the pattern was almost reversed. The poorer estates, where the *Sun* and *Star* were read, bristled with Brexit pride; but the richer folk were seriously angry at a Tory government which had messed up and, by pandering to nationalism, was putting at risk the international networks on which their businesses and livelihoods depended.[203]

But my core vote was what it always had been amongst young, aspirational, middle class graduate families who cared about their children's education and had come to the borough because of the reputation of its schools. My campaigning in the election was centred on school funding and, in particular, the fact that schools were having to make teachers redundant: a consequence of cuts which had gone beyond those of the coalition years.

Since I was on the side of the angels on the two issues which mattered to people – Brexit and schools – I had a strong following wind. What I was afraid of was a Tory

[203] "Speak out, plea to 'punchbag' bosses", *Mail on Sunday*, 30 April 2017.

campaign like that of 2015, ruthlessly focusing on the fear of Corbyn amongst 'soft' Conservatives. But it never materialised and instead Theresa May was a poor campaigner and stumbled into a confused presentation of her plans on social care. But the Corbyn factor worked against the party nationally with excited Corbynites unwilling to vote tactically, and 'soft' Tories reluctant to jump to us.

The result wasn't seriously in doubt in Twickenham, where my majority was just short of 10,000, or in neighbouring Kingston. But we failed to hold onto Richmond, where Zac Goldsmith staged a come-back and the result nationally was disastrous and summed up in the headline 'Clegg out and Cable in as Lib Dems win just a handful more seats'.[204] The hard 'Remain' vote across the country had splintered between ourselves, Labour and the Greens (who had stood aside to support me in Twickenham) and many 'Remainers' were reconciled to leaving and moving on.

June 11 2017: *It's all over and we won with a thumping majority – 9,700 and something! I did some leafleting at the station, which was fun, and some vote telling at Heatham House on the day – also fascinating. Friday, we biked to Teddington to look at a potential office, and yesterday we biked all the way to Hampton for their carnival. We got an amazing rumble of cheers from bystanders on both days! And stopped by in Lisbon*

---

[204] *Evening Standard*, 9 June 2017.

Avenue, where they were having their annual street party. It was a lovely event – people originating from all corners of the globe but getting along and being inclusive. Just what we need.

The national picture is extraordinary: Theresa May's tiny majority of 12 is gone and there is now a hung Parliament. She stays in office with a supply and confidence arrangement with the DUP, who have ten seats. This is making Ruth Davidson, who won 13 seats for the Tories in Scotland, sound anxious: she being married to her gay partner whilst the DUP are against same-sex marriage – and abortion. In social matters, it seems they are rather similar to the Catholics they so loathe. Funny old world!

16 June 2017: *Back on the treadmill! Life moves on so fast. It is now Friday night and I have been in the New Forest since Tuesday. We spent Monday going to Parliament to get V sworn in and collect our parliamentary passes, then to see the publishers at Atlantic. In between, we just had time to go to an exhibition by the Japanese artist Hokusai at the British Museum! I went home, but V had three more meetings that evening.*

The news has been dominated ever since by the most awful fire in a tower block in North Kensington in the middle of the night. It is said there will be at least 100 dead when they can reach the bodies. *It went up like a Roman*

---

* The final fatality total was less – just over 70 people – but still appalling.

candle, looking as if the cladding was highly flammable.*

No sooner had the polls closed than the speculation started on my replacing Tim as leader. He hadn't had a particularly effective campaign but, in the event, he fell on his sword for a different reason: religion. He had said in an interview that he considered homosexuality a 'sin', reflecting his evangelical Christian convictions.

Other major party figures – Charles Kennedy and Shirley Williams – had managed to reconcile their (Catholic) faith with their popularity in a secular and liberal party but, sadly, Tim couldn't find the words to extricate himself. The substantial gay contingent amongst our leading national activists exploded in outrage and Tim resigned. It was possible he saw ahead a difficult inquest on the election. Or perhaps he was just not willing to trim his deep, religious convictions. Either way, he went.

Although Tim had not come across convincingly in a general election, his judgement on the way forward for the party had been absolutely spot on: to concentrate on rebuilding the local government base and to make ourselves unambiguously the 'Remain' party with the uncomplicated objective of 'stopping Brexit'. If I now found myself stepping into his shoes, as many inside and outside the party were assuming, I would adopt and develop that approach.

However, I had very mixed feelings about the idea of the leadership. If I had competed and won a decade earlier, the party might well be in a very different place; but I hadn't. I

---

* And later was proved to be so: a shocking indictment on the cheapskate attitude of the housing management team there.

was now 74 and would be touching 80 at the end of the Parliament which would be a difficult political sell. I knew that a lot of people in the party wanted 'something new' and forward-looking, whilst I, as a veteran of the coalition, would be spending a lot of time explaining and justifying the past.

I had also already taken on various voluntary roles, locally and nationally, which would be difficult to reconcile with a big party role, including the chairmanship of the large, social enterprise bus company HCT.[205] Not least, Rachel and I were enjoying spending more time in each other's company and doing what we liked doing in both town and country, socialising with family and friends, travelling and indulging my renewed passion for writing.

June 20 2017: V went public today with his candidacy for Leader of the Lib Dems. I watched him on BBC News at 4 pm and on Channel 4 News at 7.30 in a three-way debate with Labour and Conservatives. But now not sure where he is or when he will be back. And this is what it will be like from now on.

June 20 2017: Ed Davey has not yet 'declared'. Nominations close on July 20, so there is lots of time, of course.

I started to take soundings in the party and discovered that Ed Davey was doing the same. It looked initially like a

---

[205] "Tania Mason 'Busman's Holiday' Governance and Leadership", May 2017.

competition and I was urged by my friends to rush out a 'mission statement'. Dee, in the Lords, began to organise for a serious contest. Duncan Brack, one of the party's leading policy thinkers and an enthusiastic environmentalist, crafted a manifesto. But a collision with reality occurred in the form of a poll of our activists which suggested that they wanted Jo Swinson as leader – she had won back her seat in East Dunbartonshire – with Layla Moran, the new Oxford West and Abingdon MP as second favourite and me, third, with Ed Davey and Norman Lamb further behind.

In the event, Jo did not want to stand, and was prioritising her family for the next few years. Layla was quick to appreciate the dangers of moving too soon. Ed realised that his family situation with a seriously disabled child was far from ideal and Norman realised that his Euroscepticism was a big handicap. In any event, a majority of the MPs and many peers were nominating me.

So, there was to be a coronation rather than a contest, which was not ideal since it would deprive me of legitimacy and an opportunity to deploy one of my strengths in competitive debating. My role of 'last man standing' wasn't particularly helpful in defining an exciting new phase in the party's history and the idea grew that I was taking on the role out of a sense of duty rather than because I foresaw a bright shiny future. Jo was the unanimous choice of colleagues to be my deputy; she was clearly heir apparent and my role as a transitional leader was underlined. Still, I was good at making the best of a difficult situation and buckled down to it.

The first big step was a rally of supporters to have me formally adopted. The Lib Dems do these events well. There was a large, enthusiastic, crowd and the TV cameras were present; a neutral bystander could have been forgiven for thinking that we were still in the glory days of Ashdown and Kennedy rather than a party with 12 MPs and firmly stuck in single figures in the polls.

I needed a simple message with a simple slogan to give a sense of direction (and to make the news bulletins). I coined the phrase 'Exit from Brexit' which got me off to a good start.[206] My own support for the European Union was intellectual rather than emotional, but sincere and long-standing. I also felt that, after May's uncompromising Lancaster House speech, proposing withdrawal from both the Customs Union and Single Market, we could convincingly champion the idea of another referendum – not to repudiate the last one but to confirm or disconfirm a Brexit very different from the 'soft' Brexit many people voted for. I tried also to define a centrist and social democratic vision which was pro-business but also committed to fighting inequality through taxing wealth and drawing from Macron's success. [207]

I was aware of the need to buttress the more nuanced and academic arguments about Brexit with some political 'red meat' and used the brief window of national publicity as the new leader to throw some big punches. My friends in the *Mail on Sunday* gave me a platform to denounce Brexit 'zealots' and 'jihadis'.[208] *The Guardian* gave me two

---

[206] "Cable vows to champion 'exit from Brexit'", Metro, 21 July 2017.

[207] *City AM*, 21 July 2017.

[208] "Cable warns of Brexit 'jihadis'", *Mail on Sunday*, 6 August 2017.

pages.[209] The *New Statesman* did a profile which highlighted my reaction to Theresa May's dreadful phrase about 'citizens of nowhere' which had echoes of 'rootless cosmopolitan'.[210] My throw-away line – "it could have been taken out of *Mein Kampf*" – got a headline, but was not one of my better judged remarks. The *Mirror* gave me a page to highlight the wider economic fragility of the economy with Brexit approaching.[211] With these and other interviews I had a summer of good and extensive publicity. I felt a little like a camel at an oasis drinking in the headlines in preparation for a desert ahead.

21 July 2017: *Vince has become leader by default after the others didn't compete. He was quite nervous about his acceptance speech, which followed Tim Farron and Jo Swinson, so there were overlapping thank-yous. However, as usual, he managed to introduce a couple of catchy phrases – the need for an 'Exit from Brexit' and describing Theresa as 'adult' whilst Boris was in 'short trousers' and Liam Fox 'in nappies'. Then after a short interval at party HQ with sandwiches, there was a 'hustings' at Coin Street Community Centre near Waterloo.*

Finally, a taxi home with an Observer *journalist interviewing Vince. He got a good five minutes on the 6 o'clock news, with clips from Strictly and the Mr Bean joke in Parliament.*

---

[209] Interview with Stephen Moss, *The Guardian*, 15 July 2017.
[210] Anoosh Chakelian Interview, *The New Statesman*, 7-13 July 2017.
[211] "Mountain of debt puts UK in peril again", *Daily Mirror*, 13 August 2017.

August 2 2017: *V and I escaped to see the film* Dunkirk, *which was very moving. I was tearful when all the little ships appeared on the horizon. The central story of the evacuation was amazing. But I can't help feeling that it was conceived at the height of Brexit mania as the Brits were depicted as (almost) universally jolly good chaps whilst the French were the sort of people who stole IDs off the Brits to get a place on the boat to England. But the achievement of getting around 300,000 of the 450,000 troops home was indeed miraculous.*

I write this while V deals with his end-to-end phone calls. He is trying to keep up the momentum since he became leader. He is rather mischievously nurturing a rumour that Boris Johnson might resign as Foreign Secretary over Brexit.

September 5 2017: *My brother, Hugh, died after his lung condition suddenly got a whole lot worse. I visited him last week, when Gay and I were able to wheel him outside for a breath of fresh air outside Guys and Thomas Hospital. I find it very hard to come to terms with the five of us siblings not being complete any more. As my son Max says, he was 'gentle', the middle one, perhaps a bit squashed between the strong personalities above, below and around him.*

Other than harvesting a few headlines to keep the party in the news, my first task was to get around the party and meet the activists. In the absence of a string of hustings meetings, I did a solo tour around the 20 or so venues. What it revealed was a tale of two parties. In London, Bristol, Oxford, Cambridge and Southampton there were packed meetings, buzzing with youthful energy and enthusiasm for the Brexit battles ahead. In Manchester, Leeds, Newcastle, Birmingham, Derbyshire, Kent, Cardiff, Exeter, Edinburgh, Aberdeen and Cornwall the attendees were older: mostly veterans of local government campaigning and looking to me for signs that the party could recover from its two electoral maulings.

I was aware that publicity was crucial for the party to be seen as relevant. After two years of 'cold turkey', I had lost my taste for publicity but I knew I would be judged by how much I could get into the news. My publicity offensive was helped when my novel appeared at the beginning of September, launched at the Edinburgh Literary Festival. The timing was, however, unfortunate in getting the book taken seriously as a work of fiction, albeit very light political fiction.

The *Times* gave an extensive review, but was trying to place my characters in the current political context and struggled to understand why I had made a Conservative MP, rather than a Lib Dem, my leading character.[212] The *Mail on Sunday* again gave me a big plug but tried to make a 'bonk-buster' out of the non-existent sex.[213] The *Telegraph* managed to make my return the most interesting twist in the plot.[214] I had again managed to mix up entertainment with serious issues.

---

[212] "Lib Dems are Lost in Sir Vince's Plot", *The Times*, 19 August 2017.
[213] "Vince and the VERY racy bonk-buster that's got the Commons guessing", *Mail on Sunday*, 10 September 2017.
[214] "The twist in the plot: I didn't expect to come back", *Daily Telegraph*, 6 September 2017.

Conference in Bournemouth was more optimistic than it had been for some years and I found some of the buzz and expectation that had been present in the run up to 2010. There was a feeling amongst our supporters and in the press that, with Corbyn way out left and the Tories committed to a 'hard' Brexit, there was potentially a big market for our centrist, 'Remainer', politics: even, a Lib Dem revival.[215]

There was also a feeling that I had got off to a very good start, being taken seriously as a national figure and giving clear definition to our objectives without stirring up the negatives from the coalition years. I was fortunate, too, that Tim had been very supportive and constructive with no sign of resentment at his sudden loss of power. He was an important ally, still popular in the party at large and with a nice line in political humour to cheer an audience.

In my big speech to Conference, I took what I thought was a necessary risk and trailed the thought that I could be the next PM, however improbable it might seem.[216] I think I managed to sound tongue-in-cheek and not too pompous and thought it was important to dismiss from the outset the idea that Lib Dems were only interested in winning parish council by-elections; that competing as a national party must involve competing to win not just to take part; and that I wasn't just treating the job of leader as a post-retirement hobby, but determined to make a breakthrough. It attracted predictable mirth from the satirists but I thought it was the

---

[215] Matthew Parris, "This is the moment for a Lib Dem revival", *The Times*, 16 September 2017.
[216] "'I could be the next PM': Vince Cable plots path back from wilderness", *Observer*, 17 September 2017.

right message.[217]

September 17 2017: I set off this morning to get an Observer and was rewarded with a full two-page spread on Vince and a Rawnsley headline: 'Has Vince Cable been smoking too many hallucinogenic drugs?' This is because he talks of himself as a credible Prime Minister... which is indeed what he needs to convey!

At Lib Dem conference, yesterday's highlight was Vince in conversation with Will Hutton. Jo Swinson did a good speech, but her delivery is rather self-conscious – lots of walking about and flashy gestures. However, she does cut through. Her description of Trump as a bully, a misogynist and a racist ran all afternoon on the ticker tape on the BBC News Channel. The management won the vote on the amendment to the motion on Europe, specifically endorsing a referendum once the terms of Brexit are known.

Now I needed to get to grips with the nuts and bolts of the job away from the more glamorous bits like the luxury suite at the conference hotel and the celebrity interviews. I got off to a bad start: the seemingly simple job of putting together a competent leader's office under a chief of staff. Dee had helped me to obtain the services of Alex Davies from the Rowntree Trust for a deputy role and he proved to be a superb acquisition. But for the main role I chose, from a very competitive field, was Sarah Olney who had lost her

---

[217] Andrew Rawnsley, "Has Vince Cable been smoking too many hallucinogenic drugs?", *Observer*, 17 September 2017.

seat and was looking for a job.

She was a very capable woman and had a following amongst the 'newbies' where I was felt to lack support. But it soon became apparent that the party machine would not tolerate her remaining as candidate in Richmond while also working for me and, in order to retain her position in Richmond, she was forced to resign, leaving me without a chief of staff. It took some time to recruit another: Fiona Cookson, my BIS press officer.

That episode also alerted me to the problem of the party machine, the HQ and the party committees under the party president Baroness Brinton. The party prided itself on its 'democratic' governance which meant a vast amount of time spent in endless committee meetings. The apex body, the Federal Executive, had 35 voting members, many of whom considered it their democratic duty to speak at length on every item.

The apex body was supported by an expanding infrastructure of subcommittees of similar prolixity. Elected members had been chosen from several hundred conference representatives and some had become masterful at this version of 'democracy', and often saw it as their role to put properly elected politicians in their place. Combined with the president's passion for process, the system brought out the inner Mussolini in those of us eager to get things done.

The Labour Party appeared to have the same problem, with the added ingredient of ideological venom, though I could not believe that the Tories were hobbled in this way. For the party leader the dilemma was that I was responsible for our – now very small – parliamentary party but the president and her committees were responsible for the HQ and the running of the party.

Moreover, while the elected base of the party had been devastated, locally and nationally, the HQ and the committees remained largely intact. Tim Farron had realised that power in the party had moved from Parliament to head office and based himself there. I thought that that was inappropriate for a party trying to revive as a serious political force and devoted my time to the parliamentary estate and activists and council groups out in the country.

My priorities were noted and resented and I soon had reports of mutinous head office staff. There were some good and dedicated individuals but others whose talent was mainly for office politics. I was shielded from the hostility by Alex Davies' diplomatic skills but soon began to feel it. It took the form of a campaign to weaken and oust a leader who was too old, a man and insufficiently "shouty".

The problem was made worse by the fact that the bloated political machine had to be paid for and the overwhelming majority of the party's income went towards paying the full-time staff. Although the surge in membership had greatly alleviated the looming post-election cash crisis, the party was heavily dependent on a few large donors.

Some had become totally disillusioned by having subsidised two disastrous election campaigns. The fact that their money had been wasted on a last moment blizzard of low-grade leaflets rather than investing earlier in campaign staff on the ground was not understood. Others were keen to support our anti-Brexit campaign, but insisted that the money be spent on that campaign and not on party bureaucracy.

My job as leader was to go out and get these and other donors to sign cheques. Some of the donors had little understanding of politics and assumed that my job was simply to ratchet up our poll ratings like a marketing director meeting monthly sales targets, or to copy Emmanuel Macron and sweep to power on a popular tide of centrist fervour which I would miraculously generate. Some wanted peerages and could not understand why I would not, or could not, dish them out. A few were dodgy and after recalling the scandal of Scottish businessman Michael Brown – when the party in the Charles Kennedy era had taken large sums from a fraudster – I was inclined to err on the side of caution. So, income lagged spending.

Helped by Dee Doocey and other financially literate colleagues in the Lords, I sought to launch a cost-cutting exercise and looked to former ministerial colleague Nick Harvey, whom I had encouraged to take on the role of chief executive. I was also represented at the Federal Executive by Mike Tuffrey, an accountant and former leader of the Lib Dem group on the Greater London Executive, who did painstaking work on my behalf. A few cuts were made and posts lost, but the machine fought back and only small savings were made. Nick came close to being evicted by the party machine and I had made some implacable enemies, as did my staff, who were fighting my corner, especially Alex.

September 28 2017: V here for early lunch but last seen cycling towards Sky TV at Isleworth, whilst his constituency office phoned rather plaintively to say that his 2 pm appointment had been waiting for some time. There is a string of things, ending with his weekly dancing lesson at 8.30, which he said he was going to do by car, but the car keys are still here...

Next day, a 7 am start to get the early morning train up to Manchester for anti-Brexit rally: one in the morning, then another in the afternoon. Big crowds and good vibes, though I began to think my demo days were over!

October 15 2017: Day in Cheltenham for V to do some campaigning for the local Lib Dems and to appear at the Cheltenham Book Festival, where he has long been booked, and is paired with Stanley Johnson, who has also written a political thriller. Stanley is being upbraided in the green room by his Lib Dem friends who are furious that he has suddenly changed sides in the Brexit debate (citing Juncker's speech as the reason for changing his "life-long" support for the EU); and resigned from the Europe-wide conservation movement they all belonged to, as part of his volte-face to advance Brexit Boris for PM.

He was enormously ebullient but very egotistical. The referee was a lovely author called Cathy Rentzenbrink who had to keep putting him back in his box. The train back took four hours to get us home after midnight – V has to be in central London for an 8 am breakfast to chat up potential party donors.

The decision to concentrate on parliamentary activity over headquarters management did not prove particularly rewarding. Because we had only 12 MPs, the Speaker was very reluctant to call me to speak and ask questions. At weekly PMQs, the one parliamentary event seen by the public, the Scottish Nationalist leader at Westminster was allowed to ask two questions a week, as Lib Dems had before 2010 when we were the third party. I was allowed one question every four weeks, an outrageous inequity but one for which we had no serious comeback. That was the price of electoral failure in the British system. People started to ask 'Where is Cable?', the assumption being that I wasn't trying.

It soon became clear that the only issue preoccupying Parliament was Brexit. I had asked Tom Brake to be our Brexit spokesman. He was liked and trusted by all his colleagues: a rare attribute in a political party. He had no apparent ambition to a bigger role than this, for which he was ideally suited as a committed Europhile, fluent in French, but grounded in the practical political realities of Westminster. He was also being brave politically since his seat in Carshalton was one of the few London constituencies which voted for Brexit and he risked annoying a segment of his voters who had stuck with him in 2015 and 2017 on the strength of his constituency work and general popularity.

What soon became clear to Tom and myself was that the clarity of our position also meant that we had no leverage in the parliamentary positioning. The Lib Dem vote was totally predictable. We were for 'a People's Vote' and against Brexit: period.

I soon got used to the idea that this was not a Parliament for eloquent speeches – since the Speaker would only call me or other Lib Dems very late and for a few minutes in length. Wit and subtlety of argument were not in demand. Speaking in Parliament involved endless repetition of the same core message and its value lay, not in the chamber, but in the video sent out to our core supporters that we were speaking up on their behalf.

The one opening which allowed me to do something different was whenever Theresa May made a Prime Ministerial statement, after which I would normally be called fifth and I managed occasionally to be original, at least for a while. The big prize was to get a clip on the 10 pm TV news; but that was a rarity and the main publicity was speaking to a few news obsessives and old folks' homes on the BBC News Channel.

One of the positives of our positioning on Brexit was that the parliamentary group was cohesive and largely united. Norman Lamb was exploring links with other 'soft Brexiteers' which I encouraged as a way of broadening our reach but the group (also in the Lords) disagreed only in the degree of anti-Brexit fervour with Vera Hobhouse – our new MP from Bath and a German by origin – as the most fervent.

We also had one very individualistic colleague, Stephen Lloyd – whom I liked and related to – who was a 'Remainer' but had pledged to vote in accordance with his ('Leave') Eastbourne constituency, which was to become a serious problem later. My colleagues and I tried to reach out to the fifteen or so Tories who had emerged as 'mutineers' and were taking a lot of stick in the Brexit press and the larger group of fervently pro-Europe Labour MPs. But I soon realised the extent of the damage done by the last two general elections; they had mostly written off the Lib Dems and didn't like to be too closely associated, lest they be identified as potential defectors.

With mounting frustration at the lack of opportunity to play a leadership role in Parliament, I returned to the work I used to enjoy and do effectively as a back-bencher: asking lots of questions of different ministers and looking for adjournment debates on issues which mattered to constituents.

I obtained a debate on school funding which then provided a peg for discussion with headteachers as I continued the pilgrimage I had started, visiting every school in Twickenham on successive Fridays. I also secured another on the funding of care, which was one of those crucial issues which had been kicked into the long grass to accommodate the all-consuming Brexit debate. And I took up again the cause of those businesses who had lost large amounts of money as a result of the activities of RBS and Lloyds in the aftermath of the financial crisis and had not yet been compensated.

October 21 2017: *Manage to rendezvous with V in Devon where he is doing party events and a book fair in Sidmouth. We are put in the bridal suite of the Victoria Hotel, an enormous red sandstone affair to match the red cliffs at the other end of the promenade. V leaves for Manchester. I drive through strong winds and heavy rain back to the farm.*

On arrival our friend Jennifer is on the phone with a story about V appearing on Have I Got News For You *<u>sitting in a bath</u>. Eventually, I trace it to a photo I took of him in an ancient bathtub in a hotel near Lough Conn in Ireland in 2011. We also have one of me. Lots of bubbles and very tasteful. Goodness knows how they got hold of it!*

October 30 2017: *An awards ceremony for bravery: Pride of Britain organised by the* Daily Mirror. *Nobody had* *warned me about the red-carpet entrance and the serious flow of celebs. We found ourselves in the middle of the* Strictly *cast, which was wonderful and shook hands with Anton du Beke. Also spoke to the dishy surgeon from* Holby City *and were at a table with the cast of* Coronation Street: *Gail (Helen Worth), who is delightful – and her school teacher husband, Anita Dobson opposite. Close by is Chuka Umunna and his beautiful wife.*

Prince William arrived and had a speaking part, as did Theresa May, Jeremy Corbyn and Vince, to make police awards to the heroes of the London Bridge and Borough Market terror attack.

November 1 2017: *Defence Secretary Michael Fallon has fallen on his sword. He is alleged to have repeatedly put his hands on Julia Hartley-Brewer's knee at a dinner 15 years ago. Julia herself seems to be able to laugh about it, but there is a feeding frenzy in the media ever since the Harvey Weinstein allegations.*

The issue of former Lib Dem chief executive Chris Rennard inevitably resurfaces. The long and short of it is that he was found not to have done anything to answer for 'on the balance of probabilities', but is still considered guilty in the court of (mostly female) public opinion.

I know some of the individuals involved as well as the Rennards and feel I need their side of the story. His wife, Ann, sends me a detailed rebuttal of the most serious of the allegations. V reports that there is a very bad-tempered meeting of the MPs on the subject and he is getting ground down by this stuff on early morning and late-night media on top of the more important outward-looking work he is trying to do for the party as a whole.

There was another poisonous issue circulating in Parliament and in the party and reinforced by the growing numbers of 'sexual harassment' cases exposed by women inspired by the #Me Too movement.

In November, Michael Fallon resigned as Defence Secretary after a series of allegations emerged of misconduct, including an incident some years before involving Jane Merrick, a very professional journalist I knew well enough to know she would not be exaggerating. There had been a few comments made about female civil servants feeling 'uncomfortable' when we were ministers together in BIS, but nothing specific. Then Damian Green resigned as Theresa May's deputy after a series of allegations involving porn on a computer and incidents involving other female journalists.

The Lib Dems had form in this area and the case of Lord Rennard resurfaced in the press. Jo Swinson continued to be preoccupied by the issue and the fact that Lord Rennard was still active in the Lords. She was publishing a book in which she would call for his expulsion from the party, although the original complaints and the internal investigation had gone as far as was possible under the existing rules.

I was dragged into the story since Rennard had come to help in Twickenham in the 2017 election campaign and had been photographed with a canvassing group; the photograph was circulated on social media with the accusation that he had been my 'adviser' during the campaign. He had given me a few helpful tips on target letters, but nothing more.

I had worried at the time when he appeared and had asked for advice amongst the women I worked with, including Rachel. They hadn't been unduly fussed but I realised later that there was a generational issue. Older women, who had been involved in campaigning on big women's rights issues like equal pay, sex discrimination, birth control, abortion and divorce, regarded 'handsy', flirtatious men as one of life's nuisances and had dealt with them, if necessary, with a slap on the face, a knee in the groin or the judicious use of a stiletto. Younger women were much less indulgent and regarded such behaviour as inexcusable and requiring sanctions, including exclusion from public life, especially if the man was in a position of power.

Lord Rennard would have been dealt with more severely under party rules which had come in later. But I was left explaining to fiercely professional women journalists, like Emma Barnett and Cathy Newman, why the Lib Dems had a poor history in this matter.

November 2-3 2017: *On to Newcastle. Got off to a bad start when V 'lost' his mobile phone after a C4 interview in Gateshead. After great panic, it was found in his knapsack. Then off to a grand banquet in the Civic Centre with 200 of the leading business and other 'establishment' figures from the north east. Unfortunately, the sponsors, Newcastle Airport, had left packets of milk chocolate on our chairs. V sat on his, unaware of the contents. Melted chocolate was not a good look for someone about to go on stage to speak. I escorted him to the toilets where we got rid of the worst* of it. Luckily only two other people were aware of this sideshow and he made a very good speech, without notes as usual. Was able to relax afterwards to take in the amazing banqueting hall with a large frieze round the walls of the city's history since mediaeval times.

Next day V is to speak to the Chambers of Commerce at the Trinity House, a Tudor jewel in the quay area with exquisite dark panelling and a secret door to the chapel. They are investigating whether the painting in the style of Rubens **is** a Rubens. I am more impressed by the naval battle paintings of a certain Carmichael. V goes off to speak to university students – told to expect 20, gets 200, and friendly – while I go to look at Roman stuff in the Museum of the North. Then regional Lib Dem conference and annual dinner.

V has the next morning in Sunderland where a group of young Lib Dem activists are gradually taking over the council from a dozy Labour party and then train back to London. These regional visits are fascinating and politically worthwhile, but very demanding and very frequent.

November 23-24 2017: A long night ahead doing a homeless count for the charity SPEAR in Twickenham of which I am a trustee. Got off lightly; it was 8 degrees centigrade and dry in Old Deer Park. Our little unit of three only found two people not already known about, sleeping rough under the arches of the A316, one in a tent and one just in bedding. A man with a bike was disconcerted to see us: our SPEAR staff member knew him to be a local drug dealer.

On December 1, my interview on *BBC News*, referring to Trump as an 'evil racist', caused a stir. I normally tried to avoid too much name-calling and I knew the term 'racist' was much over-used. But, in this case, Trump's use of the 'birther' controversy to discredit President Obama and other innuendo, including some obvious 'dog whistles' to racist supporters, merited the term.

The fact that the UK government was so desperate to line up trade deals with the USA post-Brexit was blurring its judgement, including turning a blind eye to the obvious abuses. Some of my friends thought I had gone OTT. I didn't normally, but if anyone merited the epithet of racist, it was Trump.

We had been celebrating my son Hugo's wedding at a hotel in North Somerset with a large turn-out from both my family and Rachel's, as well as the family of Hugo's wife Laura. It was a joyful occasion and I felt real happiness for my son, who had had years of loneliness and had now met a lovely woman who obviously reciprocated his feelings. He had also landed a really promising job in a quantum computing start-up in Silicon Valley, which had taken him out of the frustrating university politics of the UK and the endless quest for research funding.

The New Year media rounds started with Piers Morgan on *Good Morning Britain*: Trump being the subject. I had come to enjoy *GMB*, apart from the very early morning rise. Piers is a more populist version of Jeremy Paxman or John Humphrys but, like them, is a good interviewer if you engage and answer his questions. The worst kind of interview is with journalists who haven't done their homework and ask lazy, open-ended questions 'What do you think about the current state of British politics?' 'Tell us about your policies?' etc.

Piers Morgan was going after my 'politically correct' (which would now be described as 'woke') views on Trump and why I didn't see the need to embrace Trump in our national interest. I thought this was an issue where the public was on my side.

Chapter **Eighteen**
Brexit, more Brexit
and a health hiccup

Brexit, Brexit and more Brexit: and numerous meetings with supporters, business groups, student societies and whichever news outlet would give me an interview.[218] I seized on a rare slip from Nigel Farage, who seemed to indicate a willingness to take on a referendum, giving me an opening to do an 'I agree with Nigel' routine.[219] He quickly retreated.

I had more luck with a member of the public who rushed up to me after R and I had been to a '*Strictly* Experience' at the O2: 'Please save the country,' she said. I hated to disabuse her of the idea that my hands were on the levers of power!

There was, however, a Brexit debacle. I went to the Brussels meeting in March of ALDE (Alliance of Liberals and Democrats for Europe), which was the umbrella group for European Liberal parties. The group meets when there is a heads of government meeting in Brussels and I was invited to join a lunch of leaders who were also prime ministers and the three Liberal commissioners.

There were seven heads of state or government, of whom

---

[218] "He faced the music - and is still dancing", *Sunday Times*, 21 January 2018.

[219] "I agree with Nigel", *Mail on Sunday*, 14 January 2018.

Mark Rutte from the Netherlands was clearly the leading force. He was an extremely smart centre-right politician with real presence. Helped by fluency in several languages, he tended to dominate the conversation. He was also well disposed to the UK and to the Lib Dems (he had been close to Nick Clegg). The other dominant personality was the leader of the Liberal caucus in the Parliament: Guy Verhofstadt. Guy had been prime minister of Belgium and then leader of the Liberal MEPs for ten years. He was outspoken, highly articulate in English and an Anglophile, though his uncompromisingly 'federalist' views went some way beyond Lib Dem, let alone wider British opinion.

I was mobbed by the media on the way in, where Rutte joined me in expressing solidarity with the Lib Dems on Europe and that was also the mood around the lunch table – though they were quick to move on from the UK which was thought to be distracting attention from other European issues.

At the end of the meeting, the Lib Dem press office put out a press release welcoming the support of fellow Liberals in Europe for our position. But an ALDE press officer took offence at not having been consulted and wanted it to be clearer that the heads had supported us as party leaders, not as prime ministers. The press release had to be withdrawn and a totally anodyne ALDE press statement issued. I had a furious row over the phone with the press officer whose dignity had been affronted and who refused to budge.

Weeks later, I had an apology from the Secretary-General of ALDE and Rutte also made a very helpful statement of support. But the damage was done in the British press; even the normally friendly *Independent* newspaper talked about the referendum campaign being 'in tatters' and a 'humiliation'. I also later discovered that the problem was perhaps deeper than the press officer; a couple of the Liberal heads (Belgium, Luxembourg) saw the UK as a cuckoo in the European nest and weren't inclined to support our efforts to reverse Brexit.

Next day there was a test of how much damage had been done: *Any Questions* in Romsey with, *inter alia*, Diane Abbott. I needn't have worried. After a barbed comment from Jonathan Dimbleby at the beginning, the mood of the audience was very positive and on my side: presumably a Remain stronghold! I came back in the car with Diane, who was much warmer and friendlier than I had known her before. I discovered that the Brexit issue was one where she was unambiguously for 'Remain', unlike her close ally, Jeremy Corbyn.

There was even better therapy in a short spring break, a week's ski-ing in Courchevel with friends. Wonderfully restorative and I had the morale boost of doing my first ever black (advanced) run: difficult and in a strong wind, but Lib Dem peer and businessman Paul Strasburger was very patient and made sure I didn't come to grief.

A new party called Renew was formed, which triggered a round of speculation in the media about 'new parties' and critical comment about why funders were putting their money there rather than into the Lib Dems. I happened to know the backstory behind Renew: a very ambitious Lib Dem candidate in 2019 who had been affronted that the party hadn't targeted her seat and had split the local party, then broken away, attracting some funding from rich donors. It was clear that, despite the hype around Renew as the British *En Marche*, it wasn't a serious proposition. And there were 20 other parties setting up, mostly rather wacky, based on someone's whim or that of a millionaire with money to burn.

But the whole episode was unsettling. I went to see Tony Blair for advice, as his name, along with David Miliband, was being bandied about as a national saviour working through a new party. He was very well informed and still emotionally linked in to UK politics: desperately worried about the Corbyn factor, but thinking only in terms of Labour renewal.

February 22 2018: Am a last-minute replacement at a fundraising dinner in Richmond standing in for V's caseworker, Sandra, who has pulled out in protest at the presence of Jenny Tonge. Jenny T was the local MP in Richmond and quite popular but was thrown out of the Lib Dem group in the Lords for 'anti-Semitism' stemming from language she had used as part of her crusade on behalf of the Palestinians. Sandra is highly sensitive to criticism of Israel, especially given that Jenny T was excommunicated nationally (but not apparently locally). As a result, I find myself on V's staff table, listening to the office gossip.

Next day, V is embarking on one of his insanely complicated journeys: this time to Perth via Harrogate on the way up and Cambridge and Royston on the way back, places seen as important for the May council elections. As I waited at Zoe's, a minor disaster unfolded. First, he left his wash bag in Harrogate and then, rushing from the Harrogate train to the Edinburgh connection in York, left his case behind. He set out his papers on the Edinburgh train, realised that the case was missing and as the platforms were close to each other, pelted back for it, only to find that the Edinburgh train had set off without him (but with his papers).

After mobilising help from platform staff, he was eventually reunited with his papers but at the wrong Edinburgh station for his Perth train. Eventually, on the last train, he arrived in Perth, still agitated.

His mind is so often on the bigger picture, but this sort of thing isn't good for his confidence or his image. He has thankfully had a day off watching Six Nations rugby with my son-in-law, Stuart, before heading to Glasgow to speak at a dinner for Jo Swinson.

March 10 2018: *Lib Dem spring conference and we are in a magnificent penthouse suite at the Ramada Inn, Southport. Just arrived, with a heavy cold, from London via Penrith where V had a big book festival event in the Lakeside theatre and a meeting with the local Lib Dems. Set off on a circuit of receptions before V's speech rehearsal which took well over two hours and finished at 11 pm. Despite the panic, it turned out brilliantly, was well received and I felt I'd been helpful in delivering the outcome.*

Back to the farm for overdue maintenance: clearing brambles off the muck heap in the cattle yard; digging up snowdrops 'in the green' and replanting; litter picking on the road to the village. Then a visit to the local hospital to see an old friend and neighbour, now in his late eighties and very poorly. He had taught me to ride a horse more than 40 years ago. Having been brought up in the

Tanzanian tsetse fly belt, I had zero experience of horsiculture until I settled down in the New Forest in 1972.

A reminder that there was a world outside Brexit: the attack by Russian operatives using nerve agents on the Skripals in Salisbury. Theresa May made a statement in Parliament which was carefully phrased but made clear the inescapable evidence and logic linking the fatal attack back to the Putin regime which had form in this kind of extra-territorial assassination.

To gasps from his own backbenchers, Corbyn made an extraordinarily evasive response seeming to give the Russians the benefit of the very limited doubt. I got a feeling that whatever lingering sense of loyalty many of the mainstream Labour people still had over the Corbyn leadership, this had now gone.

Ian Blackford of the SNP spoke strongly in support of the Prime Minister's statement and I had no trouble following in a similar vein with strong backing for the government on this matter – at least – and for sanctions in the form of diplomatic expulsions. The episode did, however, stir up questions about some of the UK's links with Putin's cronies who owned valuable property in London and laundered dirty money through the City: an issue which provided useful political ammunition whenever I got the chance to ask a question or speak.

Local elections in May were the first test of political opinion since taking over the leadership and I spent weeks buzzing around the country to areas where we have the prospect of regaining ground or winning control – and another trip to Scotland, to the Scottish party conference in

Aviemore: a bracing change from the London heat-wave.

Given a choice between sitting around in Westminster going through the motions of parliamentary opposition and being out in the field meeting campaigners, getting publicity for local candidates and raising money for their campaigns, Westminster came a long way behind in effectiveness and satisfaction. There was a lot of tut-tutting about my regular absence from PMQs, where I was not called in any event (and other parliamentary rituals) but I thought the local priority was right.

I was delighted to see that the local campaign in my borough was fizzing with energy and the goodwill from the general election the previous year was still very live. There was a good chance of winning back control and it was good to see that there was a very favourable response on the doorsteps to the pact with the Greens which I had sought, reciprocating the help which the Greens had given me a year earlier and in Richmond. I spent much of my time out with canvassing teams locally and in other boroughs like Kingston, Merton, Haringey, Southwark or elsewhere – Cheltenham, Cambridge and Cambridgeshire, Oxford and even 'Brexity' Hull – where good things seemed possible.

The results exceeded expectations. My own borough was won by a landslide, returning the Lib Dems to power and in Twickenham the Tories were defeated in every seat. I felt a sense of vindication and the lingering bad feeling from 2015 was finally washed away. Nationally, we had net gains of 75 and three other boroughs. There was a collective sigh of relief in the party: a sense that we were at last moving forward.

But the grumbling in the Westminster village and

especially at HQ and amongst the prospective donors was getting intense: why was I not giving an inspirational story of how Brexit would be overturned by the Lib Dems and the path to Downing Street clearly mapped out? Why were we still struggling to get out of single figures in the polls when it was so obvious that, when we add up all the 'centrist' voters we should be at 50 per cent? Surely I could precipitate a general election and win by a landslide?

The local successes didn't interest them. I was becoming exasperated by the arrogance and ignorance of some of the people we had to approach to help pay the bills. I tried tapping a different market for money. I was introduced to a fabulously wealthy individual who said: "Cameron offered me a peerage in return for £1 million, but hasn't delivered. I am thinking of trying your lot". "Sorry, I don't have peerages to hand out". "Your party managed to get peerages for Lords X and Y who were less generous than I would be". (Y had become a crossbencher shortly after his elevation).

"Sorry, it doesn't work like that."

"Oh yes, it does". No peerage, no money. And indeed, the fabulously wealthy individual duly became a Tory peer.

And as the bills went unpaid, restiveness grew at HQ. Dee organised a small group of sympathetic advisers – Lib Dem peer Tom McNally, former Scottish Secretary Alistair Carmichael, House of Lords leader Lord Newby and its Chief Whip Lord Stoneham – who wanted me to make a success of the leadership. They suggested a series of thoughtful speeches on emerging issues.

For my first, I spoke on the tech giants and the new data economy and the need for a radical trust-busting policy for the data platforms. It received a respectful report in the

Guardian, but no wider pick-up, although it was one of the best things I had done for a while.[220] And there were other pieces in the press – usually when I had written them myself.[221] I had a new press officer, Mark Leftly, who was particularly good at getting me into specialist publications like those covering curry restaurant awards and building industry magazines.[222] [223]

I reassured myself that when Paddy Ashdown and Charles Kennedy had long media droughts, the expectations were lower; but I sensed that a crisis was coming. It came unexpectedly, and from a different direction, on what was supposed to be a break: a week's trip in recess to accompany Rachel on an art course in Atessa in Central Italy at the end of May. When I stepped from the Ryanair flight in Pescara, I felt ill: dizzy and unco-ordinated with blurred speech and a strange, disembodied feeling. It was later described as a 'mini-stroke'. Because the classic stroke symptoms were not there, I assumed it was some passing bug and didn't take it too seriously, pressed ahead with what turned out to be a nightmare drive to the hill-town of Atessa and struggled through several days before being sent off to a local hospital for checks and scans. Like a lot of basically healthy people,

---

[220] "Vince Cable Calls for Break-up of Google, Facebook and Amazon", *The Guardian*, 19 April 2018; "Tech Giants Must be Tamed for the Sake of a Fair Society", *City AM*, 17 May 2018.
[221] "Lords are Leaping to the Defence of British Democracy", *Financial Times*, 12/13 May 2018.
[222] "Vince Cable stands up for curry restaurants", *Spice Business*, April/May 2018.
[223] Chloe McCulloch, "Quick on his Feet", *Building Magazine*, 29 June 2018.

I tended to assume that illness is something which only happens to others.

It was only when I got back to the UK that doctors explained that an 'incident' had occurred in the brain. I had been very lucky: a bigger or longer episode and I would be dead or incapacitated. The good news was that within months or possibly weeks, with medication, I could be back to normal. The West Middlesex neurological consultant happened to be a fervent 'Remainer' and thought that a return to the political battlefield would do no harm. But there were long term questions about continuing as party leader and about how open to be with colleagues and friends.

May 28 2018: The trip to Atessa did not begin well: a very early start to get to Stansted after a night of thunderstorms. The storms had damaged the fuel depot at the airport and there was mayhem in departures. Our flight had survived but very late and we were kept on the ground for ages. And maybe the oxygen was turned low which might explain what happened next.

When we arrived in Pescara, several passengers complained of having felt ill, including V, who was very wobbly and unsteady on his feet. I got hold of some sweets and sweet drinks, thinking his blood sugar levels must be low. We then had an interminable wait for our hire car which was a small red Fiat with a very strange combined auto/manual gear change. We had to summon help to get the car started at all. There was no 'drive' position and it was necessary to go into reverse and start again whenever we stopped to combat constant slipping into low gear. We slowly made our way, in the gathering dusk, through industrial estates and other wrong turns until we found the motorway and, with the help of Google Maps, the correct turn into the mountains and eventually the hilltop town of Atessa before midnight.

V seemed better the next day, so we took in the surroundings: a palatial balcony overlooking an old part of town with swallows in abundance and a splendid campanile immediately opposite with fancy railings. The plan had been for him to visit Italian hill towns while I followed the textile art course. Our tutor Dionne Swift's minibus had room for us both so Vince came with us from the hotel to her studio on Day One and read his book, hoping that time and rest would sort out whatever was ailing him.

On Day Two, he stayed behind to go to the municipal swimming pool. When I rang after lunch, he had a blurry voice and when we met up in the early evening, he couldn't walk in a straight line. Over his protests, we went to the village's first aid clinic – 'pronto soccorso' – where they did the basic blood tests and rehydrated him.

They were sufficiently concerned to send him by ambulance to the district hospital in Lanciano to do a CT scan. I followed in a taxi, arranged by our very kind hotel proprietor. We left the hospital at 1.30 am with a computer disc to analyse in London and a prescription for drugs to counter dizziness provided by a nice young doctor called Simone, who spoke good English. Hurrah for the European health card! I had several days trying to concentrate on drawing, stitching and silk-screen printing while Vince lay on a sunbed, ploughing his way through the Elena

Ferrante quartet.

Day 6. V practised driving the Fiat to get us back to the airport via the small coast road and, despite shredded nerves, we made it. V has survived without further episodes, but I am having to think for us both on small matters.

When we got home V announced that he was better and plunged back into the parliamentary routine, keeping most of his engagements and finishing with an evening dancing lesson. But that was decisive since he couldn't keep his balance and had to stop after ten minutes. We were lucky to get an early MRI scan and a diagnosis from the consultant who explained that there was a neurological problem stemming from a minor stroke. She managed to be very positive and argued for keeping going, rather than resting, since muscles atrophy after a stroke unless fully used, and she advocated a course of physiotherapy to restore balance.

V's family rallied round but were seriously alarmed and thought V should retire from politics forthwith before more harm was done; though they accepted the reality that this wasn't going to happen any time soon.

I tried to get back into a regular routine, behaving as if nothing had happened though it was difficult to follow long meetings and I was conscious of having a 'funny' voice. Rachel and I agreed that we needed to tell Dee and my key office staff. We also told Nick Harvey as CEO of the party; and Alistair Carmichael who needed, as Chief Whip, to understand the purpose of mysterious disappearances for hospital and physio appointments. Rachel became my default chauffeur for six weeks, as I was not allowed to drive.

There was advice, which I resisted, from Dee, Rachel and others to be more open about the problem. Norman Lamb had had a similar issue and when he made it public there was a wave of sympathy and understanding. But he wasn't leading a party. I knew that, in my case, I could expect a similar response from my parliamentary colleagues, the party at large and my constituents. But my adversaries in the party would soon be making it clear that a sick man shouldn't be doing such a demanding job and their thoughts would soon find their way into the media.

I was also mindful of Olympia; I knew cancer was different but she was always adamant that, apart from the small number who had to know the truth, it was a mistake to tell the world about a serious health issue since the world would express sympathy but treat you as a 'goner'.

The next few weeks were difficult, trying to behave normally and keep to a regular schedule. I was helped by the fact that there was a by-election in Lewisham East. Campaigning with our admirable candidate, Lucy Salek, who had a deep background in development issues, was less stressful than long meetings and parliamentary events.

I went half a dozen times and encouraged the kind of by-election razzamatazz which had served the Lib Dems well in the past. We had no hope of winning in a London seat with a 21,000-plus Labour majority. But we cut it to 5,629 with the biggest swing from Labour in a decade. The result was judged a big success and I got a share of the credit for taking the campaign seriously and hard work there.

At Westminster, the story was less happy. There was an awful moment when I was speaking late at night in the chamber on some Brexit-related debate. I don't speak in Parliament from a written script but rely on memory and powers of improvisation. On this occasion, I totally lost my bearings and for what seemed an eternity I was paralysed. There weren't many MPs in the chamber and those present were either half-asleep or working on their i-phones so I was able to get back into my stride without too much attention being paid. But my confidence was seriously shaken.

A few days later, there was the big People's Vote March in London (on June 23), and I was to speak to the crowd outside Parliament alongside Chuka Umunna, Labour's David Lammy, Conservative Anna Soubry and the Green Party's Caroline Lucas, united in opposition to Brexit. There were estimates that a million people were at the march and a sizeable fraction in Parliament Square afterwards. The march was massive, good-natured and full of commitment.

The rally involved celebrities like businesswoman and anti-Brexit campaigner Gina Miller and the comedian, Tony Robinson who denounced Corbyn for not attending – to loud cheers. When it came to the politicians, I was terrified of drying up on stage, as I had in Parliament, and had memorised my lines to be sure I wasn't grasping for words. In the event it went well and the response from the audience was warm and energising. The rally overall was seen as a big success and momentum was sustained by celebrities like sports commentator Gary Lineker and comedian Rory Bremner identifying with the People's Vote campaign.

Behind the bonhomie at the People's Vote (PV) rally, there was, however, some serious factional politics which would later become disastrously destructive. There were several 'non-political' front organisations with different views about tactics and sometimes strategy, each involving strong and divisive personalities. The PV movement was heavily dominated by New Labour people: former EU Trade Commissioner Peter Mandelson and multimillionaire Roland Rudd in the background with Chuka the front of house lead and with strong day to day direction from the Labour Party's Alistair Campbell and Tom Baldwin.

The Lib Dems had a key figure in the organisation (James McGrory, a former press officer for Nick Clegg) but our presence was tolerated rather than encouraged, despite our being the one serious political party committed to the cause and providing a large proportion of the marchers and foot soldiers. It was partly that we had been written off, partly a preoccupation with internal Labour politics and Corbyn, and partly that we were seen as a threat to Labour (including by those working on a 'new party' project).

In the midst of these events, I gave speeches on housing at the Royal Institute of British Architects and corporate governance at the Institute for Public Policy Research, which were very well received by those who were there but had virtually no traction outside. People's Vote. People's Vote. Nothing else mattered.

Indeed, the national drama around Brexit was unfolding rapidly. When Theresa May presented her draft 'divorce' agreement with the EU to a cabinet meeting at Chequers on July 8, David Davis, the Brexit negotiator and Steve Baker, his deputy, resigned, followed a day later by Boris Johnson, the Foreign Secretary. The disagreement was that the Prime Minister had agreed a continuing close link with the EU through a 'common rule book' which the hard-liners would not accept. The battle lines between the Tory 'hard Brexit' (or 'no deal') and Theresa May's softer version were to define the internal debate in the Tory party until the next general election. We were essentially bystanders. We had a good slogan but no leverage.

July 17 2018: I am sitting in front of an exceedingly boring debate about the Trade Bill. Vince has bigger troubles. The Whip's Office misjudged the need for him to be at a vote last night and the government won by three votes. In his defence, four Labour MPs voted with the government, so arguably that's what allowed them to win. We were at a dinner in Barnes, ready to go if a car was sent for him.

It's the parliamentary party meeting and MPs' dinner tonight and I've texted V to say I think he should come clean with his parliamentary team about what's been going on with his health for the last seven weeks. V rang mid-morning to say he is the subject of a Twitter storm. Apparently, the Mail Online *is airing a* Where's Wally? *cartoon of Vince. Ain't politics fun?*

While the national and party campaign for a People's Vote was gaining momentum there was another personal disaster in mid-July. I was due to have a series of hospital tests at the West Middlesex as part of the monitoring of my recovery. Parliament was debating a series of technical amendments to a bill on the contingency of 'no deal' customs arrangements – to cover the contingency of no deal being negotiated – and I had no inkling that my presence was essential. So I took up an invitation to dinner afterwards with Geeta Guru-Murthy, who was married to

Philip Collins, a Labour-leaning journalist. He was one of the leading figures in the 'new party' movement who I hoped could brief me on what was happening behind the scenes. The Indian dinner was great but my text messages told me that there had been a series of close divisions, one of which the government had won by three votes.

The press coverage next day was uncomfortable but not catastrophic and there were a couple of redeeming factors. There had been quite a lot of other absentees, amongst them Tim Farron, who had been at a religious event. And Alistair Carmichael took responsibility for the lack of clarity around the whipping arrangements. I kept quiet about the hospital and encouraged media interest in the 'secret' meeting.

18 July 2018: *V back at 11.30 pm – dreadful day, of course. V didn't come clean with his fellow MPs about his health scare... Alistair is carrying the can for Cable's non-appearance yesterday.*

A storm in a teacup? Not so. HQ and the party committees hadn't had their say. We had an emotional meeting in which I was told that 'thousands' of our members were leaving in disgust (it turned out to be about a dozen). Our new members, who had joined on the back of Brexit, apparently couldn't understand or forgive the fact that I hadn't been there in a vote to 'stop Brexit' or 'bring down the government'. I doubted that many of our members were quite so ignorant of the more prosaic reality, but it was certainly true that many members were annoyed – having been misinformed that the vote was 'crucial'. We had become a single-issue party for good and, now, ill.

The party machine wasn't finished. Baroness Brinton, the party president, insisted that I speak apologetically by audio-conference to the Federal Board, the apex body of the party's labyrinthine committee structure. Most of the members were calm and reasonable. But the person I saw as one of the leading plotters screamed down the phone, demanding my immediate resignation for perpetrating one of the greatest political catastrophes in the party's history. Outside the party, the interest was in whom I was meeting secretly and to what end.[224]

July 19 2018: Red letter day. Six weeks after V's initial diagnosis, the neurologist has signed him off for three months. We are able to attend and enjoy one of his big constituency events: a fireworks concert at the Kneller Hall Royal School of Music.

The missing vote issue quickly disappeared from the news. I was able to focus on an initiative I had set in train some months earlier. Paul Strasburger had encouraged me to pay attention to what had been happening in Canada and how Trudeau had lifted the Liberal Party from a dismal third place to be the party of government in a first-past-the-post voting system, not wholly unlike the UK.

It was certainly true that we paid too little attention to the world's most successful Liberal Party and perhaps too much to continental parties – like *En Marche* – whose

---

[224] "Vince Cable missed customs bill vote to discuss anti-Brexit party", *Sunday Times*, 22 July 2018; "Cable in Secret talks with Blair Ally over New Lib-Lab pact", *Mail on Sunday*, 5 August 2018.

situation and values were often quite different. I had had an opportunity to meet Trudeau when he came for the Commonwealth heads meeting in April. He was undoubtedly charismatic and came across as very self-confident, articulate and intelligent (and much smaller than his public image). He encouraged me to work with one of his team, Tom Pitfield, to see if we could adapt the 'Canadian model' to our situation.[225]

The Canadian approach had within it one big idea: to open up leadership contests to people outside parliament in a 'primary' selection of 'supporters' (not necessarily members). In Canada, Trudeau had had a dozen or so competitors from a much bigger talent pool than the parliamentary team and the selection process had galvanised public interest in the Liberals. With only twelve MPs and, in practice, only Jo Swinson and Ed Davey likely to contest my succession, the case for a wider contest was strong. There were some obvious problems: what if we got a Trump-like maverick? How would a new leader function if outside parliament? And wasn't I casting aspersions on the heirs apparent? It seemed to me, nonetheless, that the merits narrowly outweighed the negatives. We needed a shock to the system.

I decided to push ahead with the reforms (and also the less controversial proposals for widening the support base of the party). The first reactions were predictably negative. The Federal Executive was bristling with suspicion. Ed

---

[225] Adam Payne, "How Justin Trudeau is helping Vince Cable transform the Liberal Democrats", *Business Insider*, 20 July 2018.

Davey saw the threat and declared his opposition. Jo was cannier: probably hating the whole idea but expressing support and welcoming the competition. I embarked on a summer offensive to change hearts and minds in the party. But the new initiative had further stirred the hornets' nest of opposition in the party. I read in the *Sunday Times* that "the knives are out for the Lib Dem leader, who could soon face a leadership challenge... a secret meeting of activists is due to take place when plans are expected to be discussed to replace him with a younger leader".

July 31 2018: *Summer recess is here, not before time. The New Forest is idyllic. Less chasing madly round the country; more time for family and friends – I hope. It arrives with a heatwave and a chance to swim in the sea locally at Milford-on-Sea.*

Then we drove to Burnham Market in north Norfolk to say goodbye to Hugo and Laura before they set off for California. Lovely: her clan are warm and welcoming with assorted children running around.

August 4 2018: *My first grandson arrived, after four granddaughters: Max and Maria's son, Harlan. I am relieved and delighted for them, having waited up with my daughter, Zoe, for much of Maria's very long labour. V and my son-in-law, Stuart, were a bit bemused by the intensity of our anxiety.*

August 6 2018: *For me, there was a magical moment at the London hospital: my son Max cradling his son and then getting my turn with the baby. Zoe and her girls brought a* *huge "baby shower" of gifts which we managed to transport by underground and deliver to the proud but tired parents of baby Harlan.*

V is fretting about his non-appearance on the news. I point out that Corbyn's coverage is almost all negative and May's not much better, so I wish he would switch off for a week. His reaction is to give up on the short break we have planned in Dorset and hang around in the hope of getting some TV and radio which makes me cross and makes no sense. He does get some action with a trip to Bristol for a rally, media and canvassing and then another to Newcastle.

On August 23, we attended the funeral for a friend and one of the unsung heroes of the SDP revolt, George Cunningham. He had passed away in late July. Unusually for the SDP, he was definitely not a fan of the EU and the main legacy of his parliamentary career was having (as a London-based Scot) blocked Scottish devolution for 20 years by inserting the requirement for a successful referendum to have 40 per cent of the electorate as well as a simple majority. He was a fiercely independent-minded man and an assiduous constituency MP in the council estates of Islington, which was why in 1983, and again in 1987, he was one of the very few defecting Labour MPs who came within a whisker of holding his seat. He and his wife Mavis, a formidable political campaigner in her own right, were immensely helpful and supportive to me.

September 2 2018: *Another rally, this time in Cambridge, and we go together. V is the first speaker and* is cheered to the rafters. I don't think there can be fewer than 500 people in the room and everyone seems dedicated to the cause.

The bad news is that Paddy Ashdown seems to have got wind of V's health problem and is making waves in the Lords. I suppose we should be grateful to have had a summer without endless discussion of it.

September 7 2018: The party reform proposals are publicly launched at the National Liberal Club. V is as nervous as I have ever seen him but the speech holds together well and he gets more relaxed as he goes along and there is a lot of media interest. These 'Canadian' proposals have been brewing for months and it is good to have the launch out of the way. Paddy texts V to say 'you have pulled it off', having told him to resign a few days earlier. We will see what conference thinks in a few weeks.

Next day, I took off to Iceland for a week with a fantastic group of a dozen women for a charity walk, hiking and camping across 50 kilometres of wild and rugged terrain but stunning scenery and views. It was an amazing out-of-this-world experience and we raised lots of money for Richmond Talking Newspapers. In June, I had thought I would have to pull out but V's children rallied round to keep an eye on him.

Chapter Nineteen
The beginning of the end

After all the internal party dramas, conference at Brighton was more important than usual. There was a good start at the pre-conference rally and good vibes amongst the delegates who seemingly didn't know or care about the machinations in Westminster. There was a packed audience for Gina Miller, whom I had invited to address the conference.

My motives for inviting her were twofold. The first was that she was a genuine hero of the anti-Brexit movement. Without her successful legal action, which required parliament to approve the government's Brexit Withdrawal Agreement with the EU in a 'meaningful vote', Brexit would have been done and dusted already. Second, for our almost exclusively white membership, I wanted to present a highly successful 'woman of colour' as a role model for the greater diversity which the party desperately needed.

Gina was well received, though her impeccable upper-class accent sounded a little too much like the Queen in my view. But there was a negative reaction in some quarters from people who had added 2 + 2 to make 7 and thought I was promoting her to be the new leader in the open selection system I was proposing.

She denied any such ambition a little too vehemently, making it altogether too clear that she couldn't think of a worse idea than being leader of the Lib Dems, which came across as if she was rejecting a besotted suitor. But the news clips sounded and looked good.

The key battleground was the 'consultation' which had been planned on my proposed reforms. There was a good-natured and intelligent exchange and the strengths and weaknesses of the approach I had advocated were fairly made. Paddy Ashdown spoke up strongly and very effectively in support. Otherwise, grassroots support came mainly from newer members; the established activists who were at every conference didn't like challenges to the status quo.

The proposals went off for further discussion in the party's committees and would be voted on at a special conference (as the constitution demanded) or at the next conference, in the spring. I was worried that the Federal Executive was intent upon the latter course of action when it would be easier to kick the proposals into the long grass.

September 15 2018: Arrived in Brighton on Friday morning. Magnificent suite on the first floor of the Metropole (Hilton). Vince's rally speech a triumph! We fitted in a walk along the promenade, but I have not been tempted to swim in either the sea or the hotel pool. Now in a meeting in the 'Leader's Room', putting the final touches to V's Tuesday speech. As usual, this process is like living with a crocodile: every time you think it has been put to bed, it emerges again, jaws agape. This time, I think we are nearly there...

September 17 2018: So far, no major banana skins. Paddy spoke warmly about the proposed party reforms at the end of the consultation session on Saturday. There are, of course, the 'awkward squad' – we are the Lib Dems after all – but at least in public, all is bonhomie. And Vince is performing well.

For the big speech, there was quite a lot of anticipation and media interest, not all of it friendly. I had spent too much time explaining to Piers Morgan on *GMB* that reforming inheritance tax to a tax on lifetime gifts (buried in one of our recent policy documents) didn't mean that the Lib Dems were bent on taxing everyone's Christmas presents.

My press officer Mark Leftly had also released to the press a risqué joke that had got inserted in the speech and I was interrogated at length as to its significance which, of course, killed the humour. I was inclined to take it out but that would have created a new round of press comment on why it had been dropped. So, I left it in but was so agitated by all the coming and going that I muffed the line, as I did occasionally, under stress, a few months after the 'incident'. The rest of the speech was fine and very well received around the theme of listening to and understanding Brexiteers' fears. But that wasn't the story the press wanted.[226]

September 18 2018: *A joke, inserted at the last moment, involved changing a jibe about the Brexiteers' "erotic joy" on leaving the EU to "erotic spasm". This was then widely trailed by Mark Leftly in the press office and dealt with by*

---

[226] "Faithful leave unsatisfied after Sir Vince fluffs his big line", *The Times*, 19 September 2018.

Vince in his early morning interviews as 'colourful language'. But when he came to deliver the line (near the beginning of the speech) it came out as "exotic spresm". It was, literally, as if he choked on the word. The rest was word perfect, but the damage was done, and I saw it being repeated on Channel 4 News.

There were some quite barbed cartoons even in yesterday's papers, so I dread to think what Friday will be like. And of course, the mini-stroke which resulted in the misspeak must be kept secret.

I was desperate to get away after the very fraught summer with a seemingly endless programme of Brexit rallies, speeches and debates, local visits, party reform and HQ issues to come. Rachel did us proud with a week in a very comfortable hotel in Sardinia. Bliss.

September 22 2018: *We have survived. I ran away to the farm on Wednesday and came back on Friday. Vince did* Question Time *in Dewsbury on Thursday, by which time erotic spasms/exotic spresms seemed to have been consigned to history. But it superseded all the more serious messages from his speech and will have caused some angst amongst his parliamentary colleagues, for sure.*

October 2 2018: *Imminent departure of Max and Maria and baby, Harlan, to Melbourne, Australia, where they have decided to settle in the bosom of her very close Greek-Australian family.*

I won't see them for a while. But maybe next winter? I am hoping V will have stepped down from the leadership by next summer, making a long trip possible.

October 6 2018: *We stopped for V to give an interview to the TV in support of the 'Bollocks to Brexit' poster put up by Pimlico Plumbers near Waterloo. The local Labour council wants it down on the grounds of the rude language and not having been asked for planning permission to put it up, but there is apparently a precedent for the language. V tells me he has met the boss of the company who has a very enlightened approach to apprenticeships and is supporting us over Brexit but is otherwise not noted for his progressive views.*

October 18 2018: *Welsh party conference in Aberystwyth. Rail to Newtown and then a kind party member takes us on through the beautiful Welsh countryside – but not fast. When we arrive, there is a storm and the stony beach has migrated onto the road. We have a wonderful sea view from the hotel, enjoying the wildness of it.*

Conference went very well notwithstanding the weather and there was tremendous spirit, despite our rather depleted political position in Wales. After the politics, there was a very professional cabaret with a choir that had competed on TV. Leader Jane Dodds who has had a massive job reviving the Welsh Lib Dems, volunteered her husband to drive us back to London in their Fiat 500 after the storm had closed the rail route. Five and a half hours in a foetal position in the back was uncomfortable but we were grateful for the lift and marvelled at their commitment to multi-tasking with such dedication. She holds down a big job overseeing the Salvation Army's children's homes in India and Kenya at the same time as pursuing her political career with style, enthusiasm and competence.

October 24 2018: *We are now old hands at royal banquets! The milling around was a bit hurried but we rocked up and shook hands with the Queen, Queen Maxima and King Willem-Alexander of the Netherlands and Charles and Camilla before finding our places for dinner. I was beside a nice professor and a naval attaché (replacing a no-show) who were both good company. Flowers were burnt orange colour (for the House of Orange) and exquisite; food and drink super.*

I now know the drill for toasts – do not pick up the glass until the national anthems are over. Speeches predictable: references to former trade wars but overwhelmingly friendly: wonderful trading partners, royal connections, Wilhelmina during the war, Beatrix, Willem, etc, etc.

I realised belatedly that my perfectly pronounced 'Goede Avond' (having lived in the Netherlands for two years) was wasted on Queen Maxima. She is Argentinian, not Dutch. Enormously tall, like her husband. There is a wonderful cartoon this morning of the Dutch king bending double to shake hands with our Queen, as she greets him with: "I thought you came from the Low Countries."

November 2 2018: *Back to Edinburgh, this time for Lib Dem MP Christine Jardine's annual dinner. After late votes in Westminster and a delayed flight, it is a scramble to get there. Christine and I have changed into our posh outfits in* *the City Airport loos to save time and I have broken my favourite necklace in the process. We make it by 10 pm and, while V speaks, we get a hastily warmed-up main course. A jolly event. Next day V goes off with Christine for campaigning and media and I rendezvous with my oldest granddaughter, Elsa, now in her first year at university here. She shares lodgings with six Chinese men and three other Scottish girls.*

At last, after months of phoney war, we got to crunch time on the Brexit negotiations. There was a 500-page draft of the 'divorce' agreement covering the financial payments by the UK, citizenship rights and the tricky issue of the Irish border. When Theresa May presented it to parliament on November 15, Dominic Raab (the Brexit negotiator) resigned, followed by Esther McVey, in an echo of the David Davis/Boris Johnson resignations in July.

The issues were much the same. In order to reconcile Brexit with the terms of the Northern Ireland Good Friday Agreement which precluded a 'hard' border, the government had negotiated a 'backstop' under which the UK could remain within the EU Customs Union, obviating the need for customs checks at the Irish frontier while Northern Ireland could remain within the Single Market.

Behind the specific disagreement on the backstop, which was a red rag to the bull of the DUP, who provided the government with its majority, the hardliners wanted a 'clean break' with the EU. Theresa May's somewhat plaintive argument that 'this was the best we could negotiate' did not carry conviction with the fundamentalists on her own side or with those of us who thought Brexit could be stopped if we could get to a referendum. But the main obstacle to that was Corbyn, who had so far opposed Labour endorsing it.

There were some in the business community, who were beginning to panic over the possibility of 'no deal' if no agreement could be reached at the end of the two-year timetable allowed under Article 50 of the March 2017 Brexit withdrawal legislation. The Theresa May argument that she had made 'the best of a bad job' appealed to a lot in the business community. I took to the press to argue that this was still a bad deal, especially for services and with years of negotiating uncertainty ahead.[227]

To add to the drama, Theresa May was likely to face a Tory 'no confidence' vote; the numbers were piling up. It also seemed unlikely she would get her deal through. The debate was increasingly polarising into 'no deal' versus 'no Brexit'. Much was made of the government's 'no deal preparations', which were supposed to frighten the EU into acquiescing to British demands (but weren't), though they were frightening wavering opinion in the UK.

I worried that our side was making too much of the horrors of 'no deal', heightening its credibility as an option and doing the government's job for it. I was also worried that parliament, and government, had completely ground to a halt on any other issue. Trying to break the Brexit obsession, I secured an Adjournment Debate on the problems with the South Western Railway franchise, which was causing massive disruption for a lot of my constituents.

---

[227] "Should British Business accept May's Brexit deal? No", *Financial Times*, 21 November 2018.

I also prepared a Christmas message with a properly researched and well-presented video on knife crime. But I confess to having allowed the Brexit obsession to take over; in highlighting the problems which Brexit would present for migration, I had used the example of *Strictly* stars, which provoked a reaction along the lines of: 'Is nothing sacred anymore?'[228]

November 11 2018: *V gets back to more trouble at HQ where a round of redundancies is causing people to behave even more badly than before. The chief executive Nick Harvey seems to have given up and delegated all the staffing decisions to his deputy and in V's view, the wrong people are being laid off, with the main trouble-makers still there. An hour of this stuff exhausts V more than a day of debating or writing.*

There was also a tension between engaging with the Westminster media bubble and getting out to parts of the country, where the arguments needed to be won. One of my most rewarding visits was several days in Cornwall: I was given a couple of hours for a call-in on Radio Cornwall where I was seriously taken to task for my comment that the concerns of the Brexit movement were heavily dominated by the prejudices of the older generation.

But I enjoyed these robust but genuine exchanges, unlike those in the Commons which had become endlessly

---

[228] "Is nothing free from Brexit? Oh, please leave Strictly out of it, Vince", *The Observer*, 28 October 2018; "May's crude policy is the wrong way to manage immigration", *City AM*, 11 October 2018.

repetitive, stylised and boring (not helped by Theresa May's robotic responses to questions). At the same time, ducking out of those rituals, which I did, invited critical comment. I could not help but reflect that the man who had done more than any other to win the Brexit argument – Nigel Farage – had never set foot in parliament.

December 5 2018: *The Brexit debate grinds on and on. I watched a lot of yesterday's 'business of the government' being held 'in contempt of parliament' and therefore defeated. I help to get V into London with six bottles of wine for his office party and go with him to a reception for the party's main financial donors: again, Brexit talk dominates.*

V tells me that Paddy Ashdown has been taken seriously ill following a bladder cancer operation: he has pneumonia and is in a coma. V has crossed swords with him from time to time, especially around the 2015 election, but I admire his boundless physical and nervous energy and we have never wished him ill, least of all this. But it is hard to imagine him putting up with a long, slow decline either.

December 6 2018: *V off early – I think Leicester this time – and back at 10 pm. He has enjoyed being out of the Westminster bubble, where today the machinations to derail Brexit have got very complex and fraught. I am unable to prevent him seeing a piece in the 'i' newspaper criticising him and Jo Swinson for letting the Lib Dems disappear from the scene, so he doesn't sleep well (Have they <u>seen</u> his diary?) But the article is accompanied by a* nice pic which gives me a chance to have a friendly email exchange with Jo.

Next day, V has one of his annual rituals: the Xmas card competition prizes. Most of the local infant and junior schools have entered and we pick the winners and runners-up from hundreds of entries, which is then the front of the MP's Xmas card sent to every house in Twickenham (I am starting to quibble about the cost – down to us – which runs into thousands of pounds). The prizes are House of Commons teddy bears which apparently are always a success: the children rebelled when they were given something educational. Then he went off to do some filming with sixth formers on a project studying genocide, cycled to the Sky News studio – and back to his advice surgery.

December 9 2018: *We go to Streatham for the filming of V's Xmas message. It centres on a conversation with a man called Arnold, a former gang leader who now works for a charity trying to help kids stay away from knife crime, who is very clear about the problem: "Some youngsters would rather be found by the police with a knife than by a rival gang without one." Mainly black-on-black but an upsurge in 'white' areas too.*

December 11 2018: *It's my turn to organise my Wenban-Smith siblings' annual family lunch – but V is called away to a People's Vote rally in advance of the 'meaningful vote' on Theresa May's proposals.*

Michael Heseltine is leading the London rally, but V has been asked to go to Nottingham: so clearly can't be at a family meal in Twickenham.

December 16 2018: *The 'meaningful vote' has been pulled. But the campaign goes on. V has a big rally at the ExCel Centre in London and then a meeting with European Liberals in Brussels. We settle down for a long weekend at the farm. There is one more big pre-Xmas task: Xmas cards. After family and friends, there are 500+ Twickenham deliverers and other activists, over 100 parliamentarians and a few hundred other party activists around the country and donors. We have a good production line system but as V insists on putting in personal messages, progress is slow.*

The looming confrontation over the Brexit deal was postponed to the New Year but the campaigning goes on. A big rally of thousands at the ExCel Centre shows us the strengths and weaknesses of the People's Vote campaign. The echo chamber was getting bigger and louder. I was one of the main speakers with Caroline Lucas (who sets a high bar on the audience decibel count), Chuka Umunna, Anna Soubry and David Lammy.

We were now getting more high-level Labour and Tory people involved, not just 'the usual suspects'. Margaret Beckett was the ultimate Labour loyalist: solid and dependable and dead centre in the Labour Party, but is an impressive speaker for a referendum and a good catch. Veteran Conservative politician Michael (now Lord) Heseltine was the star of the show. Unlike the rest of us, who had been timed to the second, he was given more licence and took full advantage of it. He is a really impressive performer. His involvement – with John Major (albeit more quietly) and Ken Clarke in Parliament – was beginning to crystallise into a serious Tory revolt.

The weakness, of course, was that we were cheering ourselves on and not gaining many converts (though polls showed there was a steady majority, who thought Brexit was a mistake).

I was invited to the meeting of liberal heads in Brussels, who had gathered with other heads of government to discuss the implications of Theresa May's troubles with her deal. The atmosphere was transformed from the previous occasion. The episode of the press release seemed to have been forgotten. Rutte was keen to make me feel welcome. I was given pride of place in the lunch discussions.

The fact that a second referendum was now a real possibility, as a way of breaking the impasse, was taken seriously though the consensus remained that Brexit would happen and that they need to plan for the forthcoming Euro-elections without British participation. I was greatly cheered by the meeting, where the Lib Dems' relevance was recognised more than it often was in London.

The news came that Paddy had died on December 22. I was called upon to give TV and radio tributes. They were heartfelt. He had steadily but surely built his own base in Yeovil and then lifted the party from humiliatingly low ratings in the late 1980s to the mid-teens in 1997 when I and 45 other MPs entered parliament in the big breakthrough. His leadership qualities were most evident and valued in adversity.

Many of the eulogies (and this was even truer of the later, very grand, memorial service in Westminster Abbey) focused on his role as High Representative in Bosnia and portrayed him as one of the establishment 'Great and Good', which was only one side of him. Our own relationship was uncomfortable, but I admired him greatly.

It was a great relief to go to Rachel's family in Perthshire. They are a close and loving family and very grounded. They are well off and could afford private schools but have sent the three daughters to local schools in Perth, not to make an ideological statement but because it was a sensible, practical thing to do. All the girls have flourished. They are not overtly political; Scottish patriots rather than nationalists; but with a disdain for arrogant, self-important English Tories. I always seemed to arrive there after a distracting, bad episode in London but feel better when I left.

The first outing on return was to Portsmouth. The Lib Dem council leader, Gerald Vernon-Jackson, was a very shrewd operator who had built a powerful political base in the city through sheer hard work and community activism. He had kept the base together through adverse national trends and despite a local former Lib Dem MP, Mike Hancock, whose love life and other idiosyncrasies proved a heavy cross for Gerald to bear.

He had identified a major problem in the event of a 'no deal' Brexit: backing up of lorries on the motorways if the port of Portsmouth was seriously disrupted. The visit attracted good regional media though we had to be careful to frame messages which resonated with Portsmouth's majority Brexit voters.[229]

---

[229] "Cable says government has 'betrayed' Brexit voters across the city", *The News, Portsmouth*, 9 January 2019

Chapter Twenty
The search for a deal

January 7 2019: *V is now in the thick of it again with Parliament finally exerting itself. The Speaker is sticking his neck out to allow an amendment to the Finance Bill, which the government loses.*

V is reading more and more novels at night as a form of escapism. Mine is to enter a drawing competition, so I am trying to get the entries together. Back at the farm, the badgers have started digging up the back garden. What a mess! Should I roll it flat or feed them raisins and sit up at night waiting to see them?

January 12 2019: *V is firing on all cylinders this weekend. We went together to Sheffield to do another People's Vote rally. Anna Soubry and Labour's Margaret Beckett and Mary Creagh are speaking. Our parliamentary candidate here is Laura Gordon, who had a baby only a few weeks ago: a gorgeous, happy and smiley little thing, strapped to her Mum.*

The long-awaited Meaningful Vote on the Brexit deal negotiated with the EU – the Withdrawal Bill – was finally scheduled for January 15 after the Prime Minister finally ran out of procedural dodges to avoid it. The tortuous process of finding a deal acceptable to the European Union and in London, acceptable both to the hardline Brexiters in the Conservative Party and to the rest of parliament, would come to a climax. If, as seemed likely, Theresa May was defeated, this would not just derail the negotiations with the EU but put her own position in jeopardy with mounting numbers of Tory backbenchers asking for a vote of no confidence in their leader.

The sticking point for Tory Brexiters was the 'Irish backstop' and once the DUP had pronounced the deal a betrayal of their interests, there was no way that the government could carry the deal. There was high drama in the Commons and the chamber was packed throughout the debate which consisted largely of the endless restatement of known positions and continuous interruption of Theresa May who, I have to say, was impressively calm and patient: great theatre but terrible debate. In the event, the PM's deal was crushingly defeated by 432 to 200.

My main task was to ensure that the Lib Dem voice wasn't drowned out and our support for a People's Vote reiterated on every possible occasion. I took comfort from remembering the comment of a media adviser years back that 'by the time that you are beginning to get your message across, you are utterly bored by the sound of your own voice'.

I don't know about the success of the message but I learnt to repeat our mantra without sounding too bored. I tried to perfect the rather cheeky argument that a referendum was in Theresa May's interest since she had no chance of getting the deal through parliament, but stood at least a 50 per cent chance of winning a confirmatory vote on her deal.

After provincial rallies the weekend before the big vote –

mine was in Sheffield with Margaret Beckett among others – I had an orgy of media coverage around the vote, itself. I managed to silence, for a while, the critics who bemoaned my involuntary absence from the media by securing wall-to-wall coverage on TV and radio: a dozen interviews before the vote from Andrew Marr to Piers Morgan to clips for the six and ten o'clock news; and another twenty or so after.

This sudden lurch from famine to feast owed a lot to my new press spokesperson, Clodagh Higginson (formerly Hartley), who was exceptionally effective on my behalf and was liked and respected by journalists: also a couple of energetic and smart young party press officers: Tim Wild and Dave Green. With Dee managing my office and Clodagh handling media, I was able to get out and do what I was good at doing, without being sucked into the swamp of internal, head office, infighting and plotting (which was getting worse).

January 15 2019: *The PM's deal was voted down 432 to 200 votes. A crushing defeat! I sat by William Hobhouse, husband of MP Vera, and his friends. I left the gallery at just the right moment to meet V in the Central Lobby, where he was doing BBC and ITV News. His message was: 'This is the Beginning of the End of Brexit'. After the result, the PM said she would listen to a parliamentary vote of no-confidence tomorrow and Corbyn duly tabled one.*

January 16 2019: *V was supposed to be back at 8.30 for supper, but has disappeared to see the Prime Minister. She won the vote of confidence 325 to 306 after MPs reverted to party loyalties. I did listen to the debate. The most* *powerful speech was by Tom Watson, Labour's Deputy Leader who, very politely, did a very effective character assassination of the PM. Gove responded by doing a similar job on Jeremy Corbyn. I didn't hear V, but his speech got plaudits from Watson and others. The commentators say there is no parliamentary majority for a second referendum and that, anyway, it isn't clear whether the question is 'No Brexit v May's Deal' or 'May's Deal v No Deal'.*

Theresa May went off on a charm offensive talking to the leaders of all the parties, big and small. I realised that this attempt at sweet reasonableness almost certainly didn't extend to embracing the referendum option and she reiterated her opposition. But our meeting was cordial.

I also took encouragement from the fact that the PM's team had worked out a timetable for a referendum, in the unlikely event that it were to happen. They were pessimistic about the timescale (perhaps deliberately), but we were able to have a conversation about the practicalities which got us beyond a complete and final slamming of the door. I repeated my 'cheeky' argument that we were trying to help the PM by creating a better chance for her to win than in parliament.

The Lib Dem delegation was asked to continue the discussions with David Liddington, the Deputy PM. I remembered him as Minister of State for Europe during the coalition and he was as comfortable with our membership of the EU as any Tory at that time. He was now a dogged loyalist trying to secure the least damaging Brexit possible. He was affable and did his best to establish common ground by looking in more detail at a referendum timetable which we felt was being exaggerated in order to create an argument for not doing it.[230]

But the real action was on the Labour side: 70 MPs signed up to a public letter seeking a second referendum as 'the only logical option' and Corbyn was coming under growing pressure to move away from his ambiguous position on the subject.[231] It was clear that the parliamentary Labour Party could split. But where and how?

There were two possibilities. The most far-reaching split would be for the mainstream majority to split off from the Corbynite minority. The leader of such a revolt would be Tom Watson. I had met him a few times privately and we had established a rapport. He was a serious political pro and enjoyed a reputation as a tough operator from the days when he was Gordon Brown's enforcer. His vision was of a Labour Party shorn of its militant (Momentum) wing but representing a Brownite programme and working with liberal and pro-European groups like the Lib Dems. Tom claimed to have the backing of around a hundred MPs, but was moving cautiously for obvious reasons. I never got a real feel for how serious this movement was and how far Tom was speaking for others as well as himself. But I certainly rated him.

The other potential break-away was from the Blairites. But most of the people on that wing of the party were not inclined to break from the Labour Party. The SDP

---

[230] *The Observer*, 30 January 2019.
[231] *Daily Telegraph*, 17 January 2019.

experience had been a salutary warning of the fate of even the best organised schismatic movement. Moreover, most were dismissive of the Lib Dems, as I discovered when I tried to talk to them.

One of the most outspoken rebels was MP Chris Leslie whose experience in Nottingham was of a tiny Lib Dem party usually failing to save its deposit in elections and he was strongly opposed to working with us. A much better prospect for collaboration was Streatham MP Chuka Umunna. He was highly ambitious and had been hailed in the press as leadership material. He had a certain charisma, was much admired for his looks by women (including my wife) and his British-Nigerian background made him a good advertisement for multi-racial Britain: the 'British Obama' as he had been called.

He had shadowed me when I was Secretary of State and was undoubtedly one of the stronger performers on the Labour front bench. We re-established contact when I won back my seat in parliament and met regularly to compare notes. He made it clear that he saw no future with Corbyn's Labour Party and was planning a breakaway. Although we had a good personal relationship and political differences were negligible, he had no intention of joining the Lib Dems unless it changed its name and became 'new'.

He was a strong advocate of a new 'centrist' party having been persuaded by various potential funders that the Lib Dem brand was damaged beyond repair. He was also a devotee of Macron, whom he had met. But he was smart enough to understand that without a grass-roots political infrastructure his new party would struggle and would be crippled by the 'first-past-the-post' system. He accepted that it would be politically necessary to have a collaborative 'confederation' with the Lib Dems; competition would kill both of us.

It was clear in late January that serious moves were underway to launch a new party and that Chuka, Chris and Anna Soubry were key players in it (Anna, I discovered, had a particular beef against the Lib Dems, since our activists in her constituency had unfairly accused her of not being sufficiently militant in the Remain cause). A former Lib Dem MP, Mark Oaten, who had resigned after a sex scandal, was reportedly organising the legal work behind the scenes. It was abundantly clear that a competing new party would struggle to survive, but could do us a great deal of harm by attracting our prospective funders and members who liked the idea of something new.

I determined on a two-pronged approach: the first was to be ahead of the game as far as possible, not playing catch-up; the second was to embrace the new party as friends, not enemies or competitors. The latter would be a hard sell in the Lib Dems since some of our activists had strong tribal instincts based on the belief that 'those who are not with us are against us'. Others suffered from the narcissism of small differences and would find some arcane theoretical dividing line. I briefed the press about the new party and got a headline: 'Vince's Block Brexit Party', much to the annoyance of Chuka and friends who were about to launch.[232]

Alliance building extended to other parts of the UK. I had developed a good working relationship with Ian Blackford

---

[232] *Metro*, 4 February 2019.

of the SNP (not wholly approved of by my Scottish colleagues) and with Liz Saville Roberts of Plaid Cymru. We already had good links with the Alliance Party of Northern Ireland and its impressive and courageous leader, Naomi Long. She came to London with a 'Remain' delegation including Unionists and Sinn Féin. Unlike the talkative and gregarious Naomi, the Sinn Féin leader, Michelle O'Neill – Gerry Adams' successor – was taciturn, carefully scripted and gave little away. My rather vain idea, that we could talk Sinn Féin out of its boycott of Westminster to provide a crucial seven votes, hit a brick wall of nationalist resistance. For them, Brexit was just part of a bigger struggle.

For the Lib Dems, the big test looming up was the local elections in May, which in some 'Remain' areas dovetailed with the Westminster campaign, but elsewhere was kept very distinct. I relished the opportunity to support the local activists, getting away from the endlessly repetitive Brexit exchanges in the Commons and the poisonous relationships with party HQ.

I started with Cumbria in Tim Farron's patch: a well organised and motivated local party, highly regarded Lib Dem council and popular MP, well attended lively meetings and some good conversations with local business people. North Norfolk was another self-contained visit to an area with a different political dynamic: strong Lib Dem presence and bidding to control the council; heavily Brexit; but, despite that, a lot of local loyalty to the Lib Dem MP, Norman Lamb.

January 30 2019: I have been glued to the TV for hours in the last couple of days trying to make sense of what is *happening in parliament. We have moved on from the 'meaningful vote' two weeks ago to what seem like 'meaning**less** votes', which simultaneously instruct the government to take 'no deal' Brexit off the table and mandate the government to remove the 'backstop' from the Withdrawal Agreement which the EU has already ruled out, so making a 'No Deal' more likely. And I am supposed to be well informed!*

Tomorrow we are off to Norfolk, but this afternoon I am standing in for V at a constituency event, a private viewing of the refurbished house, Sandycombe Lodge, the Twickenham home of the artist J.M.W. Turner. At that time, the area was a rural retreat from the bustle of London. Local volunteers have managed to mobilise a lot of money for what will hopefully be a big local visitor attraction.

And thence to a reception for volunteers at the local homeless charity SPEAR while V goes to Lambeth Palace for an event organised by the Archbishop.

February 1 2019: *Three events in North Walsham with the North Norfolk Lib Dems: students and Lib Dem activists in an FE college, a public meeting nearby and then a donor's dinner with a well-heeled local supporter plus TV on BBC East. V in good form and visit going well. We avoid the snow though it is visible from the train on the way up. I had stopped earlier to photograph the Kindertransport monument at Liverpool Street. Ten thousand children arrived from Nazi Germany and its occupied territories. We make such a fuss about a few hundred now.*

The hotel was hilarious: said to be where Agatha

Christie wrote her books. We had a room with a curtained four-poster bed and a freestanding ball-and-claw bath. After breakfast, our long-suffering driver – a local volunteer called Kevin – took us round an intensive day of meetings until we were allowed two hours off at teatime on the Tudor-style bed.

I try to get away from the unremitting Westminster diet of Brexit, Brexit and more Brexit. I was asked to do a piece for *City AM* on China.[233] Since I was in the cabinet during what was called the 'Golden Era' there has been a sharp deterioration in relations with China, with the UK following in Trump's footsteps. There were some bad things happening in Xi's China, for sure, but the idea that we can somehow suppress China's emergence as an economic superpower was foolish and dangerous.

There was also an emerging scenario in which Britain disengaged from the world: walking away from Europe (Brexit): the USA (Trump); Russia (Putin); China ('a threat'); Brazil (mini-Trump); and many other countries thought to be too nasty or too difficult to do business with. China-phobia became a particular bugbear of mine and I intended to spend a lot of time in future writing and speaking about it.

Then, out of the blue, I came nearly top of the Private Members' Bill draw and was immediately deluged in proposals from various campaigning groups to take up their pet causes. I had been applying for 20 years and once came

---

[233] "Don't let healthy scepticism about China become paranoia", *City AM*, 4 February 2019.

No 12 from which I launched an uncontroversial Bill with government backing to strengthen Copyright. But I was now No 3 and had a chance to pursue a high-profile bill.

I decided to go for the legalisation of assisted dying. I knew that this was highly controversial, but I was drawn to it having recently changed my view. I was originally hostile to the whole idea, seeing it as part of a slippery slope to euthanasia for people with limited capacity to resist family pressure which might not be in their own best interest. My late mother spent her last years of life alternating between confusion and depression – and had low self-esteem anyway – and would, I was sure, have signed up to euthanasia on a bad day. But the legislation envisaged by Dignity in Dying had strong protections against abuse and was aimed at those faced with an extremely undignified and painful death who decided, rationally and in full possession of their faculties, to end their lives.

I was painfully conscious that I had refused political support to a couple of my constituents who were dying of Motor Neurone Disease and had wanted my help to pass earlier attempts at legislation. I was offered a page in the *Daily Mail* to make the case and the fact that I had changed my mind on the issue gave my advocacy more credibility.[234]

Progress through parliament would, however, depend on the legislative timetable and the risk of filibustering by opponents. As it happened, there was a parliamentary debate on the subject which was a good barometer of the mood in the House. There were some very powerful and

---

[234] "Cable: Legalise assisted dying", *Daily Mail*, 9 February 2019.

deeply moving speeches from Paul Blomfield (Labour), Nick Boles (Tory) and Norman Lamb, drawing on their personal family experience. I was left feeling that this was a really powerful ethical and practical issue to which I could make a major contribution.

February 5 2019: *Kew. The conifers are amazing. I had forgotten how many enormous trees they have there. Also new to me were two Verdun benches, made from an oak grown from an acorn brought back from Verdun. And also, the Hive, a large metal structure with some sort of electrical interaction with a real hive. Anyway, it was a lovely hour and a half, having persuaded V to drive there rather than spend another hour cycling there and back in the cold.*

V rang later to tell me about an article he has written for the Mail *in support of assisted dying, having previously spoken and voted against it. He knew I was a supporter of Dignity in Dying. What did I think? So I gave him my personal dimension: I would be very keen to make absolutely sure that, if I was to help, he would have to want it and I would have to be convinced that the pain was intolerable. For myself, I like to think I am quite good at tolerating pain, but I have no experience of cancer. The way he had put it – before my input – made it sound too much like a suicide pact! Better now.*

February 9 2019: *Weekend on the farm got off to a grumpy start as V has forgotten his suit and the pamphlet he wanted to work on because he is agitated about today's People's Vote rally in Winchester. In the event the rally* *went well: full house in the United Reformed Church and strong speeches from Labour peer Andrew Adonis and V amongst others. Greatly cheered by the crowd of a thousand or more, who marched down the High Street to a rally on the steps of the town hall.*

13 February 2019: *Have my first day of training today for LEAH, a Twickenham charity that organises one-to-one home teaching of the English language to refugees, as well as classes to those who are not house-bound. I feel I have started something really positive. My role model is my Aunt Margaret, who was teaching Spanish until she was 90.*

But parliament is in a complete muddle over the Brexit stuff, making it impossible for V to plan ahead. Even such practical things as getting a car serviced and taxed are a hassle when we don't know when parliament is sitting or voting.

My big political challenge was how to respond to the Independent Group of MPs who were morphing into a new political party. So far ten: seven Labour and three Tories but there were rumours of more to come, which would make them a bigger parliamentary group than the Lib Dems. There were lots of awkward interviews around the issue of 'Why haven't they joined the Lib Dems?' with journalists trying to provoke me into making some disparaging remark about them, particularly when fairly hostile quotes from Chuka and Anna were read out. There were people in the party (not the MPs) who were spoiling for a fight or (recalling the birth of the SDP) want to 'strangle them at birth'. I was taking a gamble and could look weak and foolish if the new party got off the ground and flew. My calculation was that it would fail, and fail quite quickly, since it lacked any infrastructure outside Westminster, would face the enormous barrier of 'first-past-the-post' and did not have leaders of national stature (yet). So I was relentlessly positive, praising the defectors for their courage in breaking away and looking forward to collaborating with them.

I believed that a warm and friendly demeanour would make it easier for them to continue their journey with us when their project floundered or to negotiate a seat-sharing agreement, should that be necessary. We had a powerful lever in potentially offering to support their MPs in any general election even if they stood as independents.

There was an early test of minority party collaboration in a by-election at Peterborough, where the Brexit Party was strong and expected to win what had traditionally been a Tory-Labour marginal. I encouraged the idea of a joint 'Remain' candidate for us, the Greens and Change UK as it was now called. There was agreement to back an independent called Femi Oluwole who had been prominent at Remain rallies. But he backed out under pressure from Labour who believed he would undermine their campaign.

We went ahead with our candidate, as did the Greens, but Change UK didn't field anyone. The actual election was not for some months (early June) but, in the event, there was a good outcome: Labour retained the seat narrowly from the Brexit Party. We had a respectable result with 12 per cent of the vote, comfortably saving our deposit despite the squeeze.

February 18 2019: Put V on a train back to London but he was horribly delayed by a breakdown and news broke of people leaving the Labour Party before he arrived in London. A lot to play for. But unless a lot more MPs join them, they will sink without trace under our electoral system.

The news headlines were not about the defectors but the decision of Honda to close their Swindon factory, on top of bad news from Jaguar Land Rover and Nissan. The Japanese signalled that they were very unhappy with the tone of Brexit comments from the Foreign Secretary (Hunt) and Trade Secretary (Fox).

At last got some help to roll my back garden after it was dug up (again) by the badgers. V and I have struggled with it but now we have the proper equipment.

Still glowing: basking in the glory of having got a drawing into the final round of over a hundred entries for the Diana Armfield Drawing from Observation competition.

Back to London to see V at the end of the week, though he is away most of the time on by-election duty in Peterborough and then in Glasgow for the Scottish Lib Dems' conference.

February 21 2019: V returned from Peterborough, tired but buoyed up by the local activists and candidate, who are battling hard in difficult circumstances. The party workers he met shared his views about embracing the Independent Group in contrast to what he calls the 'usual suspects' – party apparatchiks and people on the Federal Board – who are tut-tutting. Nonetheless, whilst the fractures in the two main parties are mere splinters, not icebergs, such differences do pose existential questions for the Lib Dems.

The same people in the party also seem to be sabotaging the reforms he outlined last September to make the party into a movement with wider reach, so there may be nothing to put forward to the Spring conference in York in a month's time.

There was a day visit to Hamilton, near Glasgow, for the Scottish conference. The Scottish party was small and the numbers of MPs, MSPs and councillors were much reduced from the Charles Kennedy days. But they put on a good show with an enthusiastic well-attended conference, due in no small part to leader Willie Rennie's forceful personality. I sensed that my off-the-cuff speech was considered a bit too informal for an occasion where VIP speeches were carefully drafted, polished and delivered verbatim. Jo Swinson was more in tune with the occasion and excellent. Still, there was a lot of interest in the Scottish media which made the event really worthwhile.

Back to London and a non-political treat. I was recognised as a 'famous person' meriting a 'My Music' concert at Wigmore Hall, performed by a string ensemble of the orchestra of St John's with a baritone for my choice of arias – though, seeing that Stanley Johnson was the next 'famous' person, I wondered what the selection criteria were. I was heavy on Bach and Mozart and a bit light on challenging modern pieces, but the performance was first class and a good audience enjoyed the concert as much as I did.

But the concert was just a brief, pleasant interlude in an

increasingly fraught political situation in parliament over Brexit and in the party. With Brexit day approaching – March 31 – and with no common ground between the government, the opposition and the Brexit rebels, there was the potential for a very messy 'crashing out'. Few believed that this would actually be allowed to happen, though business groups were panicking and the government was encouraging panic over 'no deal' as a way of forcing through an agreement.

When the Prime Minister came back to parliament on March 12 with a revised proposal – which rested heavily on an aspirational document setting out the nature of a post-Brexit agreement – it was again voted down, albeit less decisively: 391 to 242. A key factor was the performance of Geoffrey Cox, the Attorney General, who clearly enjoyed his 24 hours of fame and gave a grand – to my mind, pompous – statement on his legal opinion which was, in essence, that we were still potentially trapped by the Irish 'backstop'.

The following day parliament rejected the possibility of leaving without a deal which meant that the only option available to the government was to seek an extension to the Withdrawal Agreement. Every day, we sat for hours in the chamber going over and over the same arguments and then our Lib Dem MPs had a long, daily post-mortem. I had little to say since it seemed clear to me that we had no leverage in parliament and had to stick to the same mantras about the People's Vote. I saw my main role as calming down colleagues who seemed to take the 'No Deal' threat seriously and didn't seem to see the game of bluff.

Chapter Twenty-One
Exit strategy

Things were also moving very rapidly in the party. Spring conference in York was due on March 20 and it would have to confront the issue of the Independent Group along with my reform proposals. What I hadn't realised, chasing around the country and immersed in all the diplomacy around the Independent Group, as well as Brexit, was that my own position had become precarious. There were several sources of disquiet.

The first were the 'usual suspects' in the party machine who were making a lot of hostile noises and threatening 'no confidence' votes at conference. Some of the noise was coming from friends of Jo Swinson, who was almost certainly not involved herself, but whose friends were promoting the idea that now was the time for a hand-over.

Then there were the parliamentarians and others who had been supportive but were becoming alarmed at the fact that our national rating was back in single figures with impressive, if implausible, numbers for the new party.

And there were my close friends and allies who were aware of my illness and judged that my leadership was, anyway, only transitional and that I should set my own timetable for moving on, rather than have it dictated to me. I, like my friends, was aware of the experience of Ming Campbell who, following the removal of Charles Kennedy, hadn't been able to lift the party's poor ratings and was very unfairly attacked for his age and experience of illness. He was a very decent man who had given the party some calm and seriousness after the undignified end to Charles' reign and gave unstinting support to his successors, including me.

Rachel and my family felt that I should prepare an exit strategy. Dee advised the same. She would normally have urged me to fight the hostile elements in the party, but judged that I could not be guaranteed to win and should keep ahead of the game by setting out my plans pro-actively.

We agreed a formula that I would announce at conference. I would move on when I had seen through the local elections, the Euro elections – which **would** now take place since Brexit was delayed – an emergency general election if there was one and, hopefully, the defeat of Brexit. This was sufficiently vague to keep journalists and others guessing but gave sufficient guidance to the party to prepare for a leadership contest, which would very likely happen over the summer before the autumn conference.

***March 12 2019:** V got in after midnight again as parliamentarians had to wait until after 10 pm for David Liddington to return from Strasbourg with news of the PM's last-ditch improvements to the statement of intent that sits alongside the Withdrawal Agreement. I spend a lot of today trying to follow events on TV. Geoffrey Cox, the Attorney General, did quite well answering questions. And then back to the Withdrawal Agreement again: hour after hour. The SNP leader, Blackford, makes good points but goes on far, far, too long. Now Rees-Mogg gets support for an amendment to add another five hours to the debate (beyond 7 pm).*

I am feeling thoroughly negative and V is struggling to maintain any energy or optimism in the current situation. Our poll ratings have fallen back down to 7 per cent and the Tiggers or TIGs (The Independent Group) are getting all the media attention. Their only merit appears to be that they are NEW. And Chuka Umunna is, indeed, both very personable and very handsome!

March 13 2019: *After last night's defeat of the May deal for the second time, there is a bit more hope of a People's Vote. But, first, parliament has to rule out a No Deal Brexit tonight.*

V tells me that he has decided to announce his plans for stepping down after the local and EU elections.

The conference in York was something of a relief, having decided on a plan of action. In addition, I always enjoy going back to York to see my old haunts. And I had established good links with the York Lib Dems, who were running the city in a coalition with the Tories (and apparently coming the better out of the arrangement). I gave one of my best speeches as Leader and felt sufficiently relaxed to conjure up some good jokes.

I was well aware that behind the scenes the next leadership contest was beginning. Jo was being politically very astute and presenting herself as a natural successor, enthusiastically supporting what I was doing. She was a champion of working with the Tiggers and had persuaded Anna Soubry to come and speak to a fringe meeting; by comparison, Ed Davey was being more tribal and grumpy. On the reform proposals, Jo was a strong advocate and Ed the champion of the status quo.

In the event, all the reform proposals were accepted by conference except the most controversial and interesting: the open selection for leader. I was disappointed to see it go down but not surprised after the Federal Board had effectively killed it. But it was no longer my problem. I would spend the next few months enjoying myself, campaigning in the country leaving the painful problems of donors and dealing with the dysfunctional party machine to whichever of my colleagues won the contest for a job they were so keen to do.

The immediate priority was to switch attention as far as possible to local campaigning, while everyone in Westminster was 100 per cent fixated on every twist and turn in the Brexit saga. I got wind of the problem when I met a group of Lib Dem council leaders, who were in London for a meeting of the Local Government Association. They were an interesting and varied group: from Cumbria to Portsmouth, Sutton to Hull. I found them highly impressive people who had real leadership qualities, who had had experience managing multi-million-pound budgets, and who were grounded in the realities of getting things done at a local level in the face of financial constraints and difficult politics.

But they were angry and frustrated that HQ was showing no interest in them and was preoccupied with getting our supporters onto anti-Brexit marches and energised by the latest, tactical, manoeuvres in parliament. They wanted to know what our message was for Hull and Oldham, where we once had a lot of support, but the politics was pro-Brexit. Their anger was directed at me as the party leader, but I was on their side and they knew it. I made it clear that we weren't going to change our 'Stop Brexit' and People's Vote messages, but that I wanted us to get back to local campaigning and I would lead by example. Brexit was, however, still the only issue at Westminster.

March 23 2019: *Today is the latest march for a People's Vote and this is thought to be the biggest with over a million people attending. V's children and grandchildren and quite a few of my family are present. Jo is to speak at the big rally whilst V is to start the whole thing and we are whisked by the organisers up to the VIP suite of a luxury hotel on Park Lane. Very plush. Then, suddenly, the start is brought forward by 15 minutes – it was said because of pressure of numbers – and so V's kick-off speech was truncated and largely disappeared from media attention.*

But the march was very positive, disciplined and good-natured. V's twelve-year old grandson, Charlie, marched at the front with his granddad, while I fell back. I saw Caroline Lucas joining them halfway down Piccadilly. Overall, it was a great family and political occasion, if a bit dispiriting for V (needless to say, it was Jo on the News).

The political temperature was raised a notch by another People's Vote march on the Saturday preceding the indicative votes. I discovered that I was no longer a platform speaker and had been replaced by Jo Swinson. I was beginning to appreciate the significance of the phrase 'lame duck'. I was offered the role as someone 'starting' the march and realised that this was not worth a fight. It was more useful to plan a month of local campaigning.

But in the meantime, there were the 'indicative' votes designed to establish what MPs wanted as opposed to what they didn't want. The first round of voting (March 27) was designed to narrow down the short-list of options. It was clear from the voting that one option – for a Customs Union, as proposed by Ken Clarke – was closest to majority support (six votes short of a majority). A referendum was 27 votes short. Revocation, 'No Deal' and Labour's alternative fell far short and were clearly going nowhere.

March 27 2019: V gets up at 5.30 am for the Today *programme only to be told that they have cancelled because they have a Labour backbencher who will say the same thing.*

In the Commons, the news has been overtaken by the offer from Theresa May to her rebels that she will go if they vote through her deal. Few expect it to make any difference. But then the announcement of the Indicative Vote takes an eternity as there is an hour of points of order with Bercow talking for at least half the time. We have an absolutely horrible meal in the Commons Buttery and get the train home from Waterloo to arrive at midnight.

For the first time, our group of twelve MPs showed serious signs of tension and disagreement as we discussed the second round on the April 1 (appropriately April Fools' Day). For the first time in two years, our votes could make a difference. We already knew that Eastbourne MP Stephen Lloyd would vote for the Brexit deal thanks to his rather reckless promise to his constituents. Norman Lamb was a strong supporter of 'soft Brexit' options such as a customs union and threatened to resign if we continued to oppose compromise.

Ed and Jo (supported by Bath MP Wera Hobhouse) were implacably opposed to any compromise. They argued that it would be 'the worst of all worlds'; also, that it would be seen as a betrayal by our members, many of whom had joined on this single issue. And The Independent Group was ready to take over as the least compromising opponent of Brexit in all its forms. Jo and Ed were also, no doubt, mindful of the upcoming leadership election and the motivation of our membership.

The remainder, like me, were more pragmatic and could see the merits of supporting a 'second best' option. To try to keep the group together we agreed to abstain on the customs union but vote for the referendum option.

The closest to a positive vote was for Ken Clarke's motion supporting a customs union which was defeated by only three votes. A motion by two Labour backbenchers – Kyle and Wilson – for a referendum was defeated by twelve votes, though it had the highest number in favour of any proposal (280). There were sufficient Labour opponents of a referendum to block it and the narrative was developing that support for a referendum had reached a high-water mark. Another proposal by the Tory MP Nick Boles for a new Common Market arrangement lost by 21 votes (and he then resigned the Tory whip). A proposal to revoke Article 50 – to cancel Brexit – was lost by 101 votes.

The Lib Dem abstention had been crucial to the defeat of the customs union and Norman went ballistic on TV, denouncing the party for sacrificing the national interest to party interest (as if others weren't). He was, of course, right. We could (possibly) have changed the course of history, (perhaps) sacrificing the party in the process.

I had often reflected on whether we made a historic mistake and whether I should have thrown my remaining weight behind Norman. But I was still the leader, not yet a free agent, and concluded that the longstanding decision to position the party as *the* anti-Brexit party had, and would continue to have, logical consequences of which this was merely one of several.

March 28 2019: *I arrive at the farm to find a speeding summons, having been caught on camera going too fast on one of my many recent journeys from Twickenham: a fair cop.*

After the indicative votes one thing was clear: the parliamentary support for a referendum was very strong, but just short of what was necessary. When 'Remainers' got together to discuss the situation there was an awkward gap between the slogan and the reality. One explanation was that we were 'waiting for Jeremy' who, we were told, would come over when the time was right. Carolyn Lucas was the leading proponent of this theory, and she was certainly close, at least ideologically, to the Labour leadership.

There was constant embarrassment when Lib Dems put down amendments to Brexit legislation advocating a People's Vote and whipping up a social media storm in support of it, then having to withdraw it because 'Jeremy isn't ready' (or risk a crushing defeat when Labour was whipped to oppose us or abstain). The truth was that

Jeremy was never going to support a referendum and some of our Labour friends told us as much. There was an attempt by the smaller parties including the nationalists to approach Corbyn directly and we trooped off to his office at the far end of the parliamentary estate to meet the continued repetition of the official Labour line with Seumas Milne, his media adviser, filling in any gaps. It was hopeless, a waste of time

I judged that we had to try a very different approach. One was to try to talk round the May Tories who were in danger of being trapped by the continued rejection of the deal with 'no deal' as the only alternative, which they couldn't countenance. Although they were hostile to a referendum, it might come to seem the least bad option. I wanted to play the one card which the Lib Dems could offer: to prop up the government in return for a second referendum. Some of my colleagues were very unhappy with the idea but they didn't try to stop me. I went to see Greg Clark, my successor at BIS, who had once briefly been my deputy, and asked him to float the idea with Philip Hammond and the others who were trying to keep the moderate options alive. It was clear that there was some interest, but it never came to anything.

The second initiative, which I floated in the media, was to include 'no deal' as one of the options in any referendum. This would meet the objection from Brexiteers that a referendum was simply a dodge to kill Real Brexit. Again, some of our leading activists were appalled that I was taking a risk but, without taking risks, the whole referendum idea was doomed.

April 2 2019: *After all the sound and fury, it has gone*

very quiet today while May has her five-hour cabinet meeting. The House of Commons heaved with opinions, many well expressed but, when it came to outcomes, produced a very small squeak.

So on we go. V had a late-night talk with Greg Clark who wants to know if the Lib Dems would prop up a May government long enough to have a confirmatory referendum. He had two radio interviews this morning and is relaxed about having a no-deal exit on the ballot paper. I cannot for the life of me see how this can be done since you have to have a way of eliminating one of the three options (Remain, May's Deal and No Deal) and a play-off between the last two. I spent some of the morning trying to put options on paper but didn't get very far. V says this is a non-issue.

From the beginning of April, I tried to get out of Westminster whenever I could to meet and cheer on the activists who were fighting local elections in a few weeks' time. These visits were incredibly rewarding for me, and I seemed to be welcome wherever I went. I covered about 25 council districts and several mayoral contests of interest to the Lib Dems (Bedford, Watford) usually with a rally, a fundraiser and some door knocking.

There were areas where strong 'Remain' sentiment provided a following wind: Oxfordshire (Vale of White Horse and South Oxfordshire), Bath and North East Somerset, Winchester, Cambridgeshire, the Cotswolds, St Albans, Taunton. There were some where we looked to make a revival albeit in Brexit areas: Chelmsford, Colchester, North Devon, Teignbridge (South Devon), West

Somerset, and others, where we had a strong council campaign but powerful political headwinds (Hull, Liverpool). There were some defences of established Lib Dem councils (South Somerset; Three Rivers, Oadby and Hinckley in Leicestershire, Watford, York) and others where we were trying to build from beleaguered outposts (Manchester, Kent).

As the campaign went on, confidence grew that we were going to get a good result in both 'Remain' and 'Brexit' areas. The vibes were positive everywhere. Years of retreat were over, it seemed.

April 8 2019: Every time you think the news can't get any worse, something happens to show that it can. Whilst I'm not suggesting that it is in any way as serious as bombing Christians at prayer and Westerners in hotels in Sri Lanka on Easter Sunday, yesterday it was announced that Trump is getting his state visit on June 3. I am delighted to find that Vince is declining the invitation to the royal banquet for the President and First Lady! He rang to make sure I agreed.

Meanwhile, it seems too late to make an agreement on an electoral pact with the new Change UK party over Euro seats. So stupid, as the D'Hondt system of merging constituencies used in European elections means that it is very difficult for small parties to get elected.

April 13 2019: On the train to Exeter, speeding through emerald green fields. The best of English spring with lambs in abundance as we approach the West Country. V's campaign planning has been really messed around by the ever-changing Brexit timetable. We aren't leaving the EU for the time being and there is no general election. But we are having to cope with Farage breathing hellfire and the TIGs saying that they plan to put up 70 candidates in a general election.

Now being driven from Exeter to Barnstaple by a charming German guy. The local party has insisted on an escort as they feared we might be physically assaulted by 'Leavers' if we used the train?

(Later) Done Barnstaple and excellent lunch laid on by the North Devon activists. Another magic carpet all the way to Newton Abbott. Put in a large hotel with a lovely room overlooking the estuary though the weather is grey and cold. A good, well-attended dinner to raise money for the elections. V well received and, as the council candidates queue up for photos, they are full of optimism about the election. Tomorrow, Torbay: Fawlty Towers...

April 28 2019: *Vince is getting quite a lot of publicity, as much for declining the Trump banquet invitation as for his local and Euro election campaign.*

Chapter Twenty-Two
Breakthrough at last

The results when they came in were better than even our optimistic predictions.[235] We gained over 700 seats (net) and 11 councils, the best results for a couple of decades. We had managed a vote share of just under 20 per cent and we gained ground in both 'Brexit' and 'Remain' areas.

One of our more spectacular results was in Chelmsford, where I went to celebrate the morning after a Conservative majority of 45 seats was overturned – and that in a Brexit-supporting area in Essex. Across the country, the Tories lost 1,300 seats and Labour, having expected to win seats, lost around 100 and four councils. The Greens also did well, helped by pacts with us.

May 8 2019: *Doesn't time fly when you are having fun? Today I follow V back to London. The local elections last Thursday were a triumph for the Lib Dems.*

We are having a revival. After the local elections, we are at 15 per cent in the polls instead of single figures. So gratifying for V to be able to go out on a high note, but he is hanging in until after the Euro elections on May 23 and until the end of the process to elect his successor which will not be over until August. The bureaucratic Federal Board

---

[235] "Big Parties Handed Hard Brexit Lessons from Bruising Losses", *Financial Times*, 5 May 2019; "Cable Hails Party as the Big Winners", *The Guardian*, 4 May 2019.

absolutely refuses to shorten the nomination period, despite Ed Davey having jury service.

I have a reunion of the 'Iceland Girls' on the farm to commemorate our successful 2018 hike: 13 of the 16 turn up. However, V is in TV demand and Sky has sent its cameras to the farm so I organise a walk to keep the girls off site and occupied. Perfect timing. Then the girls take V and me out for dinner at a posh local restaurant.

The local election results were terminal for Theresa May, whose position was already very precarious. She was trying to save her Brexit deal by working to reach an agreement with Corbyn and the Labour Party. Since the Labour Party was divided and its position incoherent, it was difficult to see what the negotiations could possibly accomplish, apart from the unintended and improbable consequence of making Corbyn look serious and statesmanlike. Good luck with that!

Her problems were compounded by the fact that, by postponing the Brexit date, she made it inevitable (and a legal requirement) that Euro-elections take place. The Conservatives were not prepared and faced competition from the Brexit Party, for whom this election was manna from heaven.

Fortunately, the Lib Dems had selected candidates on the off-chance that the elections would happen. And the momentum from the success in the locals was helpful. But there were serious worries. Our local organisation of deliverers and door-knockers was of limited help in these vast multi-member constituencies. And there were just over three weeks to get organised. We had only one MEP to start with – Catherine Bearder, who scraped in by a whisker in 2014 – so we could hardly do worse. But our realistic expectation was of winning two or three seats at most.

The position was further complicated by the new party – now called Change UK – which was unveiling its list of candidates, seeing this as their first chance to make an impact. Rachel Johnson was one of their 'big names'. There were now three 'Remain' parties in contention (and Labour, whose candidates tended to be staunch Europeans). We could finish up with the 'Remain' vote split four ways and a landslide for Farage and the Brexit Party, as the Conservatives were barely competing.

We needed a crunchy, distinctive message to flourish in this crowded field. There was a light-bulb moment when the party's two young press officers – Tim and Dave – came to my office with a suggestion for the campaign launch that they expected me to reject: to adopt the 'Bollocks to Brexit' slogan from Pimlico Plumbers.

In normal circumstances, and guided by my own temperament, I would have dismissed the idea out of hand. It was vulgar, divisive and would annoy all the people in the party and out who were hoping for a negotiated, soft, Brexit. But that boat had already sailed. I said yes and we soon had the new slogan on our leaflets and placards.

There was a campaign launch in a crowded London night club and the press/TV turned up in force to mock and disapprove, but also to publicise our campaign. After years of being asked by voters and commentators 'What do the Lib Dems stand for?', we now had a simple answer and it worked – at least in this context.[236]

I also floated publicly the idea of a pact with Change UK and the Greens to maximise our chances. The practical problems of organising a seat-sharing arrangement system within three weeks were immense and perhaps impossible to solve. But the mere fact of advertising our willingness to work with others was key.

I had had several good discussions, some weeks earlier, along with Alistair Carmichael and Jo, with the embryonic Change UK leadership group of Chuka, Anna and Gavin (Shuker) and they were clearly torn between co-operating and competing with us. But on this occasion, they were quicker to see the problems rather than the opportunities for co-operation and publicly poured cold water on my suggestion. As for the Greens, their social media traffic was hostile to working with us. I had a snatched conversation with Caroline Lucas on the green benches and she was non-committal.

In media interviews, I said that our overtures to other parties had been rejected, which was a pity. I had an angry call from Caroline who said I had misrepresented her – and, to be fair, she had always been the most constructive and co-operative of the leading Greens. But the impression had been left in the media that we were the grown-ups who were putting the 'Remain' cause before tribal aggrandisement. That reinforced a trend in public opinion polls that showed us as the most likely of the 'Remain' parties to win seats.

---

[236] "Lib Dems Bolstered by Simple Message", *Financial Times*, 28 May 2019; "The Secret to Stopping Brexit", *The Guardian*, 11 May 2019.

It soon became very clear that Change UK was not going to break the mould. Our support from the locals was holding up and their brief surge in the opinion polls had ebbed away. The attractions of being new were fading and their problems mounting, with flaky candidates exposed for embarrassing social media posts. There was no serious organisation beyond press conferences. There was a vacuum of policy thinking: not surprisingly as they tended to agree with the Lib Dems on everything, except their belief in a new brand.

On my visit to Scotland, their leading list candidate admitted that he had made a mistake leaving the Lib Dems for Change UK and was coming back, getting UK-wide publicity. Towards the end of the campaign, Heidi Allen, one of their impressive recruits from the Tories, and the party's interim leader, publicly acknowledged that setting up a new party in competition with us had been a mistake. Heidi was one of the few Tories selected by open primaries and she was hostile to partisan politics. She was angrily rebuked by Anna Soubry, but by then Heidi was simply reflecting reality.

Travelling around the country, I felt the return of optimism and energy in the party: MEP candidates who were beginning to wake up to the idea that they might actually get elected; activists in Scotland and London who hadn't had local elections in May and were getting the feeling that they might, at last, be on the winning side; 'Remain' strongholds like London, Bristol, Cambridge, where armchair Europeans were emerging in large numbers to offer practical help delivering leaflets or campaigning on the streets.

For me, the personal highlight was a day trip to

Gibraltar. It started well when I got off the plane in Malaga to be mobbed by a large group of somewhat tipsy, young women who were in town for a hen party. After a lot of selfies, I began to get the idea that they thought I was someone else, but the optics were great and I suppressed the doubts. Gibraltar itself was almost 100 per cent 'Remain' and there was real fear about how their delicately poised relationship with Spain would be affected. The leader of the Gibraltar Liberals made sure that we met everyone of significance on the Rock and we got wall-to-wall publicity, as well as good coverage back home.

May 18 2019: V is sleeping off the trip to Gibraltar yesterday when his flight was seriously delayed and he got in well after midnight. This followed from Edinburgh and Sheffield the day before and Bristol the day before that. V is 'box office' again with some mildly rude references to him on Have I Got News for You.

It would be good to have a day off, but Alice, the Richmond and Twickenham organiser, is insisting on a campaign day locally.

We had another boost when, sensing the possibility of a surprise result, ALDE leader Guy Verhofstadt decided to launch the whole of the European Liberal campaign in London. We had a bizarre event in a green space in North London, surrounded by multi-million-pound mansions, when almost every political journalist in Europe was clamouring for pictures and quotes. We then took the vast scrum of cameras and bodies to knock on several £5 million pound doors – all 'Remain' – and Guy went off in his election bus to Paris and Macron (part of our Liberal alliance).

The last few days of the campaign were frantic and our support surged to scarcely believable levels. It clearly wouldn't last and this was a very strange and artificial election. But momentum is almost everything in an election. We had leading Labour figures saying that they would vote for us.[237] George Osborne gave us a guarded plug in the *Standard*[238] which managed not to put off too many others.[239] Michael Heseltine and other leading Tories said they would be voting for us (but were still Tories!).

It was clear that we were going to do well. A YouGov poll based on voting intentions ten days before voting had the Lib Dems on 24 per cent and leading the Brexit party on 22 per cent and the Tories and Labour both on 19 per cent. The Greens were on 8 per cent and Change UK had disappeared to 1 per cent.[240] The boost was almost certainly temporary, but we had not been in this kind of territory since the early days of the 2010 election and 'Cleggmania'.

As well as rushing around the country, there were set piece events. The *Daily Telegraph* had also arranged a broadcast debate for me with Nigel Farage. We were both well-behaved and he was respectful, as he had been in the

---

[237] "Cashman Resigns from Labour to vote for Lib Dems", *Evening Standard*, 22 May 2019.
[238] "Our View on European Poll: Your Vote Matters", *Evening Standard*, 21 May 2019.
[239] "I'm voting Lib Dem – in Spite of Osborne", *I* Newspaper, 23 May 2019.
[240] "Poll Surge Puts Lib Dems on Top", *The Times*, 31 May 2019.

debates I had had with him going back 30 years to the days of the Referendum Party. By election day, it was clear that our two parties were going to come out on top, though I don't think either of us imagined that this was a permanent reconfiguration of British politics,

On election day itself, Clodagh and the team had arranged for me to do a lightning tour around the country, going to Scotland and the West Midlands, where there was, in both cases, an unexpected gain of a regional seat to Liverpool, where the North West might produce two – and then to Cambridge where another seat, for East England, was in the balance.

When the results came through on the Sunday (May 26) after a three-day lag, they justified the hype we had been building up. We had won 16 seats including three each in London and the south east with 20 per cent of the votes, by far our best performance in these elections (the previous peak was eleven).

Farage's Brexit party won overall with 29 seats and 32 per cent of the vote, but the 'Remain' parties taken together came slightly ahead. The results were greatly encouraging but reflected the peculiarities of this particular election and, before long, the two big parties would reassert themselves. Nonetheless, there was a victory to savour, and we had enthusiastic rallies with bemused MEPs who had never expected to be elected and didn't know how long their exciting new venture would last. There were also several big – and hopefully enduring – positives.

The first was that we had killed the idea that Lib Dem was a toxic brand. I had never believed that the 2015 and 2017 disasters were mainly because of the 'toxicity' issue but it was widely believed inside and outside the party and was tending to become self-reinforcing through endless repetition. It was now clear that people would vote for us locally and nationally if we gave them good reason to.

The second was that we had killed off the 'new party' idea. The shallowness of Change UK had been brutally exposed. We were indisputably the challenger party – at least on the 'Remain' side of the divide – and were able to develop alliances, notably with the Greens, and defectors from the major parties, from a position of strength.

The first fruit of the new reality was that Chuka Umunna asked to join us. Our personal relationship was undoubtedly a factor in getting him to come over. He had shown a very bad lapse of judgement with his new party and had made some disobliging comments about us. But I thought he was an excellent recruit: intelligent, articulate, very telegenic and with very similar values. And, not least, he added colour to our very monochromatic party. We organised a press conference at which he and I engaged in enthusiastic mutual backslapping, and he was warmly received by our activists. Others would follow, but there was an understanding that we should phase in the newcomers and save up some of the good news for the next leader.

While all this was going on, I was trying to keep up my profile locally and give leadership on some constituency issues. One was Heathrow and the plans for a third runway which had diminishing support and a weak rationale but also had the feeling of inevitability.[241] There was a big

---

[241] The Vince Cable Column, *Richmond and Twickenham Times*, 10 May 2019.

campaign in local schools, inspired by Sir David Attenborough, which I supported in visits to schools and secured me a debate in parliament on plastic recycling which I was able to relay back to the schools.[242] And I now had the freedom to write and speak on subjects which interested me outside the leader's brief, like climate change and the role of the oil and gas industries.[243]

The Lib Dem leadership contest moved to centre stage. I showed no preference publicly or privately. Jo was the better performer and presented herself well; Ed was solid, a strong base in the party as a campaigner, and had more substantial experience in government and in life as a carer for a disabled child.

There were no discernible ideological differences: both had been close to Nick Clegg in the Coalition years, both were at the extreme end of the anti-Brexit spectrum. But it was clear from the outset that Jo was going to win. Her supporters had a simple message: 'It's time for a woman.' She had a strong power base amongst the 'Me Too' women and played to it very effectively. Such was the poor party history of gender diversity that male guilt and female pressure almost guaranteed her the leadership.

May 26 2019: At Hafod y Garreg, "the oldest house in Wales": a wonderful old farmhouse and renovated cider mill set on a hillside, through several farm gates, a few miles from Hay-on-Wye. Via a lunch event yesterday with

---

[242] "Pupils' plastics protest", *Richmond and Twickenham Times,* 10 May 2019.
[243] "Oil and Gas Firms Have no Reason to Fear Divestment", *City AM*, 11 July 2019.

the Lib Dems in Crickhowell in anticipation of a by-election, though at this stage there are a few more signatures to gather on the Recall petition. Then to a panel discussion at the Festival 'Where the Light Gets In'. A strange affair: a discussion featuring Liz Truss for the Conservatives, V and a Labour MP on the proposition 'It's the economy, stupid'. As a lady in the audience complained, it was less an intellectual discussion than 'party political broadcasts'.

This afternoon, we took a long walk over the hills which became an adventure on the way back, getting lost and climbing lots of fences, to be greeted on our return by the first batch of results of the Euro-elections which look very encouraging.

May 27 2019: *Back to London early. V disappears on his bike to a constituency fair and then we head for central London to a big celebration of the Euro results at Lambeth Bridge. I greet our three new London MEPs: two women, Irina and Louisa, and one man, Dinesh Dhamija. I was particularly pleased to see him elected as he had been seriously miffed to be passed over as mayoral candidate. He is one of those mega-rich self-made men who think business success can translate automatically into political success – but he does have charm and he has worked hard for this election. He once told me he had started life as a doorstep insurance salesman.*

May 31 2019: *I arrive back to the farm and to a discussion on replacing the cattle grids. When I turn on the news, the polls have the Lib Dems leading in an early* *general election with 24 per cent. Nothing succeeds like success!*

There was one piece of unfinished business: the long-awaited by-election in Peterborough and a new one in Brecon and Radnor, which was a former Lib Dem seat. The by-election had been made possible by a recall petition to oust the Tory MP – and now candidate – who had been found guilty of claiming false expenses. Our candidate was Jane Dodds, whom Rachel and I had got to know well and was an impressive candidate with Welsh language as well as personal skills.

The area had sentimental interest for me: I had spent a summer in my student days leading walking parties in the Black Mountains and Brecon Beacons and Rachel and I had honeymooned there. I was to spend quite a bit of time there and my main contribution was to negotiate an agreement with Plaid Cymru, under which we would co-operate in the general election, and they would stand down for us in the by-election. The Greens agreed to support us, too. That help was valuable since the seat was Brexit-leaning and we needed every vote we could get.

June 28 2019: *There is a long hiatus as the country waits to hear whether Boris Johnson or Jeremy Hunt will be the next Prime Minister (almost certainly the former) and somewhat less excitement about the leadership of the Lib Dems: Jo or Ed (again, almost certainly the former). But one more big dinner at the Mansion House, courtesy of the Glaziers' annual guild dinner, V as guest of honour.*

Survived the train and drain in my gladrags; then

clapped in alongside the Master at the head of the procession. Seated next to a jolly Scot with a waxed moustache who was punctilious about matters of dress, tut-tutting at those (like V), who had turned up in black rather than white ties (though V did wear his knighthood medal, found with great difficulty, having been tucked away for four years). Apart from the inedible rare beef, dinner was very good.

V's speech was fine and very fluent, starting with jokes and moving on to the state of the economy. A bit too gentle in my opinion about the Tory party and all its works. The Master assures me that he will never vote Tory again (Brexit); I wonder whether he is serious (Corbyn as PM?). V has relented on his personal transport policy to the extent of getting a car home, for which I am very grateful.

July 11 2019: *I finally got round to voting in the Lib Dem election: for Jo Swinson, in spite of lingering doubts about her judgement. She is a better communicator than Ed, who is otherwise very sound.*

July 17 2019: *Back to Brecon and blissful Hafod y Garreg: by-election duty. We could do without all the travelling: four hours back!*

So, what's bothering me? V asking what he is going to **do,** *apart from being the local MP and writing books. Isn't that enough? It is clear that politics is very addictive. Very hard to sink back into obscurity. I have said that he must get off the stage once the new leader is in place.*

July 22 2019: *Had a goodbye lunch party for V's*

Westminster staff and Dee plus Lord Tom McNally, one of the party's wisest heads and a veteran of SDP days, who had given V a lot of help and advice. Then off to a night club on the Embankment for the announcement of the Lib Dem leadership. Jo got two-thirds of the vote; there had been a successful campaign based on the slogan 'it must be a woman'.

Our voting membership of around 106,000 wasn't too far short of the 160,000 Tories who chose the next prime minister: around two-thirds of them for Johnson, dubbed Britain's 'Poundland Trump'. Narcissism rules: everything is about him. V says he is clever and easily underestimated. But we both find the prospect deeply depressing.

July 23 2019: *V must decide soon about stepping down as an MP for Twickenham. He says not having his identity as an MP feels like swimming out of his depth. There is quite a lot of jockeying to take on his seat.*

July 24 2019: *Watched Theresa May's final PMQs. There were snide hints to Jeremy Corbyn that he should go too. Jo asked a good question in her first outing as leader. V out of sight of the cameras (making himself scarce?).*

August 1 2019: *Jane Dodds wins Brecon and Radnor by-election by a majority of 425, which is wonderful but in all likelihood less than the Green and Plaid Cymru vote would have been if they had not agreed to stand aside.*

August 13 2019: *The major decision was last week when V appeared with a drafted letter to Piers (chair of the local* *party), saying he would not want to stand for election again when the election is called. The Lib Dem HQ wants the party to be election-ready. This prompted Richmond Council's Lib Dem leader Gareth Roberts and a few others to implore him to hold his fire so as not to give the Tories too much time to flood the place with campaigners and literature, as in 2015. Simultaneously, I think V's desire to go ski-ing in January tipped the balance in favour of stepping down!*

Chapter Twenty-Three
When Brexit got 'done'

The big issues around Brexit would be confronted after the recess when Johnson had sorted out his government and tried to negotiate a better deal than May before the new October 31 exit date. It meant the pressure was off until after party conference in September.

I arranged to get myself appointed health spokesman: a useful niche to pursue issues of interest to me like mental health and social care. I received an early invitation to the NHS Confederation and to speak at their annual dinner. My comments on the need for management to show the same racial diversity as the make-up of hospital staff were, however, greeted with an awkward silence. There was much to do. Excepting Norman Lamb and Paul Burstow in the coalition, not many top Lib Dems had devoted much thought to NHS issues, and we needed to. I looked forward to a couple of years on this brief, which I could do alongside serious constituency work, which I always enjoyed and got satisfaction from.

I popped into Jo's office to ask how else I could best make myself useful. She wasn't there but her new team of advisers was. When I recognised them, my look of dismay must have shown. They looked very sheepish and embarrassed at my appearance. Nothing was said. I knew that I needed to keep clear and paddle my own canoe.

In the summer recess, there were two wonderful

overseas trips which put politics into its proper perspective. Rachel's son Max was marrying again, this time to a Greek-Australian in traditional fashion on the island of Hydra. This was my first experience of the Greek islands and it did not disappoint. There was a lot of extended family – Rachel's, mine, and the new Greek in-laws – and we managed a couple of steep climbs through the pine woods to the monastery above the town; a lot of steps but an idyllic setting.

Then off to California for my first visit to the state and specifically to San Francisco and Silicon Valley. I had a very deep sense of satisfaction seeing my younger son at last settled in a happy marriage and with challenging, well-paid work in quantum physics after years of frustration on both counts. We were also bowled over by the city and the sights of Yosemite and Tahoe. This was a holiday of a lifetime. But I should have known that politics would intrude.

Messages on the phone came in from the Whips' Office in London asking me to return immediately. All hell had been let loose on Brexit. The government was trying to prorogue parliament. The idea that the government can close parliament when it is a nuisance was supposed to have been killed off in the 17th century, but apparently not so. Constitutionalists were very agitated. But the practical issue was that parliament would be closed for most of the period until Brexit day. There would be little alternative to 'take it or leave it' for any deal, however bad, that the government secured in Brussels.

It wasn't clear why my presence in London would make any difference, but Alistair believed that we must have 100 per cent turnout, so we rebooked at great expense on

Norwegian Airlines, cutting short the holiday by a day so that I could be 'on parade'.

Before we left, there was another political headache. The local party had been told that it must have a candidate in place for the next election, *pronto*! The party president had set a target date and the box had to be ticked regardless of local circumstances. In Twickenham, I had let it be known that this was my last term, but I was in no hurry to become a 'lame duck'. And the local party did not want to advertise my departure before the next campaign started, since it believed this would attract a strong Tory campaign. I couldn't manage the issue from the other side of the world. The local party felt obliged to heed 'instructions' from HQ and so my decision to stand down got out to the press and the public in an unplanned and messy way.

I felt seriously irritated at the process, but this decision had to be made at some point and I was pleased to see that three good women had been short-listed for the seat. Munira, who was nominated, was someone I had known for over a decade: Rachel and I were at her wedding when she married my very effective constituency organiser at the time, Michael Wilson. She would do a good job. Twickenham was in safe hands.

September 10 2019: Paddy Ashdown's memorial service at Westminster Abbey. A very high-profile affair attended by four former prime ministers: Major, Blair, Brown and Cameron. Major gave the address rather well. Clegg had a speaking part, quoting Pericles on democracy in Athens, and so did Lib Dem chief executive Nick Harvey, who was less solemn and more entertaining. After shaking hands with the PMs, we were ushered to a place next to the altar steps behind the royals and with David Steel, Nick and Kate Harvey and others. A very grand event, which I suspect his widow, Jane, found rather overwhelming.

September 14 2019: To Bournemouth for Lib Dem conference. Have been breathing more easily after V's speech, which was delivered beautifully, with no glitches this year. All the main points came across really well and were well received: a good way to bow out. We were able to relax for the first conference in years: swimming in the sea (twice!) and breakfasting _together_(!).

The big debate was to commit to revoking Article 50, _if_ we have a parliamentary majority after an election (about 330 seats), a somewhat ambitious target to say the least, but a distinctive policy – if it is properly explained.

Overall confidence in the party is very high after our successes earlier in the year and with the growing number of defections, in particular Sam Gyimah from the Tories.

V thinks there is a way through to a referendum: Johnson comes back with a deal and parliament approves it, **subject to a confirmatory popular vote**.

Conference was a success for the party. Jo was enthusiastically embraced by a record number of attendees. She conveyed confidence and authority. The prospects looked good to excellent. I was really gratified by my own, warm, reception. Several previous leaders had been bundled off the stage rather ignominiously and I had at least avoided that.

The return of parliament proved to be seventh heaven

for constitutional lawyers, parliamentary draftsmen, the Speaker and those MPs who cared passionately about procedure and arcane points of order. The Benn Act, the Letwin amendment, Cooper-Boles, Spelman, Kyle-Wilson: all will merit a place in constitutional history, no doubt. I was frankly lost in all the legalistic argument; the stuff I knew and cared about – the practical business and economic consequences of Brexit – had just disappeared from the debate.

Parliament voted against a 'No Deal' Brexit but was told that this had no legal significance. The government moved a motion of No Confidence to try to precipitate an election but was defeated! The Scottish courts declared prorogation illegal, but not the English High Court. Then the following week, the English Supreme Court declared it illegal, also: unanimously. The government had to back down but not without a lot of bad-mouthing of the judiciary and widening divisions in the Tory party. The excellent Phillip Lee, Tory MP for Bracknell, was the latest to join us.

September 28 2019: Yesterday was, I hope, a watershed moment in the ongoing Boris Show(er). The supremo of the Supreme Court, Brenda Hale (our Cambridge contemporary), delivered the ruling on whether the prorogation of parliament was lawful. They said unanimously (eleven of them) that it was not. So, parliament now sitting again and going through all the usual stuff. Johnson was recalled from the UN summit overnight and is due to speak to the House of Commons. I've had the parliamentary channel on (mostly without sound!) all afternoon while I did other stuff on the computer.

September 30 2019: *My euphoria was short-lived... A wholly unrepentant Boris appeared in the Commons on Wednesday evening, calling the Benn Act the Surrender Act, and dismissing the fears of female MPs suffering from abuse as 'humbug'. The strategy seemed to be to wind up the opposition enough to produce rowdy scenes and then say: "I told you so. I was right to shut this down for five weeks".*

Parliament was going through the same old stuff: round and round the same issues. Parliament wouldn't allow a 'no deal' Brexit. The government insisted that this must be an option in its latest round of negotiations. The EU was running out of patience with repeated requests for postponement of Brexit day but equally was anxious to avoid a 'no deal' situation.

My belief had always been that the more cataclysmic predictions of 'no deal', with a collapse of communications to and from Europe, were always bluff to cajole the more nervous members of parliament and the public to sign up to some very weak agreement. The government talked about a Canada-type deal, but that now looked ambitious, and we could finish up with something like what the Brexiteers called 'WTO terms', which would still be very disruptive to some industries, and farming, where tariffs mattered. Boris duly came back to parliament a few days before Brexit Day with a new deal which wasn't very different from the old one except that the 'backstop issue' had been 'resolved' by, in effect, allowing a border across the Irish Sea.

The DUP had been comprehensively shafted – seemingly without noticing – but the Tories had the prize of leaving the Customs Union and pursuing new trade deals with the Americans, Australians and others. The economic benefits were potentially minor compared to the economic costs of leaving the EU, but the symbolism of 'taking back control' mattered.

The Bill went through, and Johnson carried out a ruthless purge of dissident 'Remainers'. Some decided to stay and fight in future as independents (Gauke, Grieve). Some retired from parliament to do other things (Philip Hammond, Amber Rudd, Oliver Letwin, Ken Clarke, Nicholas Soames). Two joined the Lib Dems (Sarah Wollaston and Antoinette Sandbach), following earlier defectors. Jo Johnson went to the Lords, while others buckled down to the new dispensation (Greg Clark, Stephen Hammond).

While all this went on, I was planning on the assumption that I would be able to do something useful and interesting on health and social care if the parliament continued, as well as the Private Members' Bill on Assisted Dying. I managed to get a debate on the funding of social care, an issue I thought had been dealt with in coalition with our agreement to implement the Dilnot Commission report, but the Tories backed off.

There was no way forward other than through a cross-party approach and I used the debate to set out what this should look like.[244] But no one was listening until Brexit was

[244] 'We Can Only Solve The Social Care Crisis By Working Across Party Lines', *Huffington Post*, 5 October 2019.

resolved. And, in any event, my role ended when Jo appointed Luciana Berger to be health spokesperson.

There was a Saturday meeting of parliament to approve the deal and the 'Remainers' were hoping that, as the Withdrawal Bill passed through parliament – Lords and Commons – there would ideally be a referendum attached and failing that, a customs union which would create enormous problems for the Tories. But at this point, Jo had a rush of blood to the head.

I had stood aside emotionally and practically from the decision-making in the party, leaving it to Jo and her team of advisers, together with some of the new MPs who had her confidence. There was a high degree of optimism, which I thought was misplaced, that the heavily 'Remain' seats would switch to the Lib Dems as they did in the Euro elections. There was talk of 70 seats and perhaps 140. Traditional Tory-Labour marginals like Putney and Finchley had suddenly become Lib Dem targets. But one concrete development was that the process I started, of negotiating a seat-sharing agreement with the Greens and Plaid Cymru, had progressed well and could cover 70 or so key seats.

The optimism spilled over into hubris when Jo decided to tell the press that we were thinking of switching our position to support an early general election. Since the SNP also favoured an early election (to avoid being caught in the political backwash from the forthcoming trial of Alex Salmond (on sexual misconduct charges), there was now enough support to achieve the two-thirds majority to end the Fixed-term Parliaments Act and secure an early election.

When we discussed the issue amongst parliamentary colleagues, there was clearly deep disagreement. I made the case against. There was still as much chance as there ever was of either getting a referendum or significant improvements to the Withdrawal Agreement. There was also every possibility that Farage would give Boris tactical support in the general election while the 'Remain' vote could be split with Labour.

We might try to present the election as a re-run of the Euro elections, but the two-party dynamic would return and this time the Corbyn factor would work heavily in the Tories' favour after a couple of years of picking him apart in the press and the awful stuff about anti-Semitism. There was strong support from Tim Farron, Norman Lamb and others, including Angela Smith who had emerged as the shrewdest and most thoughtful of the Labour defectors. But Jo had made up her mind. I had worried approaches from political friends, appealing to me to stop what they saw as a terrible mistake. But I was Yesterday's Man. This wasn't my call anymore.

October 4 2019: *I finally met the refugee from Syria to whom I am to teach English. She has a husband and three children, including a baby. The rules are to avoid getting into discussions about our pupils' backgrounds and private lives and to stick very professionally to the language teaching techniques we have learnt. She seems very bright and eager to learn and it helps that her two older children are at primary school and therefore in an English-speaking environment for part of the day.*

V has disappeared to a 'colloquium' at Oxford. I got a

call to say he had had an accident, "run over" by a cyclist who was travelling fast while V wasn't looking out crossing a road. Very shaken but not concussed.

October 10 2019: *Lunch and walking with V at Kew: he has a lot of time off when parliament isn't voting. Then we went to a strange event in a London hotel with Chinese students on a study tour. My card described me as Rachel Wenbin Smith (instead of Wenban) which has a nice Chinese ring to it, but by the time V's and the host's comments had been translated into Mandarin (and the responses translated back again), it was getting late and we made our excuses to leave.*

The problem with the Brexit stuff in parliament is that V has to be there to vote but there is absolutely no timetable and no way to plan ahead. For example, next Saturday V is supposed to be launching a canoe at a boat club in Twickenham but I am on stand-by to do the honours in his place. And we have a plan over Xmas to do a grand tour of relatives in India and Australia which is on hold, pending Brexit debates or an election which is being mooted as very possible.

V left parliament during one of the interminable debates to be met by Extinction Rebellion protesters outside. Their current stunt is to give oak trees to all MPs to plant. He comes home proudly with this tiny oak to plant in order to save the planet. I point out rather acidly that I have planted over 150 oak trees in the last 35 years on the farm.

October 18 2019: *I have managed to get away for a few*

days to Scotland to see Zoe and family. But the news tells me that Boris has brought back his new deal with parliament sitting tomorrow (so I will be going back to stand in for Vince at the boat club).

October 29 2019: *Parliament has voted for an election on a motion jointly proposed by the Lib Dems and the SNP. Who knows whether this will give Boris a majority to 'get Brexit done' or produce another hung parliament, which will probably go for a referendum to break the deadlock? The Lib Dems seem optimistic that they will do well, though V is sceptical. Of course, for us personally, it means V can look forward to a life outside parliament and, for me, that we can have more of a life together – I hope – starting with the visit to Goa and Australia.*

I wanted to support the party in the election, even though I no longer had an official role. My first election role was to help launch a big survey carried out by Best for Britain on what can be achieved by tactical voting. I had a lot of time for Best for Britain, and Naomi Smith, who ran it. Unlike the People's Vote campaign, which had imploded due to internal faction-fighting, it was professional and did excellent research. Its analysis showed that, with tactical voting by a third of 'Remain' voters, there could be a hung parliament. But the Lib Dems would get only 34 seats, way below what the party was hoping for – and this was after treating Kensington & Chelsea and City of London, where Sam and Chuka were standing, as Lib Dem gains.

Without tactical voting, there would be a healthy Tory majority and the Lib Dems would do well to get 23 seats. I made the case for tactical voting, alongside Dominic Grieve and Anna McMorrin of Labour, arguing that there were places where Lib Dems should support Labour Remainers. Since Farage's Brexit Party would not contest Tory marginals, the pressure was entirely on the opposition to unify.

I was asked to go to help in target seats, but it was soon clear that the campaign planners in HQ were living in a fantasy world. I was sent to one 'target' in the West Midlands which had been showered with money and campaign literature but where the local party activists knew from their canvassing that the seat would remain a Tory/Labour marginal and that we would do well to save our deposit. The activists were baffled as to why I had been sent and several were voting for a good (Remain) Labour candidate. Even seats with a very good campaign and good prospects, like Harrogate, were slipping away.

As the campaign progressed, it was clear that the primary motivation of 'Remain' Tories was to stop Corbyn rather than stop Brexit. Also, Jo was not coming across well, which may have partly reflected prejudice against a very confident, articulate, young Scottish woman. The "I intend to be Prime Minister" line attracted hostility and seemed fantastical. I had used it, attracting a lot of cynical humour, but her team hadn't learnt from my experience.

The party also adopted a Revoke message which was not understood and came across as if we were dropping our commitment to a referendum. Our support was sliding by the day. I concentrated my efforts in Wimbledon and Finchley, where polling gave us some hope, and Wokingham where Phillip Lee stood some chance against

John Redwood in a heavily 'Remain' seat.

In the event, the results were a disaster: Tom in Carshalton lost, as did Jo herself. The only gains were St Albans and North East Fife. We could blame bad luck, Nigel Farage and the disastrous Labour campaign which produced an 'anybody but Jeremy' reaction. But the uncomfortable truth was that a big opportunity and a strong starting position had been squandered by one big, bad decision – to precipitate an early election – and a poorly targeted, badly presented campaign. The one ray of sunshine for me was Twickenham: my successor romped home with a nearly 15,000 majority, the biggest ever achieved by Lib Dems in a general election in Twickenham or anywhere. Munira was gracious enough to acknowledge her inheritance.

So, my parliamentary career was over, though that was just a historical footnote of interest only to family and friends and some supporters in Twickenham. More importantly, Brexit would be 'done', albeit with a year of fraught negotiations to complete an agreement of minimal content beyond an agreement to diverge and then continuing ill-will over the non-enforcement of the Northern Ireland Protocol. Equally importantly, British politics had been reconfigured with a different kind of Tory party with a significant working-class element in the north of England; and the Labour Party was severely damaged in the north, as well as in Scotland, and had come to be seen as a party mainly for metropolitan graduates.

My party had been returned to the dire state of five years earlier and it would need a new generation to rebuild it, hopefully in partnership with like-minded people in other parties. It was definitely a good time to leave parliament.

December 13 2019: *We have a Conservative government for the next five years. A traumatic night for us in which Jo Swinson lost her seat by 149 votes.*

Here in Twickenham, Munira Wilson got an even bigger majority than V in 2017 – nearly 15,000, he says – which is wonderful.

December 20 2019: *The dreadfulness of the new political weather is sinking in slowly. Today, the Withdrawal Agreement Bill will get passed. Zac Goldsmith, having lost in Richmond to Sarah Olney, is becoming a Lord and keeping his job as a junior minister. Labour is in full vituperative mode; and we in the Lib Dems will have the same sort of raking over of the coals, but in a more diluted form.*

Vince did a very good article for The Guardian *about the lack of a home for the moderate middle.*

December 31 2020: *V and I find it very hard to engage at all on the political front. Today, the House of Commons will vote on Boris's 'deal', concluded on Christmas Eve. Such is his expectation management (much talk of 'No Deal') that he will dress this up as a triumph, whereas it is a thin deal, not covering services which are 80 per cent of the economy and involving lots more red tape and admin costs. We would argue that Brexit is not 'done'. There are all sorts of loose ends and hostages to fortune. But, depressingly, our future as an increasingly needy but irrelevant offshore island of Europe is assured.*

Vince in the Hat *(courtesy of Getty Images)*.

Post-Script

We were not to know when I left parliament that the country – and the world – would be enveloped for the next two years in a pandemic. Covid has dominated national life. On a personal level, Rachel and I were fortunate, after a trip to India and Australia to see family, to catch one of the last flights back to the UK. We were then profoundly grateful to be able to spend lockdown in the relative safety of Rachel's family farm and to be able to enjoy and explore moorland and forest in one of the most beautiful parts of the UK.

We benefited from the questionable decision to prioritise the safety of the old over the young, many trapped in high-rise flats or crowded accommodation coping with young children and taking risks with their own health to provide essential services. What is grandly called 'inter-generational inequality', which was already painfully evident before the pandemic in the housing market, government spending priorities and taxation, has emerged as an even uglier feature of national life.

The pandemic has led to unprecedented experiments in economic and social policy. After initial fumbling and incompetence, the government adopted sensible economic policies, prioritising essential public spending and jobs, through the furlough scheme. But there would be a reckoning afterwards. The vaccination programme was a great success, and I took some satisfaction from having made sure in government that AstraZeneca would remain a

British-based company and a key part of the life-science research base. Had I returned to parliament, I would probably have annoyed some supporters by supporting the government's emphasis on re-opening the economy and society as quickly as possible.

The period of lockdown gave me an opportunity to write weekly for the online *Independent* on subjects of my own choosing, complete *Money and Power*, a book about politicians who changed economic policy in radical ways, a timely book on China, *The Chinese Conundrum*, which makes the unfashionable case for engagement; and this book with Rachel, which has allowed us to reflect on a memorable decade of our lives and that of the country.

One of the attractions of being out of parliament is the luxury of stepping back from the political dramas of the day to spend time on the bigger picture. For me, the big challenge for this century will be how to accommodate a new super-power (China) and perhaps another (India), with all the implications this brings for the world economy, environment and political systems. I hope to make a modest contribution to the thinking about these issues.

In UK politics, I very much want to see the Liberal Democrats recover from a third bad general election result and return to a position of serious influence. As I discovered as leader, it is difficult for the party to make headway with little media exposure and only rare opportunities to shine in parliament. And now our signature policy, opposing Brexit, has gone. Ed Davey is laying the foundations for recovery with a rebuilding of the local, organisational base and a suite of well-chosen policy priorities (educational opportunity, carers and small business).

The victories in Chesham and Amersham and South Shropshire were a shot in the arm and a well-deserved reward for hard work on the ground, skilled campaigning, and specifically for Ed's having led from the front. Having been to both campaigns, I could feel the return of the old energy and fighting spirit There is now a reasonable prospect of doubling the number of MPs at the next election. But this will depend on tactical voting which, in turn, depends on tacit cooperation with other opposition parties. Beyond that is a need for electoral reform, amongst the many measures required to rebuild a decaying democracy.

Brexit has reshaped the political landscape and made a nonsense of the old left-right dialectic. Boris Johnson has remade the Tory party as the English National Party. He was initially successful but lost a lot of credibility after the exposure of gross hypocrisy and dishonesty after the 'Partygate' scandal. It remains to be seen if the damage is permanent.

The costs of Brexit are yet to percolate through, as they will. The unwillingness of the Labour Party to confront the issue creates an opportunity and a need for a party which will. There is little prospect of an early return, and there is little demand for such. But a serious re-engagement with Europe, in a new form, will become increasingly necessary and popular.

After leaving parliament against the background of Brexit and a poor national result for the Lib Dems, it is easy to be gloomy and cynical. But I recall the days when I was first adopted as a candidate in Twickenham and the party had so little support that it didn't register in the national polls. Dedicated and competent people turned the situation around. That will happen again.

And I find much encouragement in the energy, intellectual curiosity and idealism I encounter when I go to speak in schools, colleges and universities. The campaigns against racism and for the environment have resonated. I hope for the sake of our grandchildren's generation that they succeed.

And to that I just want to say 'AMEN!' Our generation has been blessed to have lived in a period of relative peace and prosperity for Britain. We and our families have been able to travel extensively for work and recreation.

As the Desiderata puts it: "With all its sham, drudgery and broken dreams, it is still a beautiful world", while we try to "take kindly the counsel of the years, gracefully surrendering the things of youth".

Recreational travel is now strictly curtailed. That includes skiing. We dance but mostly at home, with the carpet rolled back. Politics, however, allows us to 'rage against the dying of the light' for as long as we draw breath. Hopefully, for at least another decade!

The new cabinet, in the garden of 10 Downing Street, May 2010.
Vince is fourth on the left at the front, next to David Cameron
(*picture: Getty Images*).

Annex

Coalition agreement
For stability and reform
May 2010

This document sets out how we expect our coalition government to operate in practice and the basis upon which the Conservative and Liberal Democrat parliamentary parties will jointly maintain in office Her Majesty's Government.

It reflects the agreements reached by our parliamentary parties. We expect it to endure for the duration of the present parliament. The government will put a motion before the House of Commons in the first days of the government stating its intention that, subject to Her Majesty the Queen's consent, the next general election will be held on 7 May 2015, to be followed by legislation for fixed term parliaments of five years. The passage of the legislation will be subject to a whip in the parliamentary parties in both houses.

There is no constitutional difference between a coalition government and a single party government, but working practices need to adapt to reflect the fact that the UK has not had a coalition in modern times.

The coalition parties will work together effectively to deliver our programme, on the basis of goodwill, mutual trust and agreed procedures which foster collective decision-making and responsibility while respecting each party's identity.

Close consultation between the Prime Minister and

Deputy Prime Minister, other ministers and members of the Conservative and Liberal Democrat parties in both houses will be the foundation of the coalition's success. In the working of the coalition, the principle of balance will underpin both the coalition parties' approaches to all aspects of the conduct of the government's business, including the allocation of responsibilities, the government's policy and legislative programme, the conduct of its business and the resolution of disputes.

1. Composition of the government

1.1 The initial allocation of cabinet, ministerial, whip and special adviser appointments between the two parties was agreed between the Prime Minister and the Deputy Prime Minister.

1.2 Future allocation will continue to be based on the principle that the parliamentary party with fewer MPs will have a share of cabinet, ministerial and whip appointments agreed between the Prime Minister and the Deputy Prime Minister, approximately in proportion to the size of the two parliamentary parties. The Prime Minister, following consultation with the Deputy Prime Minister, will make nominations for the appointment of ministers. The Prime Minister will nominate Conservative Party ministers and the Deputy Prime Minister will nominate Liberal Democrat ministers. The Prime Minister and the Deputy Prime Minister will agree the nomination of the law officers.

1.3 Any changes to the allocation of portfolios between the parliamentary parties during the lifetime of the coalition will be agreed between the Prime Minister and the Deputy Prime Minister.

1.4 No Liberal Democrat minister or Whip may be removed on the recommendation of the Prime Minister without full consultation with the Deputy Prime Minister.

1.5 The appointment of further members of the Privy Council will be made following full consultation between the Prime Minister and Deputy Prime Minister.

2. Collective responsibility

2.1 The principle of collective responsibility, save where it is explicitly set aside, continues to apply to all government ministers. This requires:

(a) an appropriate degree of consultation and discussion among ministers to provide the opportunity for them to express their views frankly as decisions are reached, and to ensure the support of all ministers;

(b) the opinions expressed and advice offered within government to remain private;

(c) decisions of the cabinet to be binding on and supported by all ministers;

(d) full use being made of the cabinet committee system and application of the mechanisms for sharing information and resolving disputes set out in this document.

There are certain standard exceptions to the principle of consultation – the Chancellor's Budget judgements, quasi-judicial decisions and opinions of the law officers in particular. Budget judgements will require consultation with the Chief Secretary; when the Prime Minister is consulted the Deputy Prime Minister should also be consulted.

3. Functioning of the government

3.1 The establishment of cabinet committees, appointment of members and determination of their terms of reference by the Prime Minister has been and will continue to be agreed with the Deputy Prime Minister. The Deputy Prime Minister will serve, or nominate another member of the administration to serve, on each cabinet committee and sub-committee. The existence and composition of cabinet committees and sub-committees will be published.

3.2 Consistent with the civil service code, all civil servants have a duty to support the government as a whole. Special advisors may support an individual minister in relation to their government activities, but must at all times act in the interests of the government as a whole. The private offices of individual ministers, including the Prime Minister and Deputy Prime Minister, have a particular responsibility to their minister.

3.3 The general principle will be that the Prime Minister and Deputy Prime Minister should have a full and contemporaneous overview of the business of government. Each will have the power to commission papers from the cabinet secretariat.

3.4 The Prime Minister, with the agreement of the Deputy Prime Minister, has established a coalition committee which will oversee the operation of the coalition, supported by the cabinet secretariat. It will be co-chaired by the Prime Minister and the Deputy Prime Minister, with equal numbers of members drawn from the two coalition parties.

3.5 Unresolved issues may be referred to the coalition committee from any other cabinet committee by either that committee's chair (who will be a member of one coalition party) or its deputy chair (who will be a member of the other coalition party).

4. Policy and legislative programme

4.1 The principal policies of the government are set out in the coalition programme for government, of which the first part is the agreement of 11 May, and the second part is 'The Coalition: our programme for government' of 20 May.

5. Support for the government in parliament

5.1 The two parties will aim to ensure support for government policy and legislation from their two parliamentary parties, except where the coalition programme for government specifically provides otherwise. if on any future occasion any other exceptions are required they must be specifically agreed by the coalition committee and cabinet. ministers will be responsible for developing and maintaining a constructive dialogue with members of both parliamentary parties.

5.2 As a general rule, the same whip will be applied by both parties to their members. This includes legislation agreed as part of the coalition agreement. Any exceptions will be explicitly agreed by the parties, including exceptions identified in the agreement of 11 May. In all circumstances, all members of both parties will be expected to support the government on all matters of confidence.

5.3 The Chief Whip of the Conservative Party will serve as government chief whip and the Chief Whip of the Liberal Democrats will serve as deputy chief whip. The Government Chief Whip and Deputy Chief Whip will consult and co-operate with each other to ensure the delivery of the government's programme. Parallel arrangements will operate in respect of the government chief whip and deputy chief whip in the House of Lords.

5.4 Each of the parliamentary parties will be responsible for their own internal arrangements for ensuring effective parliamentary support for the government on all issues covered by this agreement.

5.5 Neither parliamentary party will support proposals brought before Parliament other than by the government unless considered and agreed by both parties. The two parties may agree in the coalition committee or in the parliamentary business committee occasions on which issues will be subject to a free vote, which will normally be the case for Private Members' Bills

6. Public appointments

On the issue of public appointments, the Prime Minister will consult with and have regard to the views of the Deputy Prime Minister.

See Vince's **2010s Divided Decade timeline** at *https://www.therealpress.co.uk /cable-timeline/*

Check out other political books from the Real Press...

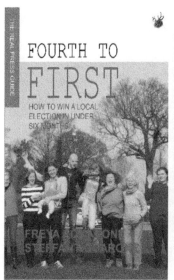